# KENNETH MUIR

*Emeritus Professor of English Literature*
*University of Liverpool*

# Shakespeare's Comic Sequence

LIVERPOOL UNIVERSITY PRESS

Published by
LIVERPOOL UNIVERSITY PRESS
123 Grove Street, Liverpool L7 7AF

CLOTH ISBN  0 85323 064 1
PAPER ISBN  0 85323 154 0

First published 1979

Text set in 10/12 pt VIP Sabon,
printed by photolithography and bound in
Great Britain at The Pitman Press, Bath

# Shakespeare's Comic Sequence

# PREFACE

This book is a natural sequel to *Shakespeare's Tragic Sequence* (1972). It may be worth while to record that although I have edited three of Shakespeare's tragedies and none of his comedies, I have been theatrically involved in many more of the comedies from 1927, when I was cast as Antipholus of Syracuse in John Masefield's production of *The Comedy of Errors*, to 1974 when I played Prospero in Nick Shrimpton's production of *The Tempest*. Altogether I have acted in seven of the comedies and directed three.

In preparing the book for the press, I have been perturbed by my failure to track down the source of ideas and phrases. One hears remarks at conferences, or reads them in articles or reviews; one may even pick them up from the essays of students, who do not always put them in quotation marks. All Arden editors have noticed that their pet ideas have passed into the common stock, so that they are no longer credited with them. If, therefore, I have been guilty of echoing not merely my elders and betters but my youngers and betters, I hope their 'indulgence will set me free'.

I am indebted to the Leverhulme Trust for their award of an Emeritus Fellowship, which enabled me to employ Josephine Pryke as a research assistant, who did yeoman service. I must also thank Mrs Joan Welford for turning my foul papers into a spotless typescript.

Although none of this book has appeared before in its present form, I have cheerfully cannibalised two chapters from *Shakespeare as Collaborator* and articles which have appeared in *Shakespeare Survey*, *Review of National Literatures* and *Trivium*. As I have recently discussed the sources of the comedies, I have excluded the subject from these pages.

KENNETH MUIR

*Liverpool, 1979*

# CONTENTS

# ABBREVIATIONS

| | |
|---|---|
| E.C. | *Essays in Criticism* |
| E.L.H. | *English Literary History* |
| M.P. | *Modern Philology* |
| N.Q. | *Notes and Queries* |
| P.M.L.A. | *Publications of the Modern Language Association* |
| R.E.L. | *Review of English Literature* |
| R.E.S. | *Review of English Studies* |
| S.A.B. | *Shakespeare Association Bulletin* |
| S.E.L. | *Studies in English Literature* |
| Sh.St. | *Shakespeare Studies* |
| S.P. | *Studies in Philology* |
| S.Q. | *Shakespeare Quarterly* |
| S.S. | *Shakespeare Survey* |
| T.L.S. | *Times Literary Supplement* |
| U.T.Q. | *University of Toronto Quarterly* |

# I · INTRODUCTION

Most of the modern critics who have written well on Shakespeare
have concentrated on the tragedies and, although there have been a
number of good books and many good chapters and articles on the
comedies, they are generally regarded as of lesser importance. Yet
Dr Johnson thought that Shakespeare's natural bent was for
comedy and Virgil K. Whitaker has recently expressed the conviction that Elizabethan comedy—not merely Shakespeare's—represents a more considerable achievement than Elizabethan tragedy.
He suggests[1] that

> after the abler Elizabethan comedies the best of Plautus and
> Terence seem pale and thin and contrived. The English plays
> have more gusto, much more action, better characterisation,
> and better dramatic techniques. They also have a far greater
> range of subject matter and of mood.

Professor Whitaker goes on to argue that Shakespeare's comedies
'are almost as untypical of the age' as his tragedies.

It is necessary to stress at the outset that it is difficult, if not
impossible, to define Shakespearian comedy because each play,
though resembling others in some respects, is unique. Whereas one
can extract a formula from Molière's masterpieces, which applies
equally to them all; or show that the English Comedy of Manners,
written by a score of writers, is concerned to satirise the manners or
morals of society from some presumed norm; or show that Shavian
comedy is designed to change society by influencing public opinion
on social, political and religious issues—no such formula can be
found to apply to Shakespeare's various experiments in the comic
mode. To adapt what I once said about his tragedies: there is no
such thing as Shakespearian Comedy; there are only Shakespearian
comedies.

It is true that every one of his comedies could be recognised as

1. Superior figures refer to notes at the end of the book (p. 203).

his, and could not possibly be mistaken for one of Dekker's, or Jonson's, or Middleton's:

> Looke how the fathers face
> Lives in his issue, euen so, the race
> Of *Shakespeares* minde and manners brightly shines
> In his well torned, and true-filed lines.

Nevertheless—much as we admire the critical constructs of Northrop Frye and C. L. Barber—it is important at this time to question their views, and possibly to modify them. It is impossible to produce a magic formula—except one so broad as to lack particularity—which can be applied with equal suitablity to *The Comedy of Errors* and *The Two Gentlemen of Verona, Twelfth Night* and *Troilus and Cressida, The Taming of the Shrew* and *The Tempest.* In other words, the differences are more important than the resemblances; and this is true even if we segregate the 'mature' romantic comedies from the 'problem' plays, and the last romances from the rest of Shakespeare's work. On a later page we shall be considering the characteristics these last plays have in common, but at the same time showing how wide the gulf there is between *Cymbeline* and *The Tempest.*

When Shakespeare arrived in London, probably in the mid-eighties, he had several possible models. John Lyly's artificial, allegorical, prose comedies were performed by the Children of St Paul's; but these plays were enjoyed by a small coterie audience who would know enough of the court gossip to interpret the allegory. They were therefore unsuitable as a model for a dramatist writing for the public theatre. Shakespeare learnt a great deal from Lyly, but he did not make the mistake of writing his kind of play. He admired and did otherwise.

Of the other university wits, Marlowe wrote only tragedy; Greene's better plays were not yet written; Peele's *Arraignment of Paris* was another play for a private audience; and, although there were many other dramatists, their extant plays, at least, were not promising as models.

The most lively comedy in Europe at the time Shakespeare came to London was Italian—the popular unscripted *commedia dell'arte*, and the more literary comedy of Ariosto, Machiavelli and others. Although we know that Shakespeare could read Italian a few years later, it is not certain that he had acquired this accomplishment by the time he wrote his first plays. In any case Ariosto's best-known comedy was available in Gascoigne's translation.

It is not surprising, therefore, that for one of his earliest comedies Shakespeare found a model in the plays of Plautus and Terence, which were studied in all Elizabethan grammar schools, praised by schoolmasters and critically respectable.

All Elizabethan critics assumed that both tragedy and comedy should be didactic—that it should mingle moral instruction with delight. It may be objected that most of them were writing in defence of the stage against its opponents and that they were not wholly disinterested, but there is no reason to doubt their sincerity. The Elizabethan theatre, indeed, was an entertainment industry, comparable to the West End stage or Broadway in the past, and to the film industry or television today. Nevertheless, nearly all the important dramatists apparently believed or hoped that members of their audience would emerge from a performance wiser than they went in. Elizabethan drama, though entirely secular, was descended from the religious and moral drama of earlier ages. The belief that drama should be didactic survived even into the age of Dryden, though by that time the gulf between theory and practice had become apparent.

It is worth considering, therefore, the way in which the orthodox Renaissance view of Plautus and Terence, from which general theories of comedy were largely derived, was related to the actual practice of comic dramatists during the hundred years after Shakespeare's birth, and to show, despite much opinion to the contrary that Shakespeare was more, and not less, didactic than Latin comic writers.

Plautus and Terence were held up as the models for comic dramatists by Renaissance critics, and their plays, particularly those of Terence, were studied in school. Not all educationists approved. Roger Ascham, for example, described Plautus and Terence as

> vtteryng the thoughtes and conditions of hard fathers, foolish mothers, vnthrifty young men, craftie seruantes, sotle bawdes, and so, is moch spent, in finding out fine fetches, soch as in London commonlie cum to the hearing of the Masters of Bridewell. Here is base stuffe for that scholar, that should becum hereafter, either a good minister in Religion, or a Civill Ientleman in service of his Prince and contrie.[2]

Ascham was replying to the kind of argument used by Sir Thomas
Elyot. Comedies, Elyot had said, were not 'a doctrinall of rybaud-
rie' but rather

> a picture or as it were a mirrour of man's life, wherein iuell is
> nat taught but discouered; to the intent that men beholdynge
> the promptnes of youth unto vice, the snares of harlotts and
> baudes laide for yonge myndes, the disceipts of seruantes, the
> chaunces of fortune contrary to mennes expectation, they
> being thereof warned may prepare them selfe to resist or
> preuente occasion. Semblably remembring the wisedomes,
> aduertisements, consailes, dissuasion from vice, and other
> profitable sentences, most eloquently and familiarely shewed
> in those comedies, undoubtedly there shall be no little frute out
> of them gathered.[3]

Professor Madeleine Doran, who refers to this passage in
*Endeavors of Art,* points out that Melanchthon, in the notes to
Erasmus's school edition, pretends that the moral to be learnt from
*Andria* is 'modest and filial behaviour on the part of a young man:
in *Eunuchus*, the dangers of bad company'.[4]

The first complete bilingual edition of Terence, by Richard
Bernard,[5] nicely illustrates the uses to which the comedies could be
put by enthusiastic schoolmasters. Bernard provided, in addition to
the translations, head-notes to each scene, phrases and sentences,
taken from the plays, which would be useful for Latin conversation—which were called *Formulae loquendi*—and useful wise
sayings or *sententiae* (for example, *senibus verba dare, difficile est*).
Apart from such detachable wisdom, Bernard claimed in his
attractively alliterated preface that the comedies were

> pithie, pleasant, and very profitable: as merrie as *Eutrapeles*,
> as grave as *Cato*, as ethical as *Plato*; he can play craftily the
> cousener, and cunningly the clowne: he will tell you the nature
> of the fraudulent flatterer, the grimme and greedie old Sire, the
> roysting ruffian, the minsing mynion, and beastly baud; that in
> telling the truth by these figments, men might become wise and
> auoid such vices, and learne to practise vertue: which was
> *Terence* purpose in setting of these comedies forth in latin,
> mine in translating them into english.

We may suspect that Bernard was more certain that the comedies

were pithy and pleasant than that they were didactic. He prefixes
each scene with an argument, although at times he is hard put to it
to extract a useful moral. He comments on Act III, scene iv of *The
Eunuch*—a scene in which the hero of that play describes with
relish how he has raped an unsuspecting girl—that

> this thing is done for this ende, that the people might by
> hearing perceive, that which with honestie could not be
> beholden with eyes.

The hero's stratagem was copied by Wycherley in *The Country
Wife*, though Horner has enthusiastically willing accomplices.
Terence does not appear to disapprove in the slightest of Chaerea's
action. It is odd that British critics who deplore Wycherley's moral
tone should regard Terence as comparatively civilised. It cannot be
maintained that this was due merely to a realisation that Roman
morals were cruder than Christian ones, for the unreproved
behaviour of the young rakes of Latin comedy would, in real life,
have been deplored by any respectable Roman citizen. Erich Segal is
surely right to argue in his book on Plautus,[6] that the whole point
of Latin comedy is that it was 'festive', that the audience delighted
in watching characters who were doing those things on the stage
which were frowned upon in real life, and that the dramatists
represented 'a temporary excess which implies everyday restraint'.
The influence of C. L. Barber is here apparent.

Because Elizabethan critics who wrote on the theatre were
replying to attacks by Gosson and others, they could not, and
would not wish to, defend it on the ground that it provided a
temporary release from the shackles of morality—what Lamb
called taking an airing from his conscience. They felt constrained to
say, and may have felt without constraint, that good drama was
essentially didactic. Plays, averred Nashe, were 'sower pils of
reprehension wrapt up in swete words'. Comedy, said Sidney,[7]

> is an imitation of the common errors of our life, which [the
> poet] representeth in the most ridiculous and scornfull sort
> that may be: so as it is impossible than any beholder can be
> content to be such a one.

Jonson, too, declared that the purpose of comedy was to delight
and teach, even agreeing with Aristotle that 'the moving of laughter
is a fault in Comedie, a kind of turpitude, that depraves some part

of a mans nature'. His own avowed aim, as expressed through the
mouth of Asper, was to correct the manners and morals of the age.
The stage was a place where the audience would

> see the times deformitie.
> Anatomiz'd in euery nerue, and sinnew
> With constant courage, and contempt of feare.

Another character, Cordatus, accepts Cicero's definition of comedy
as *Imitatio vitae, speculum consuetudinis, imago veritatis*. Despite
his derogatory remarks about laughter, in practice Jonson was less
austere. It is arguable, indeed, that in the period when he was
writing comical satire, in which there is little cause for spontaneous
laughter, Jonson was following a false trail.

The Restoration comedy of manners is descended partly from the
comedy of humours; but the attitude of the Restoration dramatists
is bedevilled by the Collier controversy. Replying to attacks on the
immorality and profaneness of their plays, the dramatists naturally
claimed that their intentions were strictly honorable and therefore
didactic. Obviously they did satirise certain characteristics of the
society they wrote about, but the heroes and heroines who are held
up to our admiration are not models of piety, fidelity or chastity.
They do the things we are restrained from doing by the chains of
morality—however lightly they weigh on us. The ambivalence can
be seen, for example, in *The Country Wife*. On the one hand,
Wycherley lashes the hypocrisy and promiscuity of society ladies
such as Lady Fidget and Mrs Squeamish, the absurdity of men who
confuse innocence and ignorance, and the contemptible nature of
fops; on the other hand, we are asked to admire the sexual prowess
of Horner and Mrs Pinchwife's adroit cuckolding of her brutal
husband. Yet the writers of the comedy of manners, indebted as
they were to Jonson, were closer in spirit than any other English
dramatists to Renaissance theories about classical comedy. It may
be recalled that this was the age of the best translation of
Terence—by Echard—and, even if Congreve found in Terence
what the critics had told him to look for, his admiration was warm
and genuine. He speaks of him in the dedication to *The Way of the
World* as 'the most correct Writer in the World' and praises the
'Purity of his Stile, the Delicacy of his Turns, and the Justness of his
Characters'.

Lope de Vega wrote some Latin verses on the didactic function of comedy and critics have tried to stress the didactic element in the Spanish comedies of the Golden Age. Edward M. Wilson, for example, argues that Calderón's cloak-and-sword plays

> though they are intended as entertainment, did not merely serve to 'amuse an idle moment in their day'. They were based on certain strict conventions of manners and upheld them: be polite, keep your word, protect the helpless, help your friends, and so forth. They also show . . . that mistakes in conduct and in the interpretation of the circumstances in which we are placed, can, and do, have disagreeable consequences.[8]

Of course, it is desirable to be polite, to be truthful, to be loyal and compassionate, though these qualities can hardly be regarded as mere conventions: and it is sometimes rather doubtful whether Calderón supported the specific conventions of the society for which he wrote. It is at least arguable that he deliberately aroused sympathy for the women who behaved in an unconventional way. No well-brought-up young lady should behave as the heroines of *La Dama duende* or *Casa con dos puertas mala es de guardar* do; but it is the jealousies of men and their rigid codes of propriety and honour which are held up to ridicule. In *No siempre lo peor es cierto* Don Pedro seems to be speaking for the author when he exclaims:[9]

> Woe to the first who made so harsh a law,
> A contract so unjust, a tie so impious,
> Which deals unequally to man and woman,
> And links our honour to another's whim!

Molière certainly inherited the view that comedy should teach as well as entertain. He argued in the preface to *Le Tartuffe* that we should *'approuver les pièces de théâtre où l'on verra régner l'instruction et l'honnêteté'*. In many of his plays he holds up to ridicule or reprobation both common and exceptional vices and absurdities, including vanity, jealousy, misalliances, hypochondria, avarice, pedantry, hypocrisy, credulity, self-righteousness, affectations of speech and promiscuity. Perhaps the *précieuses* were laughed out of some of their excesses, and perhaps some people were persuaded to put less trust in their physicians; but, on the other hand, it is unlikely that any miser became a reformed character through seeing Harpagon on the stage, that any old man was deterred from marrying a young wife from seeing *l'école des femmes,* that any hypocrite was converted to honesty, or that any dupe was saved from ruin. In the theatre, we laugh at other people, seldom at ourselves. In *Le Misanthrope,* however, Molière satirises Alceste as a misfit in society, as absurd in his self-righteousness as in his love, but no one prefers the rational, sensible compromiser, Philinte, and the society depicted in the play is as bad as Alceste pretends, so that, as the curtain falls, we may find ourselves infected with the misanthrope's feeling about the state of society.

From this brief survey, it will be seen that the chief comic writers of the Renaissance were all influenced by the theory that comedy should be didactic, although some of them, paying only lip service to this theory, came closer in practice to the actual spirit of Roman comedy.

When we turn to Shakespeare's first comedy, *The Comedy of Errors,* we find that despite his obvious indebtedness to Plautus, he is more ingenious, more complex and much funnier—but he is also more didactic. It would tax the ingenuity of commentators to extract a good lesson from either of the two Plautine plays, but Shakespeare has no difficulty in extracting two interrelated lessons from his material—the damage done to marriage by infidelity and jealousy. This is done not merely by Adriana's complaints to Luciana (II.i), the sermon addressed, as she thinks, to her erring husband (II.ii), by Luciana's advice to Adriana on the duty of submission, and by her pleading with Antipholus—the wrong one again—but more dramatically in the final scene when Adriana is convicted of nagging by her own confession to the Abbess

She did betray me to my own reproof.

He holds the balance between husband and wife. We are never directly told whether Adriana's jealousy has any real cause. Luciana, when she pleads with Antipholus, seems to assume that he is to blame; but his wild behaviour, as far as we see it in the play, is to have dinner, suitably chaperoned, with a remarkably unmercenary courtesan. Shakespeare humanised the Plautine manners and at the same time 'stooped to truth and moralised' his theme. The other early Shakespearian comedies are, in their different ways, equally didactic. Nearly all critics agree that *The Two Gentlemen of Verona* is designed to poke fun at romantic love and to lash inconstancy. Even *The Taming of the Shrew,* farcical as it is, is not without wholesome doctrine—criticism of drunkenness, hints that life is a dream, parental greed in selling daughters to the highest bidder and the foolishness of shrewishness are all presented for our edification. *Love's Labour's Lost* criticises linguistic affectations and even more obviously the aristocrats' absurd vow—absurd because they have neither the temperaments of celibates or scholars. *A Midsummer Night's Dream*, though clearly a 'festive' play, in the magic juice symbolises the absurdities of adolescent sexual desire.

In these remarks on Shakespeare's early comedies, stress has been laid on the didactic element in them. This does not mean that Mr C. L. Barber, who in his brilliant book emphasised the festive nature of Shakespearian comedy, was wrong to do so. As indeed, Mr Barber shows, all the comedies, however festive, make a relevant comment, a relevant criticism, of life. I am arguing simply that Shakespeare's comedies are more didactic than those of Plautus and Terence and that a possible reason for this is that he had absorbed the theories of the commentators and their insistence that comedy should teach as well as delight. Another reason, and possibly more potent, is that he was influenced by the didactic tradition of Moralities and Interludes.

It is unnecessary to pursue the argument through Shakespeare's remaining comedies. In all of them he shows us some characters behaving foolishly or sinfully and others behaving wisely and virtuously, and he does not leave us in doubt as to what we should be thinking and feeling. If *The Merchant of Venice*, like the old play *The Jew*, represented 'the greediness of worldly choosers and bloody minds of usurers', it also represented self-sacrificing friendship, loyalty, generosity and nobility and showed that the letter killeth. In *Much Ado about Nothing* we are constrained to laugh sympathetically at the feud between Beatrice and Benedick and to realise that their rudeness is a sign of their attraction for each other: but we are also shown the evils of Claudio's credulity.

*All's Well that Ends Well* ostentatiously teaches that virtue is the true nobility; *Measure for Measure* is almost embarrassingly full of lessons; and in the great tragi-comedies of Shakespeare's final period, as we shall see, the didactic function is even more apparent.

Shakespeare, then, has three overlapping modes of didacticism in his comedies. Sometimes he shows characters behaving as we all ought to behave—forgiving enemies, being loyal to friends, acting bravely and patiently and overcoming temptation. Members of the audience, we may hope, will be inspired by the examples set before them. Sometimes, and often in the very same plays, Shakespeare depicts characters behaving evilly or foolishly, so that no member of the audience would wish to follow their bad example—attempting murder or rape, betraying friends, falling into delusions of grandeur or sentimentality, being shrewish, jealous, credulous, fickle, sottish, proud, vain, pedantic, affected or deceitful. The third mode is perhaps the most characteristically Shakespearian: this consists of the presentation of characters with whom we are invited to sympathise but who nevertheless behave in a foolish way. If we think that the function of comedy is to improve the manners, behaviour or morals of society, this mode is likely to be the most efficacious. No spectator will see himself as Volpone or Sir Epicure Mammon, as Shylock or Malvolio; and it may be questioned whether a spectator who leaves the theatre, thanking God he is not like the characters on the stage, has been morally improved by his attendance. It is when we laugh at characters like ourselves and acknowledge the likeness that our characters may be marginally improved.

This stress on the didactic function of Shakespeare's art is necessary because many recent critics have argued, or assumed, that it was completely undidactic in character. And, it must be confessed, most critics who have argued that Shakespeare was didactic have made him more rigid and limited, more repellent even, than he obviously was. He was not, of course, a moralist or a preacher by profession or temperament, and his chief purpose was to write good plays which would be enjoyed by his audiences on several different levels. When Prospero, in the epilogue to *The Tempest,* informs the audience that his purpose was to please, the poet was referring not merely to the performance, but also to the play itself. Yet no one could deny that *The Tempest* does more than entertain.

'We hate poetry', as Keats said, 'that has a palpable design upon us'; and plays which are too blatantly didactic irritate more than they instruct. The average playgoer's reaction to *The Cocktail Party* is a case in point. What is not always recognised, obvious as it is once attention has been called to it, is that all good literature, simply by 'astonishing the mind with a new aspect of truth' must teach its readers, whatever the intentions of the author. It is possible, therefore, that Shakespeare had no theory of comedy—

though he must have discussed the topic with Jonson and been told at school what the current theory was—and that he did not set out with a conscious intention to instruct as well as delight. Yet, when all is said, the plots of his comedies are not presented in a moral vacuum; the themes which are embodied in the plays all constitute a criticism of life; and it is hardly rash to assume that the poet intended this criticism to be understood by his audience. So we get the triple paradox: first, that Renaissance critics absurdly misinterpreted the festive comedy of Plautus and Terence by pretending that what was an overturning of accepted standards was designed to teach morality; secondly, that Shakespeare, who also wrote festive comedy, nevertheless imbued his festivity with the kind of moral significance critics had pretended to find in Terence and, indeed, his morals were to be found not in detachable, and often misinterpreted, aphorisms, but in the whole substance of his comedies; and, thirdly, that confronted with what it would not be altogether absurd to call Shakespeare's saving doctrine, many critics have echoed Samuel Johnson's complaint, that he appeared to write without any moral purpose whatever, while sometimes regarding the poet's supposed freedom from didacticism as a matter for congratulation.

# II · EXPERIMENT

We have seen what models were available to a young dramatist in the last two decades of the sixteenth century. In the five comedies discussed in the present chapter—in whatever order they were written—Shakespeare can be seen experimenting to find his own individual style as a comic writer. At the beginning of his career he may have been ignorant of Italian comedy except in the guise of Gascoigne's *Supposes* but there are signs before 1596 that he knew something of the *commedia dell'arte*. Greene's two best plays—both tragi-comedies—were not yet written, and there was nothing in his earlier work which would have tempted a Johannes Factotum to imitate them. Lyly's court comedies were a minority taste, though Shakespeare learned some lessons from them. There were scores of plays written in the twenty years before Shakespeare came to town, but judging from those which have survived it seems unlikely that the lost ones could have offered a useful model.

It is not surprising, then, that Shakespeare turned to Latin drama as his first model, for Plautus and Terence were expert playwrights. He learnt from them the art of construction and already he bettered his instruction, surpassing his models in ingenuity and complexity, and by introducing the condemned Aegeon's reunion with his wife adding a new dimension to the heartless farce of the *Menaechmi*. Character, however, was subordinated to plot; and although modern critics have discovered the modern theme of a loss of identity this emerges only at moments. *The Taming of the Shrew* is also essentially a farce, but the taming plot is coupled with the plot of *Supposes*, and both are played before Christopher Sly, who is made to think he is a lord. We have a drunken tinker, living as a lord, married to a boy posing as a girl, watching a man who poses as a bully to cure a woman who poses as a shrew. Here we are presented with genuine problems of identity.

In *The Two Gentlemen of Verona* Shakespeare approached more nearly to the kind of comedy which was to be his mature concern. It is based, as Greene's *James IV,* on a foreign novel or a derivative from it. He attempted, if without complete success, to make his characters more complex than the roles dictated by the plot: the temptation and fall of Proteus is conveyed to us by soliloquies. Although the play, like most of the later comedies, is a celebration of love, it is also a satire of romantic ideas of love and of the strange quirks of human behaviour. The clowns are used brilliantly to show up the foolishness of the gentry.

Inconstancy which turns a courtier into a cad is mocked more sympathetically in the early masterpiece, *A Midsummer Night's Dream*, in which the magic juice is a symbol of the absurdities of romantic love, and Titania's love of an ass is a symbol of Venus *'toute entière à sa proie attaché'*. Yet the harmony at the end, with Titania and Oberon reconciled, and the three pairs of lovers married and blessed, makes it an ideal play for the celebration of an actual marriage.

In all these four plays there are weaknesses. Some of the verse is comparatively feeble, some scenes do not quite come off, some of the characters never come alive; but in all of them Shakespeare deploys his plots in a masterly fashion. In *Love's Labour's Lost*, on the other hand, the plot is rudimentary and the *commedia dell'arte* characters of the sub-plot are related to the main plot in a most casual way. Whereas Peter Quince's troupe are due to perform before Theseus and his leading actor gets involved with Titania, Holofernes merely has to put on the pageant of the Nine Worthies. Speed, the witty page in *The Two Gentlemen of Verona,* and the songs in that play and *A Midsummer Night's Dream* have been thought to reflect the influence of Lyly, and Lyly's influence goes deeper in the latter play. But Shakespeare avoids euphuism in these early plays, and when he does use it later it is for purposes of parody. *Love's Labour's Lost* imitates the pattern rather than the action of Lyly's plays. Shakespeare, however, chose to write mainly in verse and contrived thereby, if somewhat paradoxically, to give the illusion of colloquial speech. The play depends for its effect on its satire of affectation—the monastic affectation of the court circle, and the linguistic affectation of all the other male characters. The women are free of the latter, and a remedy for the former. In this respect the play looks forward to the masterpieces at the end of the century in which Portia, Rosalind, Beatrice and Viola outshine their masculine partners. In another respect, however, *Love's Labour's Lost* differs from all Shakespeare's other comedies—in its guying of living persons—but although this makes some passages obscure for a modern audience, it does not seriously interfere with the poetic attraction of the play, or unduly limit the targets of its satire.

It would be wrong to suggest that each of Shakespeare's plays was written to correct the weaknesses of the immediately previous one. But it is clear that although he was quite prepared to produce variations on a theme he had used before, he was never tempted to indulge in the exploitation of a previous success. Both *The Comedy of Errors* and *The Taming of the Shrew* are concerned with mistaken identity, but used with a totally different purpose. Three of the plays make use of disguise—but the disguises of Julia, of the men in *Love's Labour's Lost*, and of various characters in *The Taming of the Shrew* have little resemblance. Two of the plays are concerned with inconstancy; but in one it is regarded as sinful, in the other as comic. In two of the plays incompetent amateur actors perform before sophisticated audiences, but for very different purposes.

Although these five plays are experimental in the sense that Shakespeare was trying out different styles, they were all greatly superior to the comedies of all other dramatists of the period. Although one could welcome a revival of *Endymion* or *Mother Bombie*, Lyly's plays, underrated as they still are, lack the vitality, the humanity, the poetry and the breadth of Shakespeare's earliest attempts.

# I
# *The Comedy of Errors*

The chronology of Shakespeare's early comedies is uncertain, but there is no doubt that *The Comedy of Errors, The Two Gentlemen of Verona* and *The Taming of the Shrew* (in whichever order) were the first three. *The Comedy of Errors* and *The Taming of the Shrew* are both basically farcical, and Adriana is a shrew, though less violent than Katherina before her taming, while Luciana's speech on male supremacy is probably expanded in Katherina's final exhortation to the disobedient wives. *The Two Gentlemen of Verona* contains better poetry than either of the other two plays,

and though it is the least successful of the three it is closer in spirit
to the later masterpieces. It seems probable, therefore, that *The
Comedy of Errors* was the first to be written.

Latin comedy, as we have seen, was the natural model for one
who had undergone the grammar school curriculum and the
*Menaechmi*, the first Plautus play to appear in translation, was a
popular school text.[1] A mere translation, however, would not do, if
only because of its shortness and because of the alien morals and
manners of the Plautine world. It is notable, for example, that the
courtesan has a more important role in the *Menaechmi* than in
Shakespeare's play. In spite of Renaissance assumptions about the
moral function of comedy, discussed in the previous chapter, there
is not the faintest sign that Plautus disapproved of his hero's
conduct. Shakespeare, writing in a nominally Christian society for a
predominantly Christian audience, and, on the evidence of several
of his plays and of the sonnets, himself believing in the sanctity of
the marriage tie, goes some way to minimise the guilt of Antipholus
of Ephesus. It is not unnatural for a man who has been locked out
of his own house to seek to avenge himself by giving his wife real
cause to be jealous; and he goes, in company with another man, to
have dinner with the courtesan. As he is chaperoned, his relations in
the context of the play appear to be innocent; and, although in the
most recent productions of the play the courtesan appears as a
grotesque and repellent whore, lewd, mercenary, and vulgar, there
is no justification for this in Shakespeare's text. He refers to her as
'gentle': she has nice manners and is like a gentlewoman. She is,
moreover, singularly unmercenary. She apparently supplies dinner
to her two guests. She gives a ring worth forty ducats in exchange
for a chain; and when the chain is denied her she naturally tries to
recover the ring for 'forty ducats is too much to lose'.

Adriana is likewise treated more sympathetically than the wife in
the *Menaechmi*. The Abbess, her mother-in-law, tricks her into
condemning herself out of her own mouth by suggesting that she
had not reprimanded her husband sufficiently. Adriana replies:

> It was the copy of our conference.
> In bed, he slept not for my urging it;
> At board, he fed not for my urging it;

1. Superior figures refer to notes at the of the book (p. 203).

> Alone, it was the subject of my theme;
> In company, I often glanced at it,
> Still did I tell him it was vile and bad.     (V.i.62ff.)

The Abbess retorts that a nagging wife is worse than rabies:

> And therefore came it that the man was mad.
> The venom clamours of a jealous woman
> Poisons more deadly than a mad dog's tooth.

Although her sister protests that her criticisms of her husband were mild, Adriana admits:

> She did betray me to my own reproof.

Earlier in the play Adriana has a long speech which arouses laughter in the theatre because she addresses it to the wrong Antipholus, her brother-in-law, but which is fundamentally a serious plea about the sinfulness of adultery:

> How dearly would it touch thee to the quick
> Shouldst thou but hear I were licentious
> And that this body, consecrate to thee,
> By ruffian lust should be contaminate!
> Wouldst thou not spit at me and spurn at me
> And hurl the name of husband in my face,
> And tear the stain'd skin off my harlot-brow,
> And from my false hand cut the wedding-ring,
> And break it with a deep-divorcing vow?
> I know thou canst, and therefore see thou do it.
> I am possess'd with an adulterate blot;
> My blood is mingled with the crime of lust
> For if we two be one, and thou play false,
> I do digest the poison of thy flesh,
> Being strumpeted by thy contagion.     (II.ii.129–44)

Luciana too pleads with the wrong Antipholus on behalf of her sister, urging him, if he cannot be faithful, he should at least conceal his infidelities and be kind to his wife. These passages are far removed from the spirit of Latin comedy: although they arouse laughter because of the bewilderment of Antipholus of Syracuse, they show that Shakespeare was not wholly contented in the world of farce. Indeed, the farcical plot is set in a framework which verges

on tragi-comedy. Old Aegeon is sentenced to death in the opening
scene of the play, and he is being led to execution in the last. His
account of the disasters which have befallen his family could be
taken as the prologue to a tragedy, rather than the prologue to a
farce; and his final reunion with his long-lost wife looks forward,
over a gap of nearly twenty years, to the reunion of Pericles with
Thaisa. It is a lamentable error of taste to try and make Aegeon a
buffoon, so that the threat to his life arouses no anxiety and his
reunion with his wife no feelings of sympathy.

Although Shakespeare could not be satisfied with mere farce, he
goes far beyond Plautus in his exploitation of the farcical situation.
He complicates the plot of the *Menaechmi* in ways which reveal his
mastery of stagecraft. First, he provides the two Antipholuses with
servants, identical twins like their masters, and both called Dromio.
Secondly, he borrows from the *Amphitruo* the famous scene in
which the husband is shut out of his own house, while Jupiter is
begetting Hercules on Alcmena. Thirdly, Shakespeare sets the story
in a framework, suggested by Gascoigne's *Supposes*—translated
from Ariosto's play—in which a trade war between Ephesus and
Epidamnum leads to the death-sentence passed on old Aegeon.
Fourthly, Shakespeare invents the character of Luciana who acts as
a confidante to the wife and her critic, besides providing Antipholus
of Syracuse with a bride. Lastly, Shakespeare took from the story of
Apollonius of Tyre, which had been told by Gower and Twine
among other English writers, the reunion of Aegeon with his
long-lost wife—Diana's temple being changed into a nunnery. The
second pair of twins increases enormously the chances of error and
Shakespeare's other additions lend variety to the action.

As critics have noted,[2] the confusions caused by mistaken
identity lead to fears of enchantment, of witches and sorcerers, of
diabolical possession, requiring the ministrations of an exorcist and
even to fears that it is oneself and not the others who are deluded.
The bewilderment of Antipholus of Syracuse, and of his father at
not being recognized, exhibit the modulation of farce into something more serious:

> Not know my voice! O time's extremity,
> Hast thou so crack'd and splitted my poor tongue
> In seven short years that here my only son
> Knows not my feeble key of untun'd cares?

Though now this grained face of mine be hid
In sap-consuming winter's drizzled snow,
And all the conduits of my blood froze up,
Yet hath my night of life some memory,
My wasting lamps some fading glimmer left,
My dull deaf ears a little use to hear;
All these old witnesses—I cannot err—
Tell me thou art my son Antipholus.           (V.i.308ff.)

This is a good example of Shakespeare's early style, end-stopped, formal and eloquent, relying too much on stock epithets. At times, as in Adriana's speech quoted above, he rises above this level. The scene between Antipholus of Syracuse and Luciana, mostly written in rhymed quatrains and appropriately recalling the style of Elizabethan sonnets, descends from a charming lyricism—

Sweet mistress—what your name is else, I know not,
Nor by what wonder you do hit of mine—
Less in your knowledge and your grace you show not
Than our earth's wonder—more than earth, divine.
Teach me, dear creature, how to think and speak;
Lay open to my earthy-gross conceit,
Smoth'red in errors, feeble, shallow, weak,
The folded meaning of your words' deceit.
Against my soul's pure truth why labour you
To make it wander in an unknown field?
Are you a god? Would you create me new?
Transform me, then, and to your pow'r I'll yield—
                                              (III.ii.29–40)

but later in the same speech Antipholus indulges in absurd conceits which probably did not seem absurd to the young Shakespeare:

O, train me not, sweet mermaid, with thy note,
To drown me in thy sister's flood of tears.
Sing, siren, for thyself, and I will dote,
Spread o'er the silver waves thy golden hairs,
And as a bed I'll take them, and there lie.    (III.ii.45–9)

A few lines later the two characters drop into rhymed stichomythia.

Shakespeare was experimenting in different forms of verse,

sometimes alternating rhymed verse and blank verse in the same scene for dramatic reasons. The first scene of Act II, for example, opens in couplets so as to bring out the formal nature of the debate between Adriana and her sister about marriage, Luciana expressing the orthodox view that men should rule over their wives:

> There's nothing situate under heaven's eye
> But hath his bound, in earth, in sea, in sky.
> The beasts, the fishes, and the winged fowls,
> Are their males' subjects, and at their controls.
> Man, more divine, the master of all these,
> Lord of the wide world and the wild wat'ry seas,
> Indu'd with intellectual sense and souls,
> Of more pre-eminence than fish and fowls,
> Are masters to their females, and their lords;
> Then let your will attend on their accords.          (II.i.14–25)

Adriana scornfully taunts Luciana, implying that her willingness to be a slave prevents her from securing a husband, since men don't like their wives to be spineless. Luciana retorts that the reason why she hasn't got married is that Adriana's continual nagging and her husband's behaviour do not give her a favourable idea of matrimony. On Dromio's entrance the scene drops into blank verse, and on his departure reverts to rhyme, when the debate on marriage is resumed. Dromio's account of his interview with his supposed master has to be nearer to prose because it was necessary to convey as vividly as possible the reported conversation:

> ''Tis dinner time' quoth I; 'My gold!' quoth he
> 'Your meat doth burn' quoth I; 'My gold!' quoth he.
> 'Will you come home?' quoth I; 'My gold!' quoth he.

The doggerel verse in III.i is so distasteful to modern ears that some editors[3] have wistfully assumed that Shakespeare unwisely retained lines written by one of his predecessors. It is certainly pre-Shakespearian in style, similar to that of *Gammer Gurton's Needle* or of *Ralph Roister Doister*, written before Shakespeare was born. Presumably he thought that this kind of verse was appropriate to the knock-about comedy of the scene. The Ephesian Antipholus and Dromio are knocking at the door, while the Syracusan Dromio refuses to let them in, since his master is dining with Adriana:

| | |
|---|---|
| *Adr.* | Who is that at the door, that keeps all this noise? |
| *Dr.S.* | By my troth, your town is troubled with unruly boys. |
| *Ant.* | Are you there, wife? You might have come before. |
| *Adr.* | Your wife, sir knave, go get you from the door. |
| *Dr.E.* | If you went in pain, master, this 'knave' would go sore . . . |
| *Ant.* | There is something in the wind, that we cannot get in. |
| *Dr.E.* | You would say so, master, if your garments were thin. |
| *Ant.* | Go fetch me something; I'll break ope the gate. |
| *Dr.S.* | Break any breaking here, and I'll break your knave's pate . . . |
| *Ant.* | Well, I'll break in; go borrow me a crow. |
| *Dr.E.* | A crow without a feather. Master, mean you so? |

These lines are meant to be rattled off at a great pace; but Dromio's jokes are tedious and this is the only scene in the play that falls flat in the theatre, despite the fact that it is based on one of the most effective scenes in *Amphitruo*. Shakespeare wisely used prose for the coarsely effective account by Dromio of Syracuse of the kitchen-wench who lays claim to him.

Shakespeare was feeling his way for an appropriate form and his varying success is one sign of his immaturity. The other sign is the comparative weakness of characterisation. The characters derive what individuality they possess from the situations in which they appear. Aegeon has to be old, pessimistic and pathetic—and that is about all one can say about him. There is no discernible difference between the two Dromios and the difference between their masters is due entirely to the parts they have to play. The one from Syracuse has to be a romantic lover; he has to be afraid of witchcraft, and to be generally bewildered. His married brother has to be coarser in fibre, so that his treatment of Adriana is a cause of her jealousy, as well as its result. Perhaps Shakespeare is most successful with Luciana who is slightly more complex. She is loyal to Adriana in public, and critical in private of her jealous nagging. She defends Antipholus behind his back and remonstrates with him—or rather, with his twin—in private. She is obviously more pleased than shocked when the wrong Antipholus makes love to her, but she loyally repulses him and reports the incident to her sister. His wooing, she admits, was

With words that in an honest suit might move.

In spite of its immaturities, *The Comedy of Errors* is an admirable acting play. It does not need jazzing up, as in two recent productions at Stratford-upon-Avon.[4] Those who saw Andrew Leigh's memorable production at the Old Vic in 1927 will remember the continuous enjoyment of the audience. It was played on a bare stage without scenery and without a curtain and the speed of the action made it easy to appreciate the bewilderment of the characters on the stage.[5]

# 2
# *The Taming of the Shrew*

It used to be thought that the source of Shakespeare's play was *The Taming of a Shrew*, but most critics now believe that the indebtedness was the other way round. It is curious, however, that *A Shrew* contains an epilogue which rounds off the Christopher Sly story[6] and that, although there are echoes in it of other Elizabethan plays—a characteristic of Bad Quartos—there are virtually none of Shakespeare's.[7] It is possible that both plays were based on an earlier one, probably by Shakespeare himself. In any case *The Taming of the Shrew* was not published until 1623, some thirty years after its first performance, and much may happen to a popular theatrical script in that time.

The play has three plots—the Induction, the rivalry for Bianca's hand, and the taming of Katherina. The induction is chiefly remarkable for the portrait of Christopher Sly, with his drunken boasting, his garbled snatches from old plays—with Kyd's Hieronimo telescoped with Saint Jerome to form Saint Jeronimy—his songs, and his childish wonder at his temporary promotion to the peerage. The character is Shakespeare's first masterpiece. The plot, apparently based on a true story existing in several versions, resembles Calderón's most famous play, *La Vida y Sueno*, in which the hero, deluded like Sly, declares:[8]

> What is life? An illusion, a shadow, a tale;
> The greatest good is little; for life's a dream.

The idea of life as a dream, familiar too from many passages in Shelley's poems, was a renaissance commonplace which found its most famous expression in Prospero's words when the spirit-actors in his masque vanish:

> We are such stuff
> As dreams are made on; and our little life
> Is rounded with a sleep.

The drunken Sly, treated for a few hours as a lord, comes to believe that his previous life as a tinker was only a dream. In the Epilogue of *A Shrew* he decides to put into practice the lesson of the play he has witnessed by taming his own shrewish wife.[9]

The Bianca plot is derived from Gascoigne's *Supposes*, a translation of a famous play by Ariosto. It is concerned with assumptions about identity.[10] Lucentio and Hortensio both pose as tutors to enable them to woo Bianca. Tranio poses as Lucentio; the Pedant poses as Vincentio; and Bianca and the Widow pose as obedient wives. This plot is closely linked with the taming plot by Baptista's refusal to allow the marriage of his apparently sweet and docile daughter until he has married off the shrewish one and also by the reversal of roles at the end when the tamed Shrew is contrasted with Bianca, who refuses to obey her husband only a few hours after the ceremony in which she has vowed to honour and obey him.

The plot depends very largely on disguise, as so many of Shakespeare's later comedies do[11]—Tranio disguised as Cambio, and so on. These disguises inevitably lead to comic confusion as when the real and bogus Vincentios outface each other, or when Vincentio, seeing Tranio in Lucentio's clothes, thinks he has murdered his master.

If the Bianca plot is rather disappointing, this is not because it is lacking in dramatic skill but rather because it has less interest than the taming plot and because of the feebleness of some of the verse. The opening speech, for example, is extraordinarily clumsy compared with the opening of any of Shakespeare's other plays:

> Pisa, renowned for grave citizens,
> Gave me my being and my father first,
> A merchant of great traffic through the world,
> Vincentio, come of the Bentivolii;
> Vincentio's son, brought up in Florence,
> It shall become to serve all hopes conceiv'd,
> To deck his fortune with his virtuous deeds.[12]                (I.i.10ff.)

It has been suggested[13] that the three plots are linked together by the fact that they are all concerned with poses and supposes. This theme, as we have seen, is apparent in the Bianca plot. In the Induction, the Lord poses as a servant, induces Sly to suppose he is a lord, and makes his page pose as the tinker's wife. In the Taming plot, it has been argued,[14] Petruchio poses as a male shrew and thus persuades Katherina to accept his 'suppose' that she is not really a shrew.

Petruchio's methods of taming Katherina have aroused the horror of many modern critics. Sir Edmund Chambers, for example, said[15] that 'you can hardly refuse to shed a tear for the humiliation of Katherine' and that she 'stands for all time as a type of the wrongs done to her much-enduring sex'. John Masefield declared[16] that Katherina was 'humbled into the state of submissive wifely falsehood by a boor' and her sermon to the other wives is 'melancholy claptrap'. Sir Arthur Quiller-Couch thought[17] that 'any modern civilised man', reading the play, would find the whole Petruchio business tedious, and 'to any modern woman' it would be offensive as well.

It is true that Petruchio's avowed motive—and his actual motive at the beginning of the play—is to wed a rich wife; and apparently he does not mind about her character or appearance:

> Be she as foul as was Florentius' love,
> As old as Sibyl, and as curst and shrewd
> As Socrates' Xanthippe or a worse . . .
> I come to wive it wealthily in Padua;
> If wealthily, then happily in Padua.      (I.ii.67–9, 73–4)

His method of taming Katherina is that of a bully. He uses his superior physical strength. He arrives at the wedding in absurd clothes in order to humiliate his bride; he misbehaves atrociously during the actual ceremony; he boorishly refuses to stay for the marriage feast; he uses the methods of a hawk-tamer by starving his wife; instead of consummating the marriage he preaches Katherina a sermon on continence; he tantalises her by refusing to let her have the fashionable clothes she covets; he makes her say things they both know to be false; he makes a wager on her obedience, which he wins; and in the end she preaches to the other wives on the necessity of slavish obedience.[18] A high-spirited girl has been tamed by brutal and shameful methods into accepting slavery.

Such is the complaint of some modern critics; but, of course, such an interpretation of the play is absurd. The play is a farce and Shakespeare wrote it nearly three centuries before Nora slammed the door at the end of *A Doll's House*. On the stage, as Chambers and Quiller-Couch reluctantly admit, the play is not offensive: it is funny. The account given in the last paragraph omits some important aspects of the taming process. Apart from anything else, it is apparent that the 'high-spirited girl' at the beginning of the play is, whatever the reasons, impossible to live with. Miserable herself, she does her best to make others miserable. At the end of the play she appears to be much happier. The four best Katherinas I have seen in the last fifty years—Sybil Thorndike, Edith Evans, Peggy Ashcroft and Vanessa Redgrave—are not exactly submissive in temperament and they all enjoyed themselves in the part. Dame Edith played it in two different ways. On the first occasion, fresh from her triumphs in the Comedy of Manners, she played Katherina almost in the manner of a Restoration heroine and her final speech of submission was delivered ironically with a conspiratorial leer to the women in the audience. 'Men like to think they are our lords and masters', she implied, 'and I don't mind humouring them, children as they are; but, as you all realise, I can do what I like by giving Petruchio, this overgrown schoolboy, an illusion of authority.' I thought at the time that this way of delivering the speech was out of period and that Shakespeare cannot have intended it. But it has since been pointed out[19] that Vives in *The Instruction of a Christian Woman* had remarked that 'a good woman by lowly obeisance ruleth her husband', so that Dame Edith's interpretation may well have been right. The second time she played the part, she presented Katherina as a problem child, jealous of her sly and popular sister, hating the idea of a marriage of convenience, with its sordid mercenary basis, and not being able to find a man she could respect. She is attracted by Petruchio's virility and she submits to him only because she loves him. Dame Peggy Ashcroft and Vanessa Redgrave likewise made it plain that they had fallen in love and that they unconsciously wish to submit.

It is worth noting that Germaine Greer is one of the few women who have written in defence of Petruchio. She maintains[20] in *The Female Eunuch* that Kate

has the uncommon good fortune to find Petruchio who is man

enough to know what he wants and how to get it. He wants her spirit and her energy because he wants a wife worth keeping . . . she rewards him with strong sexual love and fierce loyalty.

Her submission is 'genuine and exciting because she has something to lay down, her virgin pride and individuality'. Petruchio is 'both gentle and strong' and Kate's address to the other wives at the end of the play 'is the greatest defence of Christian monogamy ever written'. It is surely not so much a defence of Christian monogamy as of the principle, derived from the Bible and universally accepted in the sixteenth century, of wifely obedience. As we have seen, Luciana had expressed the same ideas in *The Comedy of Errors*. We cannot know for certain whether Shakespeare himself accepted this view of marriage. It was, perhaps, somewhat undercut by the sex of the reigning monarch; but there are survivals of the subordination theory when the great heiress Portia surrenders to Bassanio, even though she soon reasserts her authority. The increasing independence of the comic heroines, who all outshine the men they are destined to marry, makes it difficult for us to imagine that their submission will be more than a formality; and in the love scenes of the final plays we are conscious of the complete equality of Florizel and Perdita, of Ferdinand and Miranda. In both cases love's service is perfect freedom.

Although Miss Greer possibly romanticises the qualities of Petruchio, Katherina is not really reduced to servitude and no audience imagines that she is. Nor do they really believe that Petruchio is a fortune-hunter, even though he starts with that ambition; and if we examine his behaviour throughout the play, we can see that those critics who write him off as a vulgar bully have missed a great deal. As soon as he hears of Katherina's reputation for shrewishness, his fortune-hunting fades into the background and he feels challenged by the task of taming her. He calls the task one of Hercules's labours. In the first wooing scene, although he indulges in plain-speaking about her reputation, he makes her know that he admires her beauty and spirit. He calls her bonny Kate, the prettiest Kate in Christendom and super-dainty Kate. At the end of the scene he speaks of

this light, whereby I see thy beauty,
Thy beauty that doth make me like thee well.

And, clearly, the attraction is mutual. She is attracted by his virility and humour; he is attracted by her beauty and wildness. In some ways the wooing resembles that of Beatrice and Benedick who are likewise individualists, distrusting equally the conventions of romantic love and the unromantic realities of marriages of convenience. All through the play we can see that Katherina's knowledge of her sister's character and the humiliation she feels that a husband must be found for her before Bianca can marry, drive her into impossible behaviour. At the same time she wants a husband, while doubting whether any man she respects will want to marry her, even with a dowry to sweeten the bargain. Those critics who find her degraded in Act V tend to ignore the much worse degradation of her situation in Act I.

Her violence towards Petruchio and her attempts to dominate are, at least in part, a means of testing him. Unconsciously she wants to submit and to accept her femininity, but she is prevented at first by her pride and by the fear that Petruchio is mainly interested in her dowry. After she has been starved and prevented from sleeping, she is willing to agree that the sun is the moon; but her relief at her own submission can be gauged from the way in which she joins in the joke:

> Be it moon, or sun, or what you please;
> And if you please to call it a rush-candle,
> Henceforth I vow it shall be so for me
> . . .
> Then, God be bless'd, it is the blessed sun;
> But sun it is not, when you say it is not;
> And the moon changes even as your mind.
>
> (IV.v.13–15, 18–20)

Anyone who heard Dame Edith Evans's address to old Vincentio as—

> Young budding virgin, fair and fresh and sweet,
> Whither away, or where is thy abode?
> Happy the parents of so fair a child;
> Happier the man whom favourable stars
> Allots thee for his lovely bed-fellow—    (IV.v.36–40)

must have been convinced that Katherina had learned to laugh.

As G. R. Hibbard points out in his admirable introduction to the play,[21] Petruchio by his outlandish behaviour has been holding up a mirror wherein his wife can see herself. In this distorting mirror she sees how impossible her own behaviour has been. Her realisation of this can be glimpsed in her sympathy with the servant who has been unjustly struck by Petruchio (IV.i.142) and with the cook (IV.i.154). Once Katherina decides to adopt the role of the obedient wife, she plays it with zest, exaggerating and parodying it as Petruchio had parodied the role of despotic husband. This, as we have seen, is apparent in her address to Vincentio; and there is nothing improbable in the assumption that her speech to the other wives is a deliberate exaggeration, as when she urges them to place their hands below their husbands' feet. The marriage, despite appearances, is based on love, mutual respect, and a kind of equality.

# 3
# *The Two Gentlemen of Verona*

Both *The Comedy of Errors* and *The Taming of the Shrew* have farcical plots, and *The Two Gentlemen of Verona*, Shakespeare's first romantic comedy, is closer to his later masterpieces. As I have suggested elsewhere,[22] although the play derives ultimately from Montemayor's *Diana*, there was probably an intermediate source, notably the *Felix and Feliosmena* which had been performed in 1585.

Shakespeare's play, despite its comparative unpopularity among critics and in the theatre, has many merits. It is well-constructed, with the situation economically and dramatically presented. By the end of the second act Proteus has followed Valentine to Milan and fallen in love with Silvia, while Julia has decided to disguise herself as a page in order to follow Proteus. In Act III Proteus betrays to the Duke Valentine's intention to elope with Silvia. In Act IV Julia takes service with Proteus and is sent by him to plead his suit with Silvia. In the last act Silvia flees to the forest, is captured by the outlaws, and then rescued by Proteus. Rejected by Silvia, he tries to force her. Valentine steps forward, Proteus forthwith repents, Valentine forgives him and offers to relinquish Silvia. Whereupon Julia faints and Proteus resumes his love for her. The denouement is preposterous and this is the reason why the play is seldom performed.

There have been numerous explanations of what has been regarded as a fatal flaw in the drama. It has been suggested, for example, that Shakespeare incorporated dialogue from an earlier play. This, of course, would not excuse him, for by borrowing dialogue Shakespeare accepted responsibility for it. Another theory is that between 1590 and 1623, when the play was eventually published, the last page of the manuscript was damaged and the editors had to fill in the gaps as best they could. Certainly, if Shakespeare wrote the scene, some lines in it are the worst he ever wrote.

> *Val.* Thou common friend, that's without faith or love—
> For such is a friend now; treacherous man, (63)
> Thou hast beguil'd my hopes; nought but mine eye
> Could have persuaded me. Now I dare not say
> I have one friend alive: thou wouldst disprove me.
> Who should be trusted, when one's own right hand
> Is perjured to the bosom? Proteus, (68)
> I am sorry I must never trust the more,
> But count the world a stranger for thy sake.
> The private wound is deepest. O time most accurst! (71)
> 'Mongst all foes that a friend should be the worst!
> *Pro.* My shame and guilt confounds me. (73)
> Forgive me, Valentine; if hearty sorrow
> Be a sufficient ransom for offence,
> I tender't here; I do as truly suffer
> As e'er I did commit
> *Val.* Then I am paid;
> And once again I do receive thee honest.
> Who by repentance is not satisfied (79)
> Is nor of heaven nor of earth, for these are pleas'd;
> By penitence th'Eternal's wrath's appeas'd.
> And, that my love may appear plain and free, (82)
> All that was mine in Silvia I give thee.
> *Jul.* O me unhappy! [*Swoons*

The sudden repentance and the instant repentance are crude enough, but they are less disturbing than the halting verse and the forced rhymes (71–2, 80–3).

A third explanation is that Shakespeare had resigned his mistress to his friend, as Valentine proposes to do, an action described in several of the Sonnets:

Take all my loves, my love, yea, take them all . . .

Shakespeare, then, was creating a Valentine in his own image. Shakespeare's emotional involvement in this conflict between love and friendship may have interfered with his dramatisation of a similar situation. But it should be emphasised that the differences between the sonnet story—whether it was biographical fact or a convenient fiction—and *The Two Gentlemen of Verona* are more significant than the resemblances. The Dark Lady seduced the poet's friend: Valentine's friend attempts to rape Silvia.

Lastly it is suggested that the theme of Love versus Friendship, popular in the early 1590s, was no longer of much interest to a later generation, and that a debate on the subject was reduced to Valentine's seven miserable lines. In this connection we are reminded of the popularity of the tale of Titus and Gysippus in Elyot's *Boke of the Gouernour*. Titus falls in love with Gysippus's betrothed, falls ill of repressed passion, and is persuaded to confess to his friend. Whereupon Gysippus agrees to relinquish his bride to Titus.[23]

> Thinke ye me suche a fole or ignorant persone that I knowe nat the powar of Venus, where she listeth to shewe her importable violence? Haue nat ye well resisted agayne suche a goddesse, that for my sake ye haue striven with her all moste to the dethe? What more loyaltie or trouthe can I require of you? Am I of that vertue that I may resiste agayne celestiall influence preordinate by prouidence diuine? . . . I confesse to you, Titus, I loue that mayden as moche as any wise man mought possible, and toke in her companye more delite and pleasure than of all the treasure and landes that my father lefte to me, whiche ye knowe was right abundaunt. But now I perceyue that the affection of loue towarde her surmounteth in you aboue measure, what, shal I thinke it of a wanton lust or sodayne appetite in you, whome I haue euer knowen of graue and sadde disposition, inclyned alway to honest doctrine, fleinge all vayne daliaunce and dishonest passetyme?

Gysippus therefore arranges for Titus to take his place in the marriage bed without the lady's knowledge, and afterwards to claim her as his wife. What she thought of this bed-trick is not recorded. However unfair to the woman, Gysippus was not handing over his bride to a man who had tried to rape her and who had previously betrayed him to the Duke. It is difficult to believe that Shakespeare admired Valentine's generosity at the expense of Julia as well as of Silvia. Valentine's behaviour is absurd, and Shakespeare meant us to think it absurd.

If we start from this assumption, we may yet believe that the ending of the play is seriously flawed, that Shakespeare did not wholly succeed in making his intentions clear. Even this is not certain, for in performance, with the author present, there may have been no difficulty.[24]

The climax of the play is surely a sardonic comment on the popular idea that friendship is superior to love and that the lover should follow Gysippus's example, even when the friend is totally unworthy. Proteus, as he confesses at the end, lacks the virtue of constancy, without which he is led into treachery, falsehood and lust. Julia, referring to her masculine clothes, also alludes to the significance of Proteus's name in the line—

> It is the lesser blot, modesty finds,
> Women to change their shapes than men their minds—

and Proteus acknowledges that man's inconstancy

> Fills him with faults; makes him run through all th' sins.

In *A Midsummer Night's Dream* the inconstancy of Demetrius is matter for mirth: in this play the criticism is much more serious.

The treacheries of love, man's inconstancy, and unintelligent sacrifices to absurd ideals, are not the only objects of satire in *The Two Gentlemen of Verona*. The knight-errant, who rejoices in the name of Sir Eglamour and is called valiant by Silvia, runs away at the first sign of danger. The desperate outlaws, on their first encounter with Valentine, after assuring themselves that he has 'the tongues', promptly make him their general and their king. By making one of the outlaws swear by Friar Tuck's bare scalp Shakespeare reminds us of the convention he is satirising.

The play was written at the height of the sonneteering craze and Proteus's advice to Sir Thurio on the wooing of Silvia, used[25] oddly by Sir Sidney Lee to prove that Shakespeare's sonnets were

insincere, shows only that Proteus was a trickster and Sir Thurio a
fool:

> You must lay lime to tangle her desires
> By wailful sonnets whose composed rhymes
> Should be full-fraught with serviceable vows.
> *Duke.* Ay,
> Much is the force of heaven-bred poesy
> *Pro.* Say that upon the altar of her beauty
> You sacrifice your tears, your sighs, your heart
> . . . and frame some feeling line
> That may discover such integrity. (III.ii.68–74, 76–7)

The word 'serviceable' indicates the way poetry is to be used for
base purposes; the epithet 'heaven-bred' displays the lip-service
paid to the arts by a philistine, and 'integrity' is an ironic comment
on the lack of integrity in Sir Thurio's counsellor.

The absurd behaviour of lovers,[26] mocked by Shakespeare in
many of his comedies, is described by Speed when Valentine falls in
love with Silvia:

> First, you have learn'd like Sir Proteus, to wreath your arms
> like a malcontent; to relish a love-song, like a robin redbreast;
> to walk alone, like one that had the pestilence; to sigh, like a
> schoolboy that had lost his ABC; to weep, like a young wench
> that had buried her grandam; to fast, like one that takes diet;
> to watch, like one that fears robbing; to speak puling, like a
> beggar at Hallowmas . . . And now you are metamorphis'd
> with a mistress, that, when I look on you, I can hardly think
> you my master.                                    (II.i.17–28)

The attempted assault on Silvia by Proteus provides a sordid
contrast to his high-flown sentiments while the down-to-earth
catalogue of the qualities and defects of Launce's girl (III.i)
contrasts with the fashionable sentiments of both gentlemen:

> She can fetch and carry . . . she can milk . . . she brews good ale
> . . . she can sew . . . she can wash and scour . . . she is proud
> . . . she hath no teeth . . . she is curst . . . she is too liberal.

Apart from the satire of received ideas, there are several ways in
which *The Two Gentlemen of Verona* is an improvement on
Shakespeare's previous comedies. First, the comics, are greatly

superior to the Dromios or Biondello, Speed being derived from Lyly's witty pages, and not therefore being particularly Shakespearian: but Launce is a splendid creation, his speeches about Crab being notable pieces of self-characterisation as well as extremely funny.[27] Secondly the verse, if one excludes that of the denouement, is generally admirable in Shakespeare's best early manner. How good it is can be seen by comparing the prolonged hysteria of Romeo's banishment speeches[28] with Valentine's restrained and effective soliloquy:

> And why not death rather than living torment?
> To die is to be banish'd from myself,
> And Silvia is myself; banish'd from her
> Is self from self, a deadly banishment.
> What light is light, if Silvia be not seen?
> What joy is joy, if Silvia be not by?
> Unless it be to think that she is by,
> And feed upon the shadow of perfection.
> Except I be by Silvia in the night,
> There is no music in the nightingale;
> Unless I look on Silvia in the day,
> There is no day for me to look upon.
> She is my essence, and I leave to be
> If I be not by her fair influence
> Foster'd, illumin'd, cherish'd, kept alive.
> I fly not death, to fly his deadly doom:
> Tarry I here, I but attend on death;
> But fly I hence, I fly away from life.            (III.i.170–87)

The third way in which this play shows an advance is in complexity of characterisation. One aspect of this is the unusual number of soliloquies. Silvia alone of the four main characters is revealed without soliloquising. As the song describes her, she is 'holy, fair and wise', sympathetic in her conversation with 'Sebastian' (the disguised Julia), indignant with Proteus, brave and loyal. Her character is sacrificed to plot when she allows Proteus to have her portrait. She has nothing to say in the last 110 lines of the play, while she is being offered to Proteus by Valentine or claimed by Thurio. Words, not unnaturally, fail her.

We are allowed more insight into the minds of the other three characters. Julia's pretended indignation with Lucetta for bringing

her a love-letter, her wish to read it, expressed in her first soliloquy
(I.ii.50–65), her tearing of the letter and her regret for so doing,
expressed in her second soliloquy, and her pretence with Lucetta
afterwards, her determination to follow Proteus which overcomes
the embarrassments of male attire (codpieces and all) and her two
soliloquies before and after she meets her unwilling rival
(IV.iv.86–103, 175–201) are the means by which Shakespeare
creates a lively and sympathetic heroine. She has been compared
with the Griselda type so common in Greene's novels and plays, but
it is by no means certain that *The Two Gentlemen of Verona* was
written after *Friar Bacon and Friar Bungay* and *James IV*.

The temptation, the fall and corruption of Proteus are revealed in
three soliloquies. He could not take Launce into his confidence
because he is ashamed of what he is doing. He falls in love with
Silvia's picture[29] and decides in his first soliloquy

> If I can check my erring love, I will                     (III.iv.209)

When we next see him, after a short scene between Launce and
Speed, he has made up his mind to a three-fold perjury. He offers
various excuses, but ends by deciding to betray Valentine's love to
the Duke. He agrees to the Duke's suggestion that he should slander
Valentine to Silvia, though he admits that

> 'Tis an ill office for a gentleman,
> Especially against his very friend.                     (III.ii.40–1)

Before the end of the play one of the two gentlemen has violated not
merely the whole code of gentlemanly conduct with regard to love
and friendship but the basic laws of civilised behaviour.

One of the most skilful scenes in the play is the one where Silvia is
serenaded. The song in which Silvia is celebrated as 'holy, wise and
fair' picks up Proteus' confession that she is 'too fair, too true, too
holy' to be corrupted by his 'worthless gifts'. The musicians are
provided by Thurio, who is being deceived by Proteus, and they are
overheard by Julia, whom we see for the first time dressed as a
page. She hears Proteus swear that she is dead and she hears Silvia
scornfully reject his suit. Neither Silvia nor Proteus knows that Julia
is present; Thurio thinks that Proteus is pleading for him and not
for himself; and the Host, who falls asleep, does not know the
identity of the page, nor why he is so melancholy and so affected by
the music. The audience alone is in possession of all the facts.

# 4
# *Love's Labour's Lost*

It took a brilliant director, Tyrone Guthrie, to establish the fact that *Love's Labour's Lost* is still a viable and delightful comedy. John Dover Wilson confessed[30] that the 1936 production of the play at the Old Vic had revealed it as a first-rate comedy of

> the pattern kind—so full of fun, of *permanent* wit, of brilliant and entrancing situation, that you hardly noted the faded jesting and allusion as you sat spell-bound and drank it all in.

Johnson had remarked[31] that 'all the editors have concurred to censure' the play and that 'there are many passages mean, childish and vulgar, and some which ought not to have been exhibited . . . to a maiden queen'. The sensitive appreciation by Walter Pater in 1878 received little support.[32] Sir Edmund Chambers complained[33] that the reader wanders 'a disconcerted alien, through impenetrable memorials of vanished humour'; Harley Granville-Barker, in one of his early prefaces, described[34] it as 'a fashionable play now, by three hundred years, out of fashion'; and H. B. Charlton maintained[35] that it 'was deficient in plot and characterisation', the four courtiers resembling 'each other in a wooden conformity' and the ladies 'as empty and as uniform as their wooers'. Here, at least, Charlton's imperfect sympathies led him into palpable absurdity—for Berowne stands out from the other suitors no less than Rosaline does from the other ladies.

In the same year as the Guthrie production two books were published—*The School of Night* by M. C. Bradbrook and *A Study of 'Love's Labour's Lost'* by F. A. Yates—which throw a great deal of light on the background of the play. It may well be that Shakespeare was writing for a private audience and that the play contains personal satire which is unique in his work.[36] The difficulty is that the scholars disagree among themselves. The name Shakespeare is supposed to have given Ralegh, Chapman and Harriot, 'the school of night' may be based on a misprint. He appears to be replying to Chapman's lines[37]—

> No pen can anything eternal write
> That is not steeped in humour of the Night—

in Berowne's claim that

> Never durst poet touch a pen to write.
> Until his ink were tempered with Love's sighs.

But it is by no means certain that Boyet was intended as a portrait of Chapman. Ralegh, the enemy of Spain, has been identified with the Spaniard Armado, whose affaire with Jaquenetta has been thought to allude to Ralegh's liaison, and subsequent marriage, with Elizabeth Throckmorton.[38] More recently it has been argued that Armado is a portrait of Antonio Perez.[39] Holofernes has been identified as John Florio, teacher of Italian, author of conversation manuals, and compiler of a dictionary, as his strings of synonyms may suggest; but he has also been identified with Gabriel Harvey, the opponent of Thomas Nashe in the controversy that followed the death of Robert Greene. There are many other disagreements. We could, perhaps, explain the critical differences on the assumption that the text as we have it represents a revision for a revival, and that new topicalities were introduced without a complete elimination of the old ones. Ralegh's banishment from court following the pregnancy of Elizabeth Throckmorton would not be topical a few years later. By then Perez was in disgrace, so that Shakespeare added some of his characteristics—his poverty, his bombastic style, and his bisexual tastes. In the same way the Nashe–Harvey quarrel by 1597 was petering into boredom and Florio may then have been substituted for Harvey. There is, of course, plenty of evidence that the play underwent some revision.

I would, however, suggest an alternative explanation of the discrepancies. Perhaps the audience was not meant to see the characters in the play as portraits of actual people, but rather to be reminded here and there by a gesture, a turn of phrase, even an accent of more than one living person.[40]

In any case, the guying of Shakespeare's contemporaries is much less important than the satire of various kinds of literary affectation—in particular, the excessive use of some of the more artificial figures of rhetoric. In this connection it is important not to equate rhetoric with artificiality or insincerity. To an Elizabethan the word had no derogatory connotation: it meant merely the art of writing and speaking. It would be quite wrong to assume that Berowne's farewell to rhetoric was Shakespeare's own. He swears to abandon

> Taffeta phrases, silken terms precise,
> Three-pil'd hyperboles, spruce affectation,
> Figures pedantical

and to woo only in simple language, as Shakespeare in his sonnets contrasts his own true, plain words with the inflated language of his rivals. But to forswear rhetoric was itself a rhetorical device and Shakespeare continued to use most of the 150 figures of rhetoric to the end of his life. The ones he tended to avoid were those which would conflict with the impression he wished to convey that his characters used the very language of men.

It is obvious that Shakespeare was satirising the affectations of those who took an inordinate pride in their inartistic use of legitimate rhetorical devices, notably Holofernes and Armado. Holofernes is a pedant, but one who makes mistakes when he quotes Latin or Italian tags. He dismisses Berowne's charming sonnet as 'very unlearned, neither savouring of poetry, wit, nor invention' and himself perpetrates an alliterative monstrosity. As he tells his admirer, Nathaniel, 'I will something affect the letter for it argues facility':

> The preyful Princess pierced and pricked a pretty pleasing pricket.

The point of the poem depends on a ridiculous conceit—adding L to sore to make sorel. Even more absurd than the poem is Holofernes's complacent conviction, overlaid with mock modesty, that he is a genius.

> This is a gift that I have, simple, simple: a foolish extravagant spirit, full of forms, figures, shapes, objects, ideas, apprehensions, motions, revolutions. These are begot in the ventricle of memory, nourish'd in the womb of pia mater, and delivered upon the mellowing of occasion. But the gift is good in those in whom it is acute, and I am thankful for it.          (IV.ii.63–9)

Holofernes's main stylistic quirk, when he is speaking rather than composing is to pour out a string of synonyms, a kind of mad Roget compiling a thesaurus:

Most barbarous intimation! yet a kind of insinuation, as it
were, in via, in way, of explication; facere, as it were,
replication, or rather, ostentare, to show, as it were, his
inclination, after his undressed, unpolished, uneducated,
unpruned, untrained, or rather, unlettered, or ratherest,
unconfirmed fashion, to insert again my *haud credo* for a
deer.                                                      (IV.ii.12–17)

The other linguistic eccentric is Armado, whose affected style is
made more ludicrous by the fact that he is a foreigner. Every one of
the rhetorical devices used in his letter to Jaquenetta can be
paralleled in the serious work of great writers, but they are
rendered absurd both by their excessive accumulation and also by
the fact that the recipient is illiterate.

By heaven, that thou art fair is most infallible; true that thou
art beauteous; truth itself that thou art lovely. More fairer than
fair, beautiful than beauteous, truer than truth itself, have
commiseration on thy heroical vassal. The magnanimous and
illustrate King Cophetua set eye upon the pernicious and
indubitate beggar, Zenelophon; and he it was that might
rightly say: 'Veni, vidi, vici; which to annothanize in the
vulgar—O base and obscure vulgar!—videlicet, he came, saw,
and overcame. He came, one; saw, two; overcame, three. Who
came? the king. Why did he come?—to see. Why did he
see?—to overcome. To whom came he?—to the beggar. What
saw he?—the beggar. Who overcame he?—the beggar. The
conclusion is victory; on whose side?—the king's. (IV.i.60–72)

Armado's conversational style is equally affected, as in his
exchanges with Moth, and even his protest at the behaviour of the
audience when he plays Hector, moving as it is, is absurd in its
vocabulary. 'Sweet' is his favourite epithet, used by him two dozen
times in the course of the play, and 'war-man' is his synonym for
'warrior':

The sweet war-man is dead and rotten; sweet chucks, beat not
the bones of the buried; when he breathed, he was a man.
                                                          (V.ii.652–3)

At this point the lords, thinking the badness of the pageant will
cover up their own humiliation, mock the actors unmercifully; and,

although the theatre audience laughs with the stage audience at the antics of Holofernes and Armado, they may also feel that, compared with the courtesy of Theseus to the absurdities of Quince's production, the lords in *Love's Labour's Lost* are lacking in manners. Indeed, the satire in the play is directed not merely against the two-dimensional figures of the underplot, but also against Ferdinand and his attendant lords.

Their initial vow to devote themselves to study and contemplation, to abstinence and celibacy, is motivated mainly by pride and a determination to be different. Berowne realises from the start that they will be forsworn 'upon necessity', as the arrival of the Princess and her entourage soon proves; the men cannot avoid seeing women, and within a few minutes they are ensnared.

The climax of the play is the masterly scene where three of the men come on in turn to read aloud the love-poems they have written to their mistresses, overlooked by Berowne who has climbed a tree on the approach of the first of the lovers. The three men hide in turn; and then Longaville exposes Dumain, the King exposes Dumain, and Berowne descends to expose the hypocrisy of the King. But the audience, knowing that Berowne, too, has fallen in love, aware that Armado's letter to Jaquenetta has been delivered by mistake to Rosaline, and aware that Jaquenetta is coming with Costard to deliver Berowne's poem to the King, waits for the turning of the tables. The preparation for this scene goes back some 400 lines, when Armado and Berowne give their letters to the illiterate Costard, who is given a guerdon and a remuneration for his services; the contents of both letters are revealed before the scene begins; and the hypocrisy of all four lovers is displayed with splendid verve. Berowne is then mocked for his bad taste in falling in love with a dark lady, Rosaline; and these attacks and Berowne's defence are appropriately in quatrains and couplets, reminding us of some of Shakespeare's own sonnets. (Berowne, on first falling in love, had credited Rosaline with the Dark Lady's promiscuity:

> A whitely wanton with a velvet brow,
> With two pitch balls stuck in her face for eyes;
> Ay, and, by heaven, one that will do the deed,
> Though Argus were her eunuch and her guard.)

The fact that he is enamoured of a woman he despises is one of the reasons why he is given the hardest penance at the end of the play.

Meanwhile, as the most articulate, as well as the most intelligent of the quartet of lovers, he is chosen to provide a salve for perjury. This speech, the finest poetry in the play, was revised by Shakespeare, as we can tell from the twenty-four lines which were included by accident in the first extant quarto and also in the First Folio. (These lines have been used in support of a theory that the play was radically revised but Shakespeare may well have written in the revised version in his original manuscript, perhaps in rehearsal.)[41] One line from the draft, however, throws light on the error of the King and his courtiers in establishing their little academe—

Learning is but an adjunct to ourself.

At the beginning of the play they regarded the acquisition of learning as a means of self-glorification, as their scorn of the vulgar, echoed by Holofernes and Armado, makes clear. Learning, apart from that, was an end in itself. It was not even what Milton scornfully described as 'a poor regardless unprofitable sin of curiosity' but the more basic sin of pride.

Berowne's apologia, and indeed the whole movement of the play, is a vindication of the educative powers of love. Perhaps, as critics have surmised, Shakespeare was supporting the Petrarchans against their opponents, the villainists against the academics.[42]

Berowne argues that the 'fiery numbers' of the poems they have written are a direct result of 'the prompting eyes/Of beauty's tutors'. Love

gives to every power a double power,
Above their functions and their offices,

enabling the lover to see, hear, feel and taste more intensely than before:

From women's eyes this doctrine I derive,
They sparkle still the right Promethean fire;
They are the books, the arts, the academes,
That show, contain, and nourish all the world.
                                (IV.iii.318–19, 327–8, 346–9)

The last line of the speech—

Who can sever love from charity?—

has been thought[43] to allude to the controversy about how best to translate *agape* in 1 Corinthians xiii. At least there is a daring identification of the two kinds of love; and this should warn us not to regard Berowne's eloquent defence as the central meaning of the play. It is (as he and his fellows recognise) special pleading, which the last scene of the play puts into perspective.

The men are tricked by the women's disguises into an inadvertent breach of faith, but, as Parolles observes, 'Who cannot be crush'd with a plot?' They can be mocked, but not seriously blamed, for this second 'perjury'. In their rudeness to the amateur performers in the pageant, they arouse an ambivalent reaction in the theatre audience—although they appear as much more intelligent than Holofernes and his fellows, they also show themselves to be deplorably lacking in courtesy to their social inferiors. They deserve Holofernes's rebuke:

> This is not generous, not gentle, not humble.

Nor can Berowne's instigation of Costard to accuse Armado publicly of making Jaquenetta pregnant be regarded as harmless fun, especially as Costard seems more likely to be the father of her offspring. Armado has not progressed beyond the verbal stage of wooing and Costard has admitted earlier that he has been 'taken' with Jaquenetta.

The entrance of Marcade, dressed in black, to announce the death of the Princess's father, transforms the tone of the last two hundred lines of the play. As Berowne says, 'The scene begins to cloud'. The Princess rightly says that they have not treated the wooing as anything more than 'pleasant jest and courtesy' and the time is too short for them

> To make a world-without-end bargain in.

The four men are given penances to test the genuineness of their love and cure them of their affectations, just as Armado has agreed to a three-year apprenticeship as a ploughman for love of Jaquenetta. The death of her father and her accession to the throne lend a new dignity and seriousness to the Princess; and Rosaline, who had praised Berowne's 'becoming mirth' and his 'sweet and voluble' discourse, now complains of his 'mocks', his 'wounding flouts' and his 'gibing spirit'. As several critics have noted, the play as a whole is a plea for good sense and balance, for the shedding of linguistic affectations and other forms of pride, and for a return to

natural forms of speech and behaviour. That is why the play ends
with the two songs of spring and winter, presented by the cuckoo
and the owl and, most implausibly, composed by Holofernes and
Sir Nathaniel. Compared with the love poems of the four aristocrats, the songs are appropriately down to earth. The spring song
reminds us of cuckoldry and the winter song is full of realistic
touches: the 'blood is nipp'd and ways be foul', there is loud
coughing in church, 'Marian's nose looks red and raw', and Joan
the kitchen-maid is 'greasy'. The play ends, as Armado says, with
the songs of Apollo. Life, shadowed by mortality, and dominated
by the rhythm of the seasons, makes us see the earlier follies of the
characters in a true perspective.

Compared with the previous comedies, *Love's Labour's Lost* has
a comparatively simple plot. It depends for its effect not on intrigue
but on language and character. Shakespeare creates more effectively than before a poetical atmosphere. As Pater puts it,

> the unity of the play is not so much the unity of a drama as that
> of a series of pictorial groups, in which the same figures
> reappear, in different combinations but on the same back-
> ground.

In some ways the play is reminiscent of Lyly, in others of the
*commedia dell'arte*; but perhaps the general tone of the main scenes
of the play is closest to Castiglione's *The Book of the Courtier*.

# 5
# *A Midsummer Night's Dream*

Professor T. M. Parrott, who was apparently unlucky in his
theatrical experiences, declared[44] that *A Midsummer Night's
Dream* was always a failure on the stage.[45] Apart from the tendency
to overload it with scenic effects, Mendelssohn and ballet, there
have certainly been some disastrous productions. One remembers a
Hollywood film of revolting vulgarity; a Puck played by a woman;
the Drury Lane production with an all-star cast, in which Edith
Evans's words in Helena's first soliloquy were drowned by the
noise of shifting scenery; a production at Stratford-upon-Avon
when Vanessa Redgrave, a glorious Rosalind, was made to play

Helena as a gawky schoolgirl; and another production at Stratford
when Mary Ure as Titania was made to mispronounce 'dewberries'
to rhyme with 'thighs', so as to demonstrate the feebleness of
Shakespeare's rhymed verse.

The last aberration was apparently caused by a misunderstand-
ing of what Walter de la Mare and John Dover Wilson had written
of some couplets in the play, but not, of course, of Titania's lovely
verses. De la Mare quoted some weak couplets from III.ii and
remarked that 'they have uncommonly little sense'. He contrasted
some good lines in the play with these and asked[46]

> Can we recall any other play written at one time and by one
> author that reveals discords in style and inequalities of mere
> intelligence so extreme? Did ever a fine poet indeed—let alone
> that pre-eminent prince of poets, Shakespeare—when once his
> imagination and gift of expression had come of age, thus
> indulge, now in excellent, and now in dull and characterless
> verse?

Whereas Dover Wilson had originally argued[47] that the weak lines
had been written some years earlier than the good ones—a theory
supported by mislineation in the quarto text at the beginning of
Act V—de la Mare went further and suggested that two authors
were responsible.[48]

> Surely, to accept as Shakespeare's, at any age, what is probably
> not merely scamped or heedless but poverty-stricken verse—
> verse that advertises a dull and stubborn pen—is more extrava-
> gant than to discredit its being his at all.

Dover Wilson delightedly accepted[49] this modification of his own
theory. And yet, as Lascelles Abercrombie argued,[50] though not
about this particular question:

> If Shakespeare did take over other people's work and convert it
> to his own use, he thereby made himself responsible for it: he
> made it his, and as his we may justly criticize it.

It is perfectly true that some passages in the play are more
'mature' than others and if we accept Abercrombie's view, as I think
we must, that Shakespeare made himself responsible for what he
included, whether his own or another's, we are driven to ask what
justification there can be for some of the lines derided by Walter de

la Mare. As Shakespeare tinkered with Theseus's speech on the lunatic, the lover and the poet, he presumably had the opportunity between 1594 and 1600 of eliminating the passages which are so obviously feeble. Possibly the scenes which read so badly had proved effective on the stage. As in parts of *Romeo and Juliet*, Shakespeare uses certain rhetorical devices to distance the characters, so that we regard them sympathetically but amusedly:

| | |
|---|---|
| *Lys.* | Ay me! for aught that I could ever read, |
| | Could ever hear by tale or history, |
| | The course of true love never did run smooth; |
| | But either it was different in blood— |
| *Herm.* | O cross too high to be enthrall'd to low. |
| *Lys.* | Or else misgraffed in respect of years— |
| *Herm.* | O spite! too old to be engag'd to young. |
| *Lys.* | Or else it stood upon the choice of friends— |
| *Herm.* | O hell! to choose love by another's eyes. |

(I.i.132–40)

This ritualistic stichomythia, with Hermia apparently determined to get a line in edgeways, prevents the audience from treating the situation tragically. Later in the scene, Shakespeare adds rhyme to the stichomythia:

| | |
|---|---|
| *Herm.* | I frown upon him, yet he loves me still. |
| *Hel.* | O that your frowns would teach my smiles such skill. |
| *Herm.* | I give him curses, yet he gives me love. |
| *Hel.* | O that my prayers could such affection move! |

Most of the scenes between the earthly lovers, from Hermia's vow in the first scene to their charming by Puck at the end of Act III are in rhymed verse. It is not difficult to see why. The behaviour of the lovers is completely irrational; they change partners, as in a dance; and the effect is almost like that of a comic opera. We are prevented from becoming too much involved in their romantic troubles by the artificiality of the form. It is in the light of this that one should consider the passages condemned by Walter de la Mare and John Dover Wilson. The passages concerned (III.ii.41–87, 122–94) are spoken after Puck has begun to anoint the eyes of the lovers. The awkward rhyming suggests that they are irrational and bewildered, puppets manipulated by Puck:

> Do not say so, Lysander; say not so.
> What though he love your Hermia? Lord, what though? . . .
> Things growing are not ripe until their season;
> So I, being young, till now ripe not to reason . . .
> Alack, where are you? Speak, an if you hear;
> Speak, of all loves! I swoon almost with fear.
> No? Then I well perceive you are not nigh,
> Either death or you I'll find immediately.
>
> (II.ii.108–9, 117–18, 153–6)

What I am suggesting is not that Shakespeare wrote badly by design, but that, when he returned to the play after the lapse of a year or two, he saw how the crudity of the rhymed verse could be turned to good account. The effectiveness of Quince's play, as of course Shakespeare knew, depended on its badness, something so badly written and badly performed that it became riotously funny. It may have been this that made Shakespeare realise that the bad rhyming of the lovers could add to the fun.

I have mentioned the irrationality of the four young lovers; and it is often assumed that the marriage of Theseus and Hippolyta—'the everlasting bond of fellowship'—is a more stable and mature relationship. Yet we should remember that Theseus had defeated his Amazonian bride in battle, and that, as Oberon enquires of Titania:

> Didst thou not lead him through the glimmering night
> From Perigouna, whom he ravished,
> And make him with fair Ægles break his faith,
> With Ariadne and Antiopa?

Although we laugh at the inconstancy of the four young lovers, we are meant to suppose that they, like Theseus and Hippolyta, marry and live happily ever after. The lovers have, of course, behaved irrationally before they are anointed with Puck's magic juice. Demetrius had turned from Helena, who returned his love, to pursue Hermia who loves another man. So, at the beginning of the play, Helena loves Demetrius, who loves Hermia, who loves Lysander. Both men love Hermia and Helena is left in the cold. In the middle of the play, both men love Helena, and Hermia is left in the cold. At the end of the play, Jack has Jill. But in the middle acts both men behave irrationally:

> Not Hermia but Helena I love:
> Who will not change a raven for a dove?
> The will of man is by his reason swayed,
> And reason says you are the worthier maid.
> Things growing are not ripe until their season:
> So I, being young, till now ripe not to reason;
> And touching now the point of human skill,
> Reason becomes the marshal to my will,
> And leads me to your eyes.                    (II.ii.113–21)

He is not swayed by reason; and Berowne's argument that true knowledge is obtained from women's eyes is here treated as absurd. Nor are the immortals any more rational. Titania has separated from Oberon on account of his infidelity and jealousy. Oberon is jealous of her love for Theseus and she in her turn is jealous of his love for Hippolyta. He wishes for her Indian Boy and, being denied, makes her fall in love with an ass. Titania's ear becomes enamoured by Bottom's braying, her eye is enthralled by his form, while all the time she imagines she is in love with his 'fair virtue'. Bottom himself comments that 'reason and love keep little company together nowadays'. In other words, Shakespeare presents Titania's infatuation—Beauty's love for the Beast—as only an extreme example of love's irrationality. Another example—wryly commenting on the fate of Romeo and Juliet—is afforded by the alacrity in suicide displayed by Pyramus and Thisbe. 'Lord, what fools these mortals be!' has a wider application than Puck intended.

The final comment is that of Theseus. When Hippolyta mentions the strangeness of the lovers' account of the happenings in the wood, Theseus replies

> More strange than true. I never may believe
> These antique fables, nor these fairy toys.
> Lovers and madmen have such seething brains,
> Such shaping fantasies, that apprehend
> More than cool reason ever comprehends.
> The lunatic, the lover, and the poet
> Are of imagination all compact.
> One sees more devils than vast hell can hold,
> That is the madman. The lover, all as frantic,
> Sees Helen's beauty in a brow of Egypt.
> The poet's eye, in a fine frenzy rolling,

> Doth glance from heaven to earth, from earth to heaven;
> And as imagination bodies forth
> The forms of things unknown, the poet's pen
> Turns them to shapes, and gives to airy nothing
> A local habitation and a name.
> Such tricks hath strong imagination
> That, if it would but apprehend some joy,
> It comprehends some bringer of that joy;
> Or in the night, imagining some fear,
> How easy is a bush supposed a bear?               (V.i.2–22)

Shakespeare's original intention was to have Theseus compare only the lover and the lunatic. Then he inserted the lines about the poet, probably in the margin. Theseus satirically compares poets to lunatics and equally frantic lovers. The 'fine frenzy' and the rolling eye recall the divine fury of which critics from Plato to Sidney had spoken. The poet's creations, resulting from imagination, have no more connection with the real world than the delusions of the madman and the lover. Theseus, as Blake pointed out,[51] is not Shakespeare's mouthpiece. He is, in fact, doing what Sidney at the end of his *Apology* urged people not to do: 'no more to scorn the sacred mysteries of poesy; no more to laugh at the name of poets, as though they were next inheritors to fools; no more to jest at the reverend title of a rhymer'. He is really a Philistine. Shakespeare, as we know from the sonnets, did not see Helen's beauty in a brow of Egypt; and, as Hippolyta properly points out, the strange story told by the lovers happens to be true:

> All the story of the night told over,
> And all their minds transfigur'd so together,
> More witnesseth than fancy's images,
> And grows to something of great constancy;
> But, howsoever, strange and admirable.        (V.i.23–7)

There is, perhaps, an additional irony. In his previous plays—historical, comical, tragical—Shakespeare had kept reasonably close to real life. The audience had been made to swallow plenty of improbable fictions, such as the two pairs of identical twins wearing identical clothes in *The Comedy of Errors*—but there had been no absolute impossibilities. When Mercutio discourses on Queen Mab, no one imagines that his account is more than fantasy.

But in *A Midsummer Night's Dream* Shakespeare took a leaf out of
Mercutio's book and exhibited fairies on the stage, fairies quite
different from those in which some of his audience believed, and
fairies who were sometimes large enough to embrace a donkey, and
sometimes small enough to be called Moth and Mustardseed. The
audience, moreover, is asked to accept the magical effects of
Oberon's juice, the 'translation' of Bottom, and side by side with
such things, and throwing them into relief, the earthy absurdity of
the amateur actors. Shakespeare relies only on his poetry to create
the wood near Athens and the strange things that happen under the
moon.[52] He 'gives to airy nothing A local habitation and a name'.
What Theseus intends as a gibe against poetry is a precise account
of Shakespeare's method in this play; and, of course, the poet who
creates

> Forms more real than living man,
> Nurslings of immortality,

may yet be making a valid comment on real life. Although the lover
may find his Rosalind is a Cressida and the poet may falsify or
sentimentalise reality, if his imagination is properly disciplined, the
forms he creates will directly (as with Hamlet) or indirectly (as with
Ariel) be a true reflection of reality.

The sense of reality, of truth to life beneath the fantasy, is
conveyed by the complex structure of the play—more complex
than that of any of the previous comedies. In this respect Shakespeare learnt from two of his immediate predecessors, Greene and
Lyly. The framework is provided by the marriage of Theseus and
Hippolyta. The events of the play take place in the days immediately before the marriage; the mechanicals are rehearsing a play for
the wedding festivities; Oberon and Titania have come to bless the
married couple, which they cannot do till they themselves are
reunited; and, finally, there are the four young lovers, whose
emotional entanglements are straightened out in time for them to
be married at the same time as Theseus and Hippolyta. The plots
are welded together primarily by the Oberon–Titania plot; and it is
through the fairies that the play is linked with the world of the
audience. Oberon's praise of the 'fair vestal, throned by the west' is
one such link. Another is the final blessing of the three couples in
the play which, almost certainly, applied at the first performance to
a couple in the audience. A third link is provided by the suggestion

that the atrociously bad summer has been caused by the quarrels between Oberon and Titania.

> the green corn
> Hath rotted ere his youth attain'd a beard;
> The fold stands empty in the drowned field,
> And crows are fatted with the murrion flock;
> The nine men's morris is filled up with mud,
> And the quaint mazes in the wanton green
> For lack of tread are undistinguishable.                    (II.i.94–100)

The audience is able to accept the fairies and their supernatural powers largely, of course, because of the supernatural quality of the poetry, but partly through the mediation of Peter Quince and his troupe. Bottom's misadventures, his unruffled behaviour when Titania makes advances to him, and the splendid soliloquy—confusing the Pauline words[53]—when he recovers his human shape convince us in the theatre of the truth of the strange events we have witnessed:

> I have had a most rare vision. I have had a dream, past the wit of man to say what dream it was. Man is but an ass if he go about to expound this dream. Methought I was—there is no man can tell what. Methought I had—but man is but a patched fool, if he will offer to say what methought I had. The eye of man hath not heard, the ear of man hath not seen, man's hand is not able to taste, his tongue to conceive, nor his heart to report, what my dream was. I will get Peter Quince to write a ballad of this dream. It shall be called 'Bottom's Dream' because it hath no bottom.                     (IV.i.202ff.)

This soliloquy, the remarks of the lovers when they awaken, Hippolyta's comments on their story, Theseus's remarks on the actors as 'shadows', and Puck's epilogue which begins 'If we shadows have offended' may lead us to have disturbing thoughts about the nature of reality and of human life as an insubstantial pageant. At the end of the play we feel like Demetrius:

> Are you sure
> That we are awake? It seems to me
> That yet we sleep, we dream.                                (IV.i.189–91)

But the play is primarily a critique of love: the irrationality of adolescent passion, the function of imagination as an ingredient of love, and the necessity of consecration. As John Russell Brown points out,[54] our wavering acceptance of the illusion of drama is an image of accepting the truth of love.[55]

# III · MATURITY

The plays discussed in this chapter—with the exception of that splendid *pièce d'occasion, The Merry Wives of Windsor*—represent the fine flowering of Shakespearian comedy, and, indeed, of any comedy. Less satiric than Jonson or Molière, less continuously witty than Congreve, less cerebral than Shaw, less funny than many lesser writers, Shakespeare presents us with a variety of lively and attractive characters, with whom audiences become friends, and he invests them with the riches of his poetry. One has only to compare *Twelfth Night* with the Italian prose comedies which it most resembles, or *As You Like It* with *Rosalynde*, or the casket story with what Shakespeare makes of it, to see what a difference this makes—not just the verse, of course, but the transformation afforded by the poetic imagination.

The plays are all different, but one can isolate certain features they have in common. Songs are used, suggested perhaps by Lyly's practice, but used not merely as interludes. In *As You Like It*, for example, the songs are an essential means of creating the atmosphere of the greenwood; and in *Twelfth Night* the songs of Feste are used variously to provide the *carpe diem* attitude of the revellers, to satirise Orsino's love-melancholy so delicately that the victim remains unaware of it, and to end the play with a song on the vanity of human wishes. Touchstone and Feste were both played by Robert Armin and it is interesting that Touchstone is not given any of the songs in *As You Like It*. It is usually thought that Kemp's leaving the Lord Chamberlain's Company and Armin's joining it accounts for the difference between Dogberry and Feste.

The plays have incidental satire but they are primarily concerned with love; with the obstacles to happiness, and with the final attainment of happiness in marriage. *Much Ado*, despite the song's warning that men are deceivers ever, ends with two marriages—with three if Margaret is foolish enough to marry Borachio; *The Merchant of Venice* and *Twelfth Night* with three, and *As You Like It* with four. Marriage is the right true end of love;

the heroines are virgins and they remain so until after marriage. Shakespeare does not deal with adulteries—innocent or otherwise—or with marital disharmony. *The Merry Wives of Windsor* is an exception to this generalisation; but Ford's jealousy is comic, the chastity of the wives impregnable, and Falstaff's intentions more mercenary than amorous. Even this play ends with one marriage—of sweet Anne Page. The couples in the plays—except for Touchstone and his incongruous bride—are well matched, and we are led to assume that they will be happy.

Not that the plays end with happiness for all, but in performance we do not worry about the fate of the forsaken William, or of Sir Andrew, a sadder, poorer and not much wiser man, or of Feste who cheers others but cannot cheer himself. Antonio's life is saved by Portia, but it is doubtful whether the gaining of her as a friend will quite compensate him for his partial loss of Bassanio. The other Antonio is more obviously frustrated.

Apart from these characters who are tacitly excluded from the general harmony, there are in these plays evil men who threaten the comic resolution, and outsiders who cannot fit into Arden or Illyria. Shylock and Don John are evil, although the Jew arouses our sympathy in a way which Elizabethans would hardly have understood. Both *The Merchant of Venice* and *Much Ado about Nothing* can be played as tragi-comedies. Jaques has lost the capacity to engage in real relationships with other people because of his cynicism; and Malvolio's self-love which turns to hatred drives him from his stewardship in Illyria. Oliver and Frederick who begin as villains, have comic, and not wholly credible, fifth-act repentances.

All the plays have multiple plots, the sub-plots being structurally, and in most cases thematically, related to the main plots. Structurally, Antonio enters into his bond with Shylock to enable Bassanio to woo Portia in proper style, and Portia repays the debt by appearing at the trial. Shylock's vindictiveness is exacerbated by Jessica's elopement with a Christian. Thematically the plots are linked by the contrast between personal and commercial values. Claudio falls out of love, and Benedick into love, by a misinterpretation of what they see and hear, and Beatrice makes Benedick choose between love and friendship. Malvolio's self-love (which makes him a victim of Maria's plot), Orsino's sentimental love-melancholy, and Olivia's sentimental mourning for her brother are three of the aberrations held up for our inspection in *Twelfth Night*.

In each of these plays the heroine is disguised—Portia as the learned doctor, Rosalind as Ganymede, Hero as her cousin, Viola as Cesario and Anne Page so that only her lover is able to pick her out—not to mention the disguisings of Nerissa and Jessica ('in the lovely garnish of a boy'), of Margaret and Celia, of Ford as Brook, of Falstaff as Mother Prat, of Feste as Sir Topas. Disguise is, indeed, one of Shakespeare's favourite dramatic devices, used as early as *The Taming of the Shrew* and *The Two Gentlemen of Verona*, and as late as *The Tempest* with Ariel's multiple roles. Shakespeare never uses disguise to deceive the audience, but rather to extract irony from the contrast between their knowledge and the characters' ignorance.

The disguise of women as men—and in the Induction to *The Taming of the Shrew* of a boy as a woman—was perhaps initially suggested by the fact that there were no actresses on the Elizabethan stage. But it would be quite wrong to imagine that Shakespeare used this kind of disguise to cover up the clumsiness of male impersonators—that it would be easier for a man to play Cesario and Ganymede than Viola and Rosalind. The actor in *Twelfth Night* had the double task of pretending to be a woman pretending to be a man; and in *As You Like It* the triple task of a man pretending to be Rosalind, pretending to be Ganymede, pretending (for Orlando's edification) to be Rosalind.

*The Merry Wives of Windsor* is unlike the other four comedies and is the only one of all Shakespeare's comedies with an English setting, and even that is distanced in time. Just as Latin comedies had Athenian settings, so Shakespeare chose Italy or France or Illyria for his, and in so doing escaped some of the problems of verisimilitude, even if he fell into geographical blunders. This strategy, which gave him freedom to manoeuvre, was suggested by the Italian novels he frequently used; and although the sources of *As You Like It* and *Twelfth Night* were English tales, they had foreign settings; and the latter appears to exhibit some knowledge of one or more Italian plays.

It is worth noting that many of Jonson's comedies (*The Alchemist, Bartholemew Fair, Epicoene*) are set in London and that *Every Man in his Humour*, originally written with Italian names and settings, was afterwards refurbished as a London comedy. This

better suited Jonson's unromantic and satirical comedy. Shakespeare's comedies of love were more suited to France and Italy
because such settings freed him from the trammels of naturalism.


# 6
## *The Merchant of Venice*

In some ways *The Merchant of Venice* appears to be the most
straightforward of Shakespeare's plays, a kind of fairy story, with a
beautiful princess, a handsome suitor and an ogre. It is often the
first play to be studied in British schools; and perhaps the children's
unsophisticated reaction to the play is more sensible than that of the
many critics who have tried to impose their own perverse interpretations on it—interpretations which have in turn imposed on
theatrical directors and on the general reader also. A brief account
of some of these may help us to regain a saner perspective on the play.

First, it is suggested that Shakespeare was guilty of anti-semitism,
as deplorable as that displayed in the tale of Chaucer's Prioress.
This was the view of the New York School Board, naturally
sensitive to the large Jewish population in the city, when it banned
the play from all schools under its jurisdiction. It is the view, too, of
a recent pamphlet by an American scholar[1] who argues that till the
memory of the concentration camps has faded, the play ought not
to be performed. One may sympathise with this attitude; but the
charge that Shakespeare was anti-semitic is nevertheless absurd. It
is doubtful whether he had ever seen Jews, though some who had
been baptised apparently practised their own religion in secret. In
any case, Shylock is condemned neither for his faith nor his blood,
but because he is a usurer, who attempts to murder Antonio. There
were apparently no Jewish usurers in Elizabethan London: the
money-lenders were mostly Puritans, and it has been argued by
Siegel[2] and other critics that the Puritans were Shakespeare's real
target. Lorenzo marries Jessica and no one thinks the worse of him.
This is very different from recent racial theories: a modern Jessica
and her children would have ended their lives in Belsen or
Auschwitz.

1. Superior figures refer to notes at the end of the book (p. 205).

It is true that the play was written soon after the execution of Dr Lopez, the Portuguese doctor who was accused of attempting to poison Queen Elizabeth. Lopez was a Jew by descent, but he was a Christian convert. He was probably innocent, but the case did reactivate the anti-semitism which was endemic in Europe during the middle ages. Henslowe put on a revival of Marlowe's *The Jew of Malta*, with its villainous hero, and Shakespeare may have been asked to exploit the popular feelings. He may even (as Dover Wilson suggested)[3] have been asked by his patron to write an anti-Jewish play, since Southampton's friend, Essex, was the main advocate of Lopez's guilt. Faced with the threat of torture, Lopez confessed. In June 1594 he was dragged to Tyburn on a hurdle, prevented by the brutal mob from making a dying speech, and then castrated, disembowelled and quartered while still alive. *The Jew of Malta* was performed during the week of Lopez's execution. The melodramatic Barabas who poisons Christians for fun and ends up in the boiling cauldron prepared for others was naturally a popular entertainment at this time and (in a sense) *The Merchant of Venice* can be regarded as a rival show. Shakespeare seems to have based it on an old play entitled *The Jew* which according to Stephen Gosson represented 'the greediness or worldly choosers and bloody minds of usurers'. It has been assumed from this reference, by many critics, that the pound of flesh plot was already combined with that of the caskets; but others have pointed out that neither Morocco nor Arragon can be properly regarded as greedy.[4]

On the surface, then, *The Merchant of Venice*, with its pun on Lopez and *lupus*—

Thy currish spirit was governed by a wolf—

might seem to be the kind of propaganda required by the Essex faction. But through the mouth of Portia Shakespeare hinted that people on the rack confess to crimes they have not committed:

I fear you speak upon the rack,
Where men enforced do speak anything.

At about the same time, Shakespeare inserted a scene in the play of *Sir Thomas More* and, as Dover Wilson suggested,[5] he was here able to state more openly what he thought of racial intolerance. More tells the mob who are rioting against foreigners:

> Grant them removed and grant that this your noise
> Hath chid down all the majesty of England,
> Imagine that you see the wretched strangers
> Their babies at their backs, with their poor luggage
> Plodding to the ports and coasts for transportation
> And that you sit as kings in your desires,
> Authority quite silenced by your brawl
> And you in ruff of your opinions clothed
> What had you got? I'll tell you: you had taught
> How insolence and strong hand should prevail,
> How order should be quelled, and by this pattern
> Not one of you should live an aged man:
> For other ruffians as their fancies wrought
> With self same hand, self-reasons and self-right
> Would shark on you, and men like ravenous fishes
> Would feed on one another.                              (72–87)

He goes on to tell them that if they themselves were to be banished
and were to seek sanctuary on the continent, they would deserve to
be treated in the same way as they were proposing to treat the aliens
in London:

> Would you be pleased
> To find a nation of such barbarous temper
> That breaking out in hideous violence
> Would not afford you an abode on earth;
> Whet their detested knives against your throats,
> Spurn you like dogs, and like as if that God
> Owned not nor made not you, nor that the elements
> Were not all appropriate to your comforts
> But chartered unto them, what would you think
> To be thus used? This is the strangers' case
> And this your mountainish inhumanity.                  (130–40)

The phrase 'spurn you like dogs' recalls Antonio's treatment of
Shylock:

> You spurned me such a day,
> Another time you called me dog.

Shakespeare (it is fairly obvious) was not anti-semitic and his views
on immigrants are more humane than those of most people today.
    The second aberration of criticism is the exact opposite of the

first. It is assumed that Shylock is the tragic hero of the play. Heine thought[6] that Shakespeare was far in advance of his age in his realisation that Shylock's crimes were the result of the intolerable wrongs he had suffered. Antonio spits upon Shylock's gaberdine and treats him as a dog. Shakespeare (it is argued) is condemning the Christians who indulge in racial prejudice. The Christians come as far short of their religious professions as the Jew does of his. Shylock is robbed by his daughter and he demands his pound of flesh only after he has been driven mad by the treatment he has received. This view of Shylock is encouraged both by the emancipation of the Jews and by the way the part is played by famous actors. Henry Irving, for example, said with regard to his own interpretation:[7]

> I look on Shylock as the type of a persecuted race, almost the only gentleman in the play and the most ill-used . . . Shylock was well-to-do . . . and there is nothing in his language, at any time, that indicates the snuffling usurer.

He introduced a scene where he knocks on his own door and waits for his daughter to open it, not knowing that she has eloped; and he aroused sympathy at the end of the trial scene on the words 'I am not well'.

This interpretation will hardly bear examination. The bargain with Antonio is not made in 'a merry sport' (as Irving himself admitted). Shylock gives away his real motives in his address to the audience when he sees Antonio approaching. He confesses that he hates him for his attitude to the Jews, for his condemnation of usury, and for his free loans which brought down the interest rates.

> If I can catch him once upon the hip,
> I will feed fat the ancient grudge I bear him.

Even the speech on the common humanity of Jew and Christian, splendid as it is, is often sentimentalised, for Shylock is using this common humanity not to encourage fair dealing but to justify revenge:

> Hath not a Jew eyes? Hath not a Jew hands? . . . fed with the same food, hurt with the same weapons, subject to the same diseases, healed by the same means, warmed and cooled by the

> same winter and summer as a Christian is? If you prick us, do
> we not bleed? If you tickle us, do we not laugh? If you poison
> us, do we not die? And if you wrong us, shall we not revenge?
> If we are like you in the rest, we will resemble you in
> that.                                                          (III.i.52ff.)

St John Ervine's sequel, *The Lady of Belmont,* in which after the
lapse of a few years, only Portia and Shylock have retained their
integrity, is an interesting play but it is not a valid interpretation of
Shakespeare's.

Leo Kirschbaum, himself a Jew, rightly pointed out[8] that the
Court is extraordinarily merciful to Shylock. His own actions have
landed him in a situation where all his lands and goods are liable to
confiscation, and his life is at the mercy of the state. First of all, the
Duke pardons him his life. Then instead of taking all his goods, he
declares that half the goods shall go to Antonio, as his intended
victim, the other half to the state. But, he adds, if he is humble, this
may be reduced to a fine. Portia, the exponent of mercy, then asks
Antonio 'What mercy can you render him?' Antonio, who has just
escaped a horrible death at Shylock's hands, urges the Duke to
remit the fine on the state's half of Shylock's goods. The other half,
the part which is Antonio's due, he proposes to keep in trust, not
for himself, but for Lorenzo and Jessica, on two conditions: first,
that Shylock shall make a will in favour of Lorenzo and Jessica: and
secondly that he be baptised as a Christian.

It is this last condition which has revolted an age less certain of
the validity of its faith. But to the Elizabethan Christian, it was the
only way by which Shylock, if at all, could escape eternal damnation. It was an additional act of mercy on Antonio's part, not a
piece of cruelty which negated the mercy he had previously shown.
Shylock, in the opinion of most of Shakespeare's audiences, must
have got off very lightly.

Shylock, then, is not the hero of the play. He is a villain. Stoll
thought the Elizabethans would regard him as a *comic* villain.[9] But
even though the character may be based on the Pantalone of the
*commedia dell'arte*, he is surely more tragic than comic, and
perhaps more a figure of melodrama than of tragedy. André Gide
was ill-advised to speak[10] of the frightful injustice inflicted on such
a villain, and to argue that to provide a really happy ending Shylock
ought to have been given his money back.

When one considers that before the expulsion of the Jews from England, they could not bequeath money to their heirs since it was confiscated by the Crown and that in their lifetime they were outrageously taxed, the comparative humanity of the Venetians is remarkable.

The third wrong line of approach to the play is that followed by Sir Arthur Quiller-Couch—or Q, as he called himself—in his introduction to the play.[11] He complains that Shakespeare blundered in not contrasting the goodness of the Christians with the badness of the Jew. Apart from Portia, the Christians are an unpleasant crowd. Lorenzo is a prodigal, Gratiano a fop and Bassanio a fortune-hunter who proposes to marry Portia so that he can repay Antonio's loans. In real life, Quiller-Couch asserted, he would not have chosen the leaden casket.

This interpretation is wrong whichever way we look at it. On the one hand, it would not be realistic to make all the Christians good and all the Jews bad. On the other hand, to treat all the characters in a romantic story of this kind as though they belonged to a modern psychological drama is absurd; and 'real life' is not the same as drama. This is one reason why productions in modern dress—such as the recent one at the National Theatre—are ill-advised. They encourage the audience to assume that the play is closer to realism than to fantasy and to ask the wrong sort of question. History, in any case, has altered our responses to any play containing Jewish characters.

It is obvious, then, that Bassanio is a spendthrift and that when he borrows money from his friend he stresses the fact that Portia is wealthy; but it is equally obvious that he is genuinely in love with Portia. To treat him as though he were a cold-blooded fortune-hunter—like the man who marries Isabel Archer in *The Portrait of a Lady*—is surely obtuse.

Then there are those critics who believe that Portia broke her oath to her father by letting Bassanio know which casket he should choose.[12] The other suitors choose without a musical accompaniment. While Bassanio is choosing, the song declares that Fancy—as opposed to true love—dies. This means that one should not judge by appearances, that one should realise that 'all that glitters is not gold'. It is argued by some that Portia went further and influenced Bassanio's thoughts subliminally:

> Tell me where is Fancy *bred*,
> Or in the heart or in the *head*,
> How begot, how nouri*shed*
>     Reply reply.
> It is engen*dred* in the eyes
> With gazing *fed*; and fancy dies
> In the cradle where it lies
> Let us all ring Fancy's knell;
> I'll begin it—Ding, Dong, bell.          (III.ii.63–71)

The five rhymes—*bred, head,* etc.—would suggest *lead* and hence the leaden casket; and the knell might remind Bassanio of a leaden coffin.

This theory, ingenious as it is, is not really credible. We must believe Portia when she swears that she will never be forsworn. J. Dover Wilson was surely right when he argued[13] that the song was Shakespeare's dramatic shorthand for informing the audience of Bassanio's silent thoughts which lead him to choose the right casket.

The next distortion worth recording is that of Mr G. Midgley,[14] who imagines that the secret of Antonio's melancholy at the beginning of the play, of his almost suicidal resignation at the trial, and of his isolation at Belmont is that he has a homosexual passion for Bassanio, and that he knows that marriage will bring his intimate friendship to an end. He has never told his love to Bassanio, but he comes near to admitting it in the trial scene where he calls himself a tainted wether of the flock, meetest for death, and seems glad to die for Bassanio's sake.

I have said this is a distortion, though there is some truth in it. Shakespeare's other Antonio in *Twelfth Night* 'adores' Sebastian, as he specifically confesses. What is understated in *The Merchant of Venice* is stated explicitly in the later play. But we need to remember that Elizabethan friendships were frequently passionate, though usually platonic; and to remember also that the main purpose of Antonio's melancholy is to prepare the audience for disaster. In the last scene he appears delighted at the return of his galleys, and he may realise that Portia is not the sort of woman to cut Bassanio off from his bachelor friends.

These approaches to the play all fail to a lesser or greater degree because they attempt to use the text as a sociological or psychological casebook instead of a poetic drama written four centuries ago in certain unrealistic conventions. But the interpretations I have outlined, however wrong they are, may nevertheless help us to get on the right lines. So also may the last two I wish to discuss, both Freudian.

Freud, a lifelong admirer of Shakespeare's plays (which he thought were written by someone else)[15] tried to explain anti-semitism not by economic jealousy or by the refusal of the Jews to assimilate themselves to the countries in which they lived—though these are both contributory factors—but by the fact that the peoples of Western Europe are unwilling converts to Christianity from Paganism, and they transfer their unconscious hatred of the Christian religion to the Judaism from which it sprung. This would account for the way the Christians in the play behave to the Jews. It has, moreover, been suggested that Antonio hates Shylock because he subconsciously realises that his profit-making trading ventures are not morally different from Shylock's usury. Elizabethan adven-turers in the sometimes piratical voyages to the New World hoped to obtain a profit of more than a hundred per cent. When Portia comes into the court, she asks 'Which is the merchant here and which the Jew?' It has been suggested by Harold Goddard that underlying her apparently superfluous question is an undertone of meaning.[16] The play, he says, was sometimes called *The Jew of Venice*. Shakespeare means us to be aware of the resemblance between the commercial morals of Shylock and Antonio.

The objection to such an interpretation is that the Churches condemned usury more than profiteering; and I can see no evidence in the text of the play that Antonio, even unconsciously, recognises his resemblance to Shylock, and still less that an Elizabethan would think along these lines.

Freud also has an interesting interpretation of the casket-scenes. He argues[17] from Bassanio's line—

Thy paleness moves me more than eloquence—

that gold and silver are symbolically loud, while lead is dumb. Dumbness is a well-known dream-symbol of death. A striking pallor is another such symbol, and the paleness of lead reminds us of death. The very fact that lead reminds Morocco of the grave makes him pass hurriedly to the other caskets. Freud therefore suggests that the caskets really represent three women and that the leaden casket represents the Goddess of Death:

Man rebelled against the recognition of the truth embodied in the myth and constructed a substitute in which the third of the sisters is not death but the fairest and most desirable of women ... Nor was this substitution in any way difficult: it was prepared for by an ancient ambivalence, it fulfilled itself along the lines of an ancient context which could at that time not long have been forgotten. The Goddess of Death, had once been identified with her ... The great Mother-Goddesses of the oriental peoples, however, all seem to have been founts of being and destroyers, goddesses of life and of fertility, and death-goddesses.

By means of this myth, man is able to pretend that he chooses death; he does not have it forced upon him against his will

Choice stands in the place of necessity, of destiny. Thus man overcomes death, which in thought he has acknowledged. No greater triumph of wish-fulfilment is conceivable. Just where in reality he obeys compulsion, he exercises choice; and that which he chooses is not a thing of horror, but the fairest and most desirable thing in life.

It is very improbable that Shakespeare intended this; and although the effectiveness of the casket-scenes, not on the plane of realism, but on the poetic plane, may be due to the fact that they link up with some such archetypal myth, this interpretation is extra-literary and extra-dramatic.[18]

It has been mentioned above that the pound of flesh plot may have been linked with the caskets plot in the hypothetical source play. Yet one modern director, Sir John Gielgud, in 1932, and again in 1938 when he himself played Shylock, presented the caskets story as fantasy and the bond story realistically. In fact, as Granville-Barker points out[19] in his preface, both plots are wildly improbable and there is some tension between the verisimilitude of the characters and the improbability of their actions. In real life, it need hardly be said, Antonio would not wager a pound of flesh with a known enemy; such a bond would not be legally enforceable in a civilized state—as Venice clearly is—and, if it were, Shylock would not be allowed to shed the blood necessarily involved. Nor, of course, would the court be quite so ignorant of the laws of Venice. The atmosphere of fantasy matches that of the caskets plot:

a father who imagined that a suitable husband could be obtained by such means would be regarded as insane. The element of fantasy needs to be stressed, not as a weakness, but as a defining characteristic.

It is true, as critics have pointed out,[20] that there is a contrast between the worlds of Venice and Belmont, the one being concerned with trade, usury and hatred, the other with leisure, love and music. Not that the worlds are completely separate: there is the music of the carnival in Venice, which Shylock characteristically dislikes, Lorenzo and Antonio, in their different ways, are in love, and Portia comes disguised to the city.

Shakespeare sacrificed plausibility, as a romantic and poetic dramatist is bound to do, for the sake of other things. On one level, he had to make his trial scene as exciting as possible: the danger to Antonio had to seem real and the tables had to be turned on Shylock at the last possible moment. This meant that Bellario had to be better acquainted with the Venetian laws than were those concerned with their administration. The confounding of Shylock by the quibble on shedding a drop of blood, when he could have been thwarted by the law against aliens seeking the life of a Venetian citizen, is more dramatic and more in accordance with poetic justice. For Shylock had demanded the letter of the law: he had refused three times the sum he had lent Antonio; he had refused to provide a surgeon; and he had refused Portia's eloquent plea for mercy. He had made it clear that he was motivated not by a desire for justice, but by revenge. He had demanded the letter, and he was appropriately defeated by the letter, of his bond. Love conquers hatred; mercy 'seasons' justice; in a sense the New Testament supersedes the Old.[21] This is one reason why the baffled usurer is appropriately a Jew, though it should be noted that Portia, in her speech on mercy, appeals to the common element in Judaism and Christianity—and, indeed, in all the major religions.

It is difficult to understand those critics who believe that Shylock was treated unfairly, and that all Portia's talk about mercy was humbug since the court shows no mercy to Shylock. In fact, as we have seen, he is treated very leniently. According to the letter of the law, both his life and goods were forfeit, but his life is spared and he is left with some of his fortune. His compulsory conversion to Christianity, so repugnant to our feelings, would have enabled him to escape an eternity of torture in hell.

The rings plot, which originates in the trial scene, is a means of making use of the disguises and of leaving a knot to be untied in the last act; but it is linked thematically as well with the pound of flesh plot, for both are concerned with pledges. If Bassanio and Gratiano kept their promises to their wives not to part with their rings, they would be guilty of ingratitude and discourtesy. Bassanio could not decently refuse when Antonio's appeal is added to Portia's request. We learn from this plot, as from the other, that the spirit is more important than the letter.

The caskets plot is also linked with the pound of flesh plot. The favoured suitor causes Antonio to sign the bond with Shylock, and his bride rescues Antonio in the trial-scene. Both plots, moreover, illustrate the falsity of money values. It has been calculated that there are some three hundred references to commerce and bargaining in the course of the play;[22] and as C. S. Lewis argued,[23] there is a contrast between 'the crimson and organic wealth' in Bassanio's veins, 'the medium of nobility and fecundity' and the 'cold, mineral wealth in Shylock's counting-house'. Bassanio instinctively avoids the caskets made of gold and silver.

But, as we have seen, there are some critics who suppose that the Bassanio Shakespeare depicts, the prodigal and fortune-hunter, would have chosen the golden casket. How could Portia's father suppose that only the true lover would choose the leaden casket? We have to leave out of consideration the kind of reasoning which might be adopted by cunning suitors, who would assume that Portia's portrait would be found in the least suitable casket, or, by a process of double bluff, in the golden one after all.

Portia's father assumed, we may suppose, that most suitors would be deterred by the hard conditions imposed. Those who took the risk of choosing set a high value on the prize, whether of Portia herself or of her fortune. But not all who took the risk would be worthy of Portia: some might be mainly interested in her fortune and some might be unsuitable in other ways, being proud, foolish or libertine. The caskets themselves and the inscriptions on them were designed to eliminate such suitors. In the terms of the story, the golden casket would be chosen by the immature man who could not distinguish between appearance and reality, who did not realise that 'all that glisters is not gold'. He may doubt whether he deserves Portia, so he will be deterred by the inscription on the silver casket; but he is likely to be attracted by the inscription on the gold casket—'Who chooseth me shall gain what many men desire'—and repelled by the idea that Portia's portrait is contained in the leaden casket, which reminds him of a coffin. It turns out that it is the golden casket which contains a skull.

Another kind of unworthy suitor will reject the gold casket because of the inscription on it. He would hate to be classed with the multitude and repudiates 'what many men desire'. He is attracted by the inscription on the silver casket because he loves himself more than Portia and is convinced that he deserves her. It is significant that Arragon dismisses the leaden casket without thought.

The true lover rejects the gold casket because he can distinguish between appearance and reality and he rejects the silver casket because, being a true lover, he knows he does not deserve Portia. He will choose lead because he knows that the lover must give and hazard all he hath.

Shakespeare in the scenes in which Morocco and Arragon make their choice has revealed to the audience the inscriptions on the caskets and their contents. It was therefore dramatically desirable to avoid going over the same ground when Bassanio comes to choose. We are not given the reasoning by which he reaches his decision during the singing of 'Tell me where is fancy bred?' His speech shows merely that he is mature enough to distinguish between appearance and reality, so that he rejects the golden casket; he gives only a perfunctory reason for rejecting the silver casket and an equally perfunctory one for choosing the leaden one. Yet the audience is convinced that the caskets have selected the right husband for Portia, that Bassanio is not merely or mainly a fortune-hunter, that he values Portia more for her beauty and virtues than for her wealth, and that he is a true lover.

By what means the audience is convinced has been brilliantly analysed in a little-known article by A. R. Cripps.[24] His main point was to show the significance of the opening dialogue between Portia and Bassanio. The inscription on the leaden casket—'Who chooseth me must give and hazard all he hath'—is not literally true. He is not risking his life or his fortune: he is only risking his chance of marriage. For the inscription to be imaginatively true, Portia would have to be all in all to the suitor, and she would have to return his love, for the marriage would otherwise be an unhappy one. Since, therefore, the suitor's future happiness depends on choosing the right casket, in the very act of choice he is hazarding all he has. If he is a true lover he will know this. But he has also to be convinced that Portia returns his love, so in the opening lines, before he confronts the caskets, Portia has to let him know, directly or indirectly, that she wants him to choose the right casket; and she herself wants to make sure that he is not a fortune-hunter and that he loves her alone.

She asks him to pause a day or two before he hazards. She tells him that she does not wish to lose him:

> One half of me is yours, the other half yours,
> Mine own I would say; but if mine, then yours,
> So all is yours.

By this classical slip of the tongue—analysed as such by Freud in his *Introductory Lectures*[25]—Portia lets Bassanio know that she is his, that she wants him to win her hand, and that therefore he is hazarding everything. Her next step is to find out whether Bassanio is genuinely in love. When she confesses that she is delaying his choice of the caskets lest she should lose him, Bassanio replies

|  | Let me choose; |
| --- | --- |
|  | For as I am, I live upon the rack. |
| *Por.* | Upon the rack, Bassanio! then confess |
|  | What treason there is mingled with your love. |
| *Bass.* | None but that ugly treason of mistrust, |
|  | Which makes me fear th'enjoying of my love: |
|  | There may as well be amity and life |
|  | 'Tween snow and fire, as treason and my love. |
| *Por.* | Ay, but I fear you speak upon the rack, |
|  | Where men enforced do speak anything. |
| *Bass.* | Promise me life, and I'll confess the truth. |
| *Por.* | Well then, confess, and live.           (III.ii.24–35) |

The treason Portia fears could be that Bassanio is a fortune-hunter. It is particularly necessary, for the sake of the audience, that he should clear himself of this charge, for in the very first scene of the play he has told Antonio that the Lady of Belmont is a wealthy heiress. Portia is convinced that, since they love each other, Bassanio will hazard everything for love and choose the right casket:

Bass.                                         'Confess' and 'love'
          Had been the very sum of my confession:
          O happy torment, when my torturer
          Doth teach me answers for deliverance!
          But let me to my fortune and the caskets.
Por.      Away then! I am lock'd in one of them:
          If you do love me, you will find me out.

                                              (III.ii.35–41)

Although in real life this may not be the safest way of finding a
suitable husband for one's daughter, in the world of folk-lore and
myth there could be no other way of winning the hand of the Lady
of the Beautiful Mountain.

On the surface *The Merchant of Venice* seems to be a strange
blending of two impossible tales with two improbable ones; but
Shakespeare uses them with extraordinary skill to illuminate a
number of eternal problems by attaching them to archetypal myths:
man's confrontation of death (as Freud argued); the quest for the
golden fleece, mentioned by Bassanio; perhaps the story of Midas.
Shakespeare dramatises, as so often in later plays, the contrast
between appearance and reality, the struggle between good and
evil, the difference between law and justice, the necessity of mercy.
As we can see from Portia's devotions on her journey back to
Belmont, Shakespeare hints perhaps at the nature of Christian
marriage. Over all, as we are reminded in the last act, there is the
ordered and meaningful universe symbolised by the music of the
spheres, which sinful man cannot hear; but the little candle at
Belmont remains as a symbol of a good deed in an evil world.

We began by repudiating a number of interpretations of the play
but it will have been observed that they are not so much wrong as
selective and partial. It is possible from the text of the play to show
that Shakespeare, at moments, sympathised with Shylock. As every
good dramatist must, he allowed his characters to speak for
themselves. A director of the play should not try to impose one or
other of these partial interpretations on his production. It is
perfectly legitimate to suggest that there are homosexual overtones
in Antonio's feelings for Bassanio, but to make this the centre of the
production would be foolish. When Jessica elopes with Lorenzo we
ought to think of her escaping from the ogre's den; when we hear of
her selling Shylock's ring our sympathies are alienated; but they

swing back to her when she and Lorenzo await Portia's return in the moonlight at Belmont. It would be as wrong for the director to make Jessica cruel and unfeeling as to deny Shylock his moment of pathos. *The Merchant of Venice* is in some ways one of the simplest of Shakespeare's plays; but, as with all the others, we ignore its complexities at our peril.

# 7
# *Much Ado about Nothing*

The date of *Much Ado about Nothing* can be fixed with unusual accuracy. It was performed while Kemp (who played Dogberry) was still a member of Shakespeare's company, but too late for Francis Meres to know of its existence when he listed Shakespeare's plays in *Palladis Tamia*. So 1598 was the date of its first performance; and it was printed, probably from Shakespeare's manuscript, two years later.

It is hardly anyone's favourite comedy and it is not so frequently performed as *As You Like It* or *Twelfth Night*, doubtless because the main plot is so much less interesting than the underplot. The Hero–Claudio plot, written mainly in verse, is combined with the Beatrice–Benedick plot, written mainly in prose. In our degenerate days it is natural for audiences to prefer prose to verse, but it is possible that Shakespeare, towards the end of the sixteenth century, went through a phase when he thought that the increasing subtlety of his actors demanded a style nearer to colloquial speech—some of Shylock's best speeches, all of Falstaff's, most of Beatrice, Benedick and Rosalind are in prose.[26]

The plots are linked together in various ways. The bringing together of Beatrice and Benedick is a means of passing the time between the day of Hero's betrothal and her marriage; Benedick is chosen by Beatrice to avenge her cousin's honour; and Benedick is a close friend of Claudio's, so that Beatrice's demand poses a favourite problem—posed earlier in *The Two Gentlemen of Verona*—of Love versus Friendship.

The play is also unified by imagery. As in *Macbeth,* the dominating image is one of clothes, and the most frequent figure of speech is antithesis.[27] Clothes are used as a symbol of the difference between appearance and reality, and hence of hypocrisy. In the first scene, for example, Beatrice says that Benedick 'wears his faith but as the fashion of his hat'; Benedick calls courtesy a turncoat; in the second act Benedick says that Beatrice is the infernal Ate in good apparel; and Beatrice asks if Pedro has a brother since 'Your Grace is too costly to wear every day'. Benedick contrasts the amorous Claudio with the man as he used to be:

> I have known when he would have walk'd ten mile afoot to see a good armour, and now will he lie ten nights awake carving the fashion of a new doublet. (II.iii.18ff.)

Pedro has a speech in Act III on Benedick's fancy for strange disguises. Borachio has a long dialogue with Conrade, apparently irrelevant to the matter in hand, on the subject of fashion:

> *Bor.* Thou knowest that the fashion of a doublet, or a hat, or a cloak is nothing to a man.
>
> *Con.* Yes, it is apparel.
>
> *Bor.* I mean the fashion.
>
> *Con.* Yes, the fashion is the fashion.
>
> *Bor.* Tush, I may as well say the fool's the fool. But seest thou not what a deformed thief this fashion is . . . Seest thou not, I say, what a deformed thief this fashion is, how giddily 'a turns about all the hot bloods between fourteen and five and thirty, sometimes fashioning them like Pharaoh's soldiers in the reechy painting, sometime like god Bel's priests in the old church window, sometime like the shaven Hercules in the smirched worm-eaten tapestry, where his codpiece seems as massy as his club?
>
> *Con.* All this I see; and I see that the fashion wears out more apparel than the man. But art not thou thyself giddy with the fashion too, that thou hast shifted out of thy tale into telling me of the fashion?
>
> *Bor.* Not so neither. (III.iii.108ff.)

The climax of the many references to appearance and reality is the scene in church, when Claudio repudiates his bride. Hero is compared to a rotten orange, 'but the sign and semblance of her honour', blushing like a maid, although she is immodest:

O, what authority and show of truth
Can cunning sin cover itself withal!
Comes not that blood as modest evidence
To witness simple virtue? Would you not swear,
All you that see her, that she were a maid
By these exterior shows? But she is none.
Out on thee! Seeming! I will write against it:
You seem to me as Dian in her orb,
As chaste as is the bud ere it be blown;
But you are more intemperate in your blood
Than Venus, or those pamp'red animals
That rage in savage sensuality.             (IV.i.34–9, 55–60)

In a later speech Claudio drops into the favourite figure of antithesis, a figure most apt for the contrast between appearance and reality:

O Hero, what a Hero hadst thou been,
If half thy outward graces had been placed
About thy thoughts and counsels of thy heart!
But fare thee well, most foul, most fair! Farewell,
Thou pure impiety and impious purity!             (IV.i.99–103)

The two plots are linked together in another way. It has often been observed that the over-all theme of the play (as Masefield put it) is 'the power of report, of the thing overheard, to alter human destiny'.[28] It is true that the complications of the play are all due to overhearing, although it could be argued that Claudio might, even without the detective work by the watch, have learnt his mistake, and Beatrice and Benedick might have allowed their unconscious love for each other to rise into consciousness. But there are at least seven examples of rumour in the course of the play:

1. In the second scene Antonio tells Leonato:

The Prince and Count Claudio, walking in a thick-pleached orchard, were thus much overheard by a man of mine: the Prince discovered to Claudio that he loved my niece your daughter, and meant to acknowledge it this night in a dance.

In this case, the servant had misheard, for Pedro had offered to pretend to be Claudio, to woo Hero for him.

2. In the next scene Borachio has overheard, correctly, that Claudio hoped to marry Hero, and that Pedro was going to woo for him.

3. In the scene of the dance there are a whole series of misunder-standings, partly owing to the fact that the characters are masked:

(*a*) Hero, instructed by her father, apparently thinks that Pedro is wooing for himself, but it is not explained what her reactions are when he pretends to be Claudio, as this takes place off stage.

(*b*) Don John, for reasons which are never explained, thinks that Pedro woos for himself.

(*c*) Benedick thinks that Beatrice does not recognise him, and she calls him the Prince's Fool.

(*d*) Borachio pretends that Claudio is Benedick, and tells him that Pedro is wooing Hero for himself; and this, in spite of their previous arrangement, is forthwith believed by Claudio.

(*e*) Benedick, who is not aware of the arrangement between Pedro and Claudio, naturally believes that Pedro has wooed for himself.

The purpose of all these confusions—and their improbability is not so apparent in performance, is to soften up the audience, so that they are willing to accept as plausible Don John's deception of Pedro and Claudio.

4. In the third scene of Act II, Benedick overhears that Beatrice is dying of love for him, and he promptly decides that her love must be requited.

5. In the first scene of Act III, Beatrice hidden by the woodbine coverture, overhears that Benedick is in love with her. She forth-with decides to return his love:

> What fire is in mine ears? Can this be true?
> Stand I condemn'd for pride and scorn so much?
> Contempt, farewell! and maiden pride adieu!
> No glory lives behind the back of such.
> And Benedick, love on; I will requite thee,
> Taming my wild heart to thy loving hand;
> If thou dost love, my kindness shall incite thee
> To bind our loves up in a holy band;
> > For others say thou dost deserve, and I
> > Believe it better than reportingly.          (III.i.107–16)

She uses, as Petruchio does, the image of the tamed hawk.

6. Borachio is overheard making love to Margaret, whom the watchers think is Hero; and Borachio, telling the tale of his deception of Pedro and Claudio to Conrade, is overheard by the

Watch. This leads to his arrest, and the acquittal of Hero.

7. On the Friar's advice, a report is circulated that Hero is dead, so as to cause Claudio to feel remorse. This remorse becomes overwhelming when it is proved that she was falsely accused. But it is typical of Claudio's self-centredness that when he hears that Hero was innocent he is more concerned about his own feelings than about her supposed death. And when he agrees to marry her cousin he has the significant lines:

> I do embrace your offer; and dispose
> For henceforth of poor Claudio.

The plots, then, are linked together structurally, imagistically and thematically, so that complaints about lack of unity have little justification. There remains the feeling of many readers that the two plots don't really harmonise since the main plot is largely conventional—depending on the convention employed by Shakespeare in *Othello* and *Cymbeline* that the calumniator of female chastity is *always* believed, though in real life he would not be—and the sub-plot is much more realistic. Moreover, Hero is a nonentity and Claudio is a cad; whereas Beatrice and Benedick (though absurd) are attractive figures to whom an audience warms.

There are several possible answers to these complaints. The first answer is one that has to be made over and over again to Shakespeare's armchair critics: that his plays were meant to be acted, not read, and that the test we should apply should be a theatrical one—Does it work in the theatre? The convention of the calumniator believed always *does* seem to work. We may think Claudio is a credulous fool, but Pedro's equal credulity prevents us from having too harsh an opinion of him.

Nor is it unusual in Shakespeare's plays for him to present his characters on different levels of reality. It has often been noticed that Katherine and the scenes in which she appears are much more vital than those relating to the wooing of Bianca. Just as in painting, an artist will relegate some figures to the background, and just as a photographer will keep his central theme in sharp focus, while the rest of his composition may be comparatively blurred, so the dramatist can vary his treatment of characters in the same play.

The characters in this play range from the purely conventional to the purely human. Don John (for example) announces himself as a villain, a true example of motiveless malignity, who does evil for the sake of evil. Although we could (I suppose) ascribe his villainy to the results of his bastardy, it is not really possible to regard him as anything but a conventional stage villain. Or consider Margaret. At one point in the play she is apparently the mistress of the debauched Borachio, who for some unexplained reason is willing to pretend she is Hero, and call Borachio Claudio (unless this is a textual error).[29] At another point in the play, she is a witty lady-in-waiting, on almost equal terms with Beatrice and Hero. She cannot be present in the church scene—if she had been she would have exposed Borachio's plot—though it is quite unnatural that she should not be present. When Leonato says that Margaret was hired to the deed by Don John, Borachio protests that she is completely innocent:

> No, by my soul, she was not;
> Nor knew not what she did when she spoke to me,
> But always hath been just and virtuous
> In anything that I do know by her.     (V.i.286–9)

In the next scene, she engages in a witty exchange with Benedick; and at the end Leonato says (in relation to the slander of Hero)

> But Margaret was in some fault for this,
> Although against her will, as it appears.

Leo Kirschbaum, in *Character and Characterisation in Shakespeare,* argues that psychologically the two Margarets are completely incompatible.[30] She is a flat character; but in the course of performance we do not notice the discrepancies, and Shakespeare was not troubled by the difficulties his readers might encounter.[31]

Hero and Claudio are more realistically presented, but they are still conventional figures, and this prevents us from being too involved emotionally at Hero's distresses. Indeed, the audience is never in doubt that things will come right in the end. The very title of the play *Much Ado about Nothing* tells them as much. The chief song has as its refrain,

> Converting all your sounds of woe
> Into hey nonny-nonny.

Borachio, moreover, has been arrested by the watch before the church scene; and it is only the loquaciousness of Dogberry which prevents the slander from being exposed before the marriage scene.

So the audience knows that Hero's name will eventually be cleared.

Dogberry is, indeed, a masterly character, one which is beautifully functional, but which is much more than functional. He has to be pompous, loquacious, fond of long words, very much on his dignity, semi-literate, and a bungler; otherwise he would get at the truth much sooner, and Leonato would not hasten to get rid of him on the morning of the marriage. On the other hand, he has to have some glimmerings of intelligence, or he would not have eventually arrived at the truth. On this functional basis, Shakespeare creates a wonderful portrait of a Jack-in-office, much less competent than Verges, whom he bullies and despises. He is the true ancestor of Mrs Malaprop, but much more plausible than her, who having been brought up as a lady would not be likely to make such absurd mistakes. All Dogberry's mistakes, taken individually, are the sort of mistakes one still hears from local politicians in England. Dogberry uses *desartless* for *deserving, senseless* for *sensible, decerns* for *concerns, odorous* for *odious, aspicious* for *suspicious, comprehended* for *apprehended*. Shakespeare may have known such a man; but he had probably read a book by his acquaintance William Lambard, on the duties of constables, so that one gets a curious mixture of Elizabethan practice with the wildest fantasy. Funny as the Dogberry scenes are, they are best played without too much farcical business; for as with all the best comic characters, there is an element of pathos about Dogberry, as when he is called an ass by one of his prisoners:

> Dost thou not suspect my place? Dost thou not suspect my years? O that he were here to write me down an ass! But, masters, remember that I am an ass; though it not be written down, yet forget not that I am an ass. No, thou villain, thou art full of piety, as shall be proved upon thee by good witness. I am a wise fellow; and, which is more, an officer; and, which is more, a householder; and, which is more, as pretty a piece of flesh as any is in Messina; and one that knows the law, go to; and a rich fellow enough, go to; and a fellow that hath had losses; and one that hath two gowns, and everything handsome about him. Bring him away. O that I had been writ down an ass!                                                        (IV.ii.69ff.)

For a modern audience, the rejection of Hero in church makes it difficult to retain any sympathy for Claudio. Prouty seeks to defend him by suggesting that it was merely a marriage of convenience.[32] Since Hero was not a virgin, her father had broken a contract, and a public exposure was therefore permissible. This is all very well. But there is one line only in Claudio's part to suggest that he was thinking of Hero's dowry. His first question to Pedro, when he reveals that he is thinking of the marriage is 'Hath Leonato any son, my lord?' Otherwise Claudio is presented as an abnormally shy, sentimental lover.

Shakespeare had to have a public repudiation. There were theatrical necessities for it—one has only to think what the play would be like without this climactic scene. There were also perfectly good dramatic reasons for a public repudiation. Claudio's action has to seem so atrocious that Benedick—his bosom friend—is willing to challenge him to a duel. The repudiation, and the following scene between Beatrice and Benedick, are a means of showing the innate good sense of Beatrice, her warm-heartedness and intuitive understanding; and they are a means of precipitating the confession of love.

The Mueschkes make the good point[33] that the theme of the play is Honour: 'Honour is the warp of the three hoaxes [perpetrated in the course of the play], hearsay is the weft, and illusion spins the web.' They go on to suggest that

> The repudiation scene, examined with the courtly code of honour in mind, is much more than a *coup de théâtre*. In terms of Renaissance mores, it is a scene of poignant disillusionment and despair. In the conflict between appearance and reality, between emotion and reason, tension increases when lover turns inquisitor and father turns executioner. Here, in a conflict between good and evil, truth clashes with error in a charged atmosphere of contradictory moods and shifting relationships while the outraged moral sense oscillates between absolute praise and absolute blame. Here, when malice triumphs, shame so submerges compassion and slander, mirage, and perjury are accepted as ocular and auditory proof. Incensed by defiled honour, men argue in absolutes shorn from any rational mean, and under the aegis of the courtly code act and react with prescribed cruelty.

In other words, Shakespeare's aim is to criticise the accepted code of honour; and (it may be argued) when Beatrice demands that

Benedick should challenge Claudio she also is enslaved by the conventional code. For if Benedick kills Claudio, it will prove only that he is a more accomplished swordsman; and if Claudio kills Benedick it will do nothing to prove the guilt of Hero. It is the dim-witted watch, and the pompous self-important Dogberry who restore Hero's reputation. As St Paul says:[34] 'God hath chosen the foolish things of the world to confound the wise; and God hath chosen the weak things of the world to confound the things which are mighty; and base things of the world and things which are despised, hath God chosen, yea, and things which are not, to bring to nought things that are.'

The behaviour of Claudio—and, indeed, of Pedro—in the scene of the challenge exhibits once again the limitations of the code. Their treatment of Leonato is bad enough, but their light-hearted ragging of Benedick shows a callousness to the memory of Hero, and cannot quite be expiated by the ritual mourning which follows the revelation of her innocence.

Beatrice and Benedick are obviously the two characters who are most vital and real—the ones who are the least conventional. Least conventional in a double sense: in the way they are drawn, and in their reacting against the romantic conventions of the society in which they live. They alone, of the characters in the play, are three-dimensional.

Superficially, it might seem that Beatrice and Benedick who detest each other are tricked into loving each other by overhearing that each is dying for love of the other. But it is fairly obvious that they are in love with each other from the start: that is the reason why they are continually attacking each other.[35] Beatrice and Benedick have several reasons for not admitting to their love. Both (it is clear) are unwilling to make themselves ridiculous, and they are too intelligent and unsentimental to indulge in the gestures of conventional romantic love. It is possible (as Prouty suggests)[36] that they are equally in revolt against marriages of convenience. Beatrice, moreover, thinks of Benedick as a philanderer. When Pedro says 'you have lost the heart of Signior Benedick', Beatrice replies:

> Indeed, my lord, he lent it me awhile; and I gave him use for it, a double heart for his single one; marry, once before he won it of me with false dice, therefore your Grace may well say I have lost it.

The speech is rather obscure; but it seems to imply that Benedick at one time had made love to Beatrice, and she felt his intentions were not serious. Both are proud and apparently self-sufficient. Benedick boasts, not very seriously, of the way women fall in love with him; but he declares to others that he will die a bachelor, and to himself:

> One woman is fair, yet I am well, another is wise, yet I am well; another virtuous, yet I am well; but till all graces be in one woman, one woman shall not come in my grace.
>
> (II.iii.31ff.)

Beatrice similarly says:

> He that hath a beard is more than a youth, and he that hath no beard is less than a man; and he that is more than a youth is not for me, and he that is less than a man I am not for him. Therefore I will even take sixpence in earnest of the berrord, and lead his apes into hell.
>
> *Leon.* Well, then go you into hell?
> *Beat.* No; but to the gate, and there will the devil meet me, like an old cuckold, with horns on his head, and say 'Get you to heaven Beatrice, get you to heaven; here's no place for you maids'. So deliver I up my apes and away to Saint Peter for the heavens; he shows me where the bachelors sit, and there live we as merry as the day is long. (II.i.31–41)

It was speeches like this that so shocked Gerard Manley Hopkins that he called Beatrice vain and unchaste.[37] Beatrice does not talk like a mid-Victorian lady, but there is not the faintest suggestion in the play that she is unchaste, and few will agree with Hopkins's epithet 'vile'. Nor, I think, is Beatrice vain; but she is proud. It has been suggested that Hero's lines describing her cousin—

> Nature never framed a woman's heart
> Of prouder stuff than that of Beatrice.
> Disdain and scorn ride sparkling in her eyes,
> Misprising what they look on; and her wit
> Values itself so highly that to her
> All matter else seems weak. She cannot love,
> Nor take no shape nor project of affection,
> She is so self-endeared— (III.i.49–56)

are based on a character representing pride in *The Faerie Queene*.[38]
But we must remember that Hero is deliberately exaggerating, as
she knows that Beatrice is overhearing her. The lines cannot be
taken as an accurate portrait. Yet both Beatrice and Benedick are
absurd in their self-sufficiency. *Much Ado about Nothing* may be
regarded as a subtler version of *The Taming of the Shrew*,
transposed from farce to high comedy—and, of course, Benedick
needs to be tamed as well as Beatrice. As we have seen, Katherina's
violence is at least partly due to the fact that she hates equally the
artificialities of romantic love and the humiliations of marriages of
convenience, in which she is bound to suspect that the suitor is after
her fortune—as indeed Petruchio admits from the start. But the
struggle between the Shrew and her tamer is carried out in terms of
farce. In *Much Ado*, Beatrice, instead of being physically violent, is
aggressive with her tongue, and she chooses as her victim the man
she really loves. She is cured and tamed, not by physical violence
and semi-starvation, but by hearing the truth about herself, and
about Benedick. The irony is that Hero and the others who talk
about Benedick's love for her think they are lying, although they are
telling the truth; and Pedro and Claudio think they are lying when
they speak of Beatrice's love for Benedick.

By the end of the play we realise that all the characters in the
play, except the Friar, have been laughed at: the watch for their
stupidity, Dogberry for his self-important illiteracy, Leonato for
being more concerned with his own honour than with his daughter's life, Claudio and Pedro for their credulity in being deceived by
an obvious villain, for the cruelty of their code of honour, and for
their failure to recognise that Beatrice and Benedick are in love;
Beatrice and Benedick for their pride and self-sufficiency. It is not
only Dogberry who should ask to be writ down as an ass.

Bernard Shaw has pointed out how much the witty repartee
depends on style. The passage occurs in a review of a performance
of the play in 1898:[39]

> Shakespear shews himself in it (sc. *Much Ado*) a commonplace
> librettist working on a stolen plot, but a great musician. No
> matter how poor, coarse, cheap, and obvious the thought may
> be, the mood is charming, and the music of the words
> expresses the mood. Paraphrase the encounters of Benedick
> and Beatrice in the style of a bluebook, carefully preserving

every idea they present, and it will become apparent to the most infatuated Shakespearean that they contain at best nothing out of the common in thought or wit, and at worst a good deal of vulgar naughtiness ... Not until the Shakespearean music is added by replacing the paraphrase with the original lines does the enchantment begin. Then you are in another world at once. When a flower-girl tells a coster to hold his jaw, for nobody is listening to him, and he retorts, 'Oh, youre there, are you, you beauty?' they reproduce the wit of Beatrice and Benedick exactly. But put it this way. 'I wonder that you will still be talking, Signior Benedick: nobody marks you.' 'What! my dear Lady Disdain, are you yet living?' You are miles away from costerland at once. When I tell you that Benedick and the coster are equally poor in thought, Beatrice and the flower-girl equally vulgar in repartee, you reply that I might as well tell you that a nightingale's love is no higher than a cat's. Which is exactly what I do tell you, though the nightingale is the better musician.

Shaw, of course, exaggerates, because he was campaigning for Ibsen. It was only in his later years, after all his plays had been written, that he confessed that his own masters were Verdi, Mozart and Shakespeare; and by a curious irony his own plays are being performed now, not for their ideas, but for their style.

In all love comedies the union of the hero and heroine must be delayed by obstacles of one kind or another—'The course of true love never did run smooth.' The obstacles can be external, as for example the opposition of parents who have other plans for their children. Or they may be psychological, the unwillingness of one or other to marry. In Congreve's masterpiece, *The Way of the World*, Millamant is afraid that (as so often in her society) marriage will destroy his love for her. And when she is finally cornered, she tells her lover:[40]

I shall expect you shall solicit me, as though I were wavering at the gate of a monastery, with one foot over the threshold ... I should think I was poor if I were deprived of the agreeable fatigues of solicitation.

Then she lays down an elaborate list of conditions for her surrender, including the provisos that she shall not be called such names as 'wife, joy, jewel, spouse, sweetheart, and the rest of that nauseous cant in which men and their wives are so fulsomely familiar . . . Let us be very strange and well bred, as strange as if we had been married a great while, and as well-bred as if we were not married at all.' Millamant, like Beatrice, uses her wit as a shield, because she is in fact very vulnerable and sensitive. In a great modern comedy, Shaw's *Man and Superman*, it is the woman who chases the man, chases him halfway across Europe in a motor-car; in *Much Ado* both the hero and the heroine apparently wish to remain single, and the marriage at the end is a satisfactory one because it fulfils their unconscious wishes. A modern dramatist has written[41] a sequel to *Much Ado* in which Beatrice and Benedick, after their marriage, continue to fight each other as they had done before. But the continuation of the merry war (as Shakespeare calls it) does not mean that their marriage would not be a success. They will enjoy the wise-cracks, and use them as a private method of courtship, long after Claudio and Hero have exhausted the pleasures of romantic hyperbole. (Indeed, if one were to treat the matter realistically—and it would be perverse to do so—one could imagine Hero reminding Claudio too often of the way he repudiated her in church.)

In 1891, when Ellen Terry was playing with Irving in *Much Ado about Nothing*, she commented on her own performance:[42]

> I must make Beatrice more *flashing* at first, and *softer* afterwards. This will be an improvement upon my old reading of the part. She must be always *merry* and by turns scornful, tormenting, vexed, self-communing, absent, melting, teasing, brilliant, indignant, *sad-merry*, thoughtful, withering, gentle, humorous, and gay. Gay, Gay! Protecting (to Hero), motherly, very intellectual—a gallant creature and complete in mind and feature.

This brings out well the gaiety and complexity of the character, but it is arguable that Ellen Terry was tempted to play too much for sympathy.

The climactic scene in the play is the one in which Benedick and Beatrice first confess their love for each other. Hero has been repudiated in church by the man she was to marry. Hero faints. In this situation the behaviour of Beatrice and Benedick is contrasted with that of the other characters. Whereas Leonato behaves like an hysterical old fool, first believing that Hero is guilty and wishing that she would die, and later uttering threats against the Prince and Claudio, Beatrice and Benedick are concerned for Hero. Beatrice knows instinctively that she is innocent, and Benedick asks some of the questions which the audience are waiting to be asked. (No one, however, seems to realise that Don John's story of a thousand secret encounters can scarcely be true, since Beatrice and Hero, until this last night, have shared a bed.) The Friar puts forward his plan of pretending that Hero has died, and suggests that the wedding-day is but postponed. Benedick naturally suspects that Don John is at the bottom of the plot to defame Hero, since Claudio and Pedro are honourable men. Everyone leaves the church, except Benedick and Beatrice, who is still weeping for her cousin.

Since they learned that they were loved by the other, Beatrice and Benedick have not met in private, and the audience have been waiting for their meeting for about half an hour of playing-time. In the scene which follows, Benedick is forced to choose between love and friendship. After he has promised to do anything in the world for Beatrice, and she asks him to kill Claudio, he first exclaims 'Not for the wide world'. When John Gielgud and Peggy Ashcroft appeared on Broadway, one of the critics regarded the production as a failure—though it was the best I have ever seen—because the audience laughed at this point. The critic thought the audience laughed because it was obvious that Gielgud's Benedick would not hurt a fly, let alone his friend. But although the scene as a whole is a poignant and dramatic one, there are several lines which are intended to be funny, and this is surely one of them. It is right that the audience should laugh when Benedick offers to do anything that Beatrice wants and refuses the very first thing she asks.

# 8

## *The Merry Wives of Windsor*

*The Merry Wives of Windsor* is unique in several ways. It is Shakespeare's one entirely farcical play;[43] it is his only bourgeois play;[44] it is the only one of his plays written predominantly in prose; and it is perhaps the only one which depends to any great extent on topical satire.[45] Whether Sir Thomas Lucy or William Gardiner, or neither, was the model for Justice Shallow,[46] what exactly was the business about the post-horses,[47] which Garter investiture was the occasion of the play, are questions not beyond all conjecture, but they are problems which can interfere with one's enjoyment of the play.

The characteristics of the play have been variously explained—by the influence of the Comedy of Humours,[48] by Shakespeare's feeling that prose, rather than verse, was a suitable medium for Windsor citizens, if they were anything like his Stratford neighbours, and by the royal, if legendary, command for him to write a play to exhibit Falstaff in love. At least we can be sure from the various loose ends that the play was written in something of a hurry, and it may well have been adapted at short notice to suit a special occasion.[49] But if one excludes the scenes which have been rendered obscure by our having lost the key to their precise topical meaning, the play as a whole, as all audiences realise, is expertly theatrical, and it deserves more than the grudging commendations it often receives from literary critics. The minor plot, the rivalry of three men for the hand of 'sweet Anne Page', is brilliantly executed. As Abraham Slender, the father's choice, is Shakespeare's most exquisite fool, and Dr Caius, the mother's choice, is a middle-aged French physician, the audience approves of the girl's elopement with her own choice, Fenton. The original audience would be delighted to welcome the reappearance of Mistress Quickly from the *Henry IV* plays, now accepting bribes from all three suitors and incongruously playing in the masque as the Queen of the Fairies.[50]

This plot is joined to the plot in which Falstaff is gulled by the facts that Anne's mother is one of the Merry Wives and that the elopement is made possible by the disguises adopted for the final tricking of Falstaff—the duped parents had been more sensible in their dealings with the fat knight than they are in their treatment of their daughter.

Although, as G. R. Hibbard points out, *The Merry Wives of Windsor* can be regarded as a comic revenge play in a bourgeois setting,[51] the play is essentially a farce. The characters, therefore, are two-dimensional, though they are given enough reality for the roles in the play. Bardolph, Pistol and Nym are drawn perfunctorily; Shallow is much less interesting than he had been in *2 Henry IV*; Sir Hugh Evans and Doctor Caius are amusing stereotypes; but Ford is a masterly study of comic jealousy and Slender a delightful portrait of engaging imbecility. Mistress Quickly, metamorphosed from the owner of a not very respectable tavern into a housekeeper and spare-time bawd, is as entertaining as ever and her Malapropisms are even better—canaries, rushling, alligant and fartuous are some of her attempts at gentility—but the revision of the play has landed her with the improbable role of the Queen of the Fairies. The main transplant from *Henry IV* is, of course, Falstaff himself and most critics have deplored his deterioration. It is true that his retorts to Shallow in the first scene are extremely feeble, that he is foolish to imagine himself as a lover, still more foolish to write identical letters to women who are friends and neighbours and that he is gulled three times by the Merry Wives. But it should be remembered that in *Henry IV* he overestimates his influence over Hal, that early in Part I he is tricked at Gadshill and ragged about the episode afterwards, and that at the end of Part II he is banished. In *Henry IV* he talks himself out of the many difficulties into which he lands himself and he has a whole succession of superb speeches—on his recruits, on honour, on sherris, on Shallow's early years—which are more memorable than his discomfitures. Yet the Falstaff of *The Merry Wives of Windsor* is not deprived of all his resources. His soliloquy after being ducked in the Thames and his account of his experience to the disguised Ford are as good—or nearly as good—as the best things in *Henry IV*; but there are fewer of them.

> But mark the sequel, Master Brook—I suffered the pangs of three several deaths: first, an intolerable fright to be detected with a jealous rotten bell-wether, next, to be compass'd like a good bilbo in the circumference of a peck, hilt to point, heel to head; and then, to be stopp'd in, like a strong distillation, with stinking clothes that fretted in their own grease. Think of that—a man of my kidney. Think of that—that am as subject to heat as butter; a man of continual dissolution and thaw. It was a miracle to scape suffocation. And in the height of this bath, when I was more then half-stew'd in grease, like a Dutch dish, to be thrown into the Thames, and cool'd, glowing hot, in that surge, like a horse-shoe; think of that—hissing hot. Think of that, Master Brook. (III.v.99–108)

All the scenes between Falstaff and 'Master Brook' are brilliantly

funny with a triple irony. Falstaff does not know that he is revealing
to the jealous husband his attempts to cuckold him, nor does he
know that Mistress Ford is gulling him; Ford does not know that
his wife is innocent and he has to pretend to be delighted with
Falstaff's narrow escapes.

The conclusion of the play sends the audience away contented.
Falstaff is punished, but forgiven; Ford is cured, at least for the time
being, of his jealousy; Page and his wife are both foiled in their rival
plots to foist an unsuitable husband on Anne, and both are
reconciled to the marriage they had opposed. It is only by comparison with the more poetic comedies of Shakespeare's maturity, with
their greater subtlety and profundity, that the play is seen to be
lacking.

# 9
## *As You Like It*

As *you* like it? Does the title suggest (as some critics have supposed)
that Shakespeare was deploring the taste of his audience at the
Globe, or was he happily proclaiming that their taste corresponded
with his own? Most great writers begin by giving their public what
it wants and end by making the public want what they choose to
give. Before the end of the sixteenth century, Shakespeare was in
this happy position, though he kept up the pretence in his titles and
sub-titles—*As You Like It, Much Ado about Nothing, What You
Will*—that the boot was on the other foot.

The same irony is apparent in his dramatisation of Thomas
Lodge's *Rosalynde*, a euphuistic novel which, despite its charm and
elegance, is entirely artificial and removed from reality. The
characters never condescend to mere conversation: they orate to
each other. Although Shakespeare follows Lodge's plot fairly
closely, there are no verbal echoes of his dialogue. His aim, it soon
becomes clear, was different from that of Lodge: he was not trying
to write a straight pastoral, but to it use for his own dramatic
purposes.

The very first speech should alert us to what he is doing. Orlando
is informing Adam, his old retainer, of facts which he already
knows, and which Orlando knows that he knows:

> As I remember, Adam, it was upon this fashion bequeathed me
> by will but poor a thousand crowns, and, as thou say'st,
> charged my brother, on his blessing, to breed me well; and
> there begins my sadness.

This violates one of the most elementary rules of play-writing.[52]
There is no other exposition in all Shakespeare's works which is so
unashamedly crude.[53] As he had already written some seventeen
competent plays, and as a writer of comedy was at the height of his
powers, we are entitled to wonder why he should revert to such an
unashamedly primitive technique—more primitive than that of his
earliest experimental plays. The speech is, in fact, a way of
preparing us for the tone of the rest of the play. Shakespeare is
pretending that he is presenting a corny tale of a bad elder brother
and a good younger brother, a tale which will end, as such tales do,
with the good brother marrying a princess and living happily ever
after. For good measure he introduces a usurping Duke and his
exiled brother who lives in the greenwood like Robin Hood. On the
face of it, the play is naïve in the extreme; but it is really as
sophisticated as those of Marivaux.

Orlando, of course, defeats Charles the wrestler, who has been
bribed to break his neck; but Shakespeare is careful to remind us
that we are in a world of fiction by making Celia comment on Le
Beau's account of Charles's prowess, 'I could match this beginning
with an old tale'. Rosalind, with the initiative expected of a
fairy-tale princess, hints to Orlando that she has fallen in love at
first sight:

> Sir, you have wrestled well, and overthrown
> More than your enemies.

Before long, Rosalind and Celia (disguised as Ganymede and
Aliena), go off with Touchstone to the forest of Arden and
Orlando, to escape being murdered by his brother, makes the same
journey with Adam. Meanwhile we have been introduced to the
exiled Duke and his entourage, and they are depicted not without
irony. However much they profess to believe in the superiority of
the forest life to that of the court, however much Amiens extols the
greenwood and the jolliness of its life, we know that they will hurry
back to court as soon as they get the chance. The only one of their

number who does not, Jaques, has mocked the insincerity of his fellow-exiles.

Yet we are prevented from accepting Jaques's comments as authorial by the fact they are undercut by the Duke, by Orlando and by Rosalind. The Duke accuses him of being a reformed libertine,[54] satirising the vices he once enjoyed; when Orlando is invited to rail against mankind, he gently reproves Jaques; and when Rosalind hears his affected account of his particular brand of melancholy, she laughs at him:

> A traveller! By my faith you have great reason to be sad. I fear you have sold your own lands to see other men's; then to have nothing is to have rich eyes and poor hands . . . I had rather have a fool to make me merry than experience to make me sad—and to travel for it too!

Even Jaques's set speech on the seven ages of man, suggested probably by the motto of the Globe theatre, cannot be taken as Shakespeare's considered opinion on human life; for its melancholy outlook is contradicted by the play as a whole, as well as by the situation which evokes it—for Orlando, courteously received by the outlaws, has gone out to fetch the exhausted Adam and courtesy, charity and fellow-feeling are apparently excluded from Jaques's philosophy of life.

The attitude we are forced to adopt to the outlaws is a complex one and the same complexity is apparent in the other versions of pastoral with which Shakespeare treats.[55] The oldest matter of pastoral, dating back to Greek and Latin poetry, and still flourishing in Shakespeare's day in the eclogues of Spenser and Drayton, is that of a love-sick shepherd in love with a scornful shepherdess. The love of Silvius for Phebe is in this convention, and it is in the scenes in which they appear that Shakespeare comes nearest to the spirit of his source. Yet he provides a suitable antidote to the convention in the very scene in which the pastoral lovers are introduced when Rosalind intervenes:

> And why, I pray you? Who might be your mother,
> That you insult, exult, and all at once
> Over the wretched? What though you have no beauty—
> As, by my faith, I see no more in you
> Than without candle may go dark to bed—

Must you be therefore proud and pitiless?
Why, what means this? Why do you look on me?
I see no more in you than in the ordinary
Of nature's sale-work. 'Ods my little life,
I think she means to tangle my eyes too!
No, faith, proud mistress, hope not after it;
'Tis not your inky brows, your black silk hair,
Your bugle eyeballs, nor your cheek of cream,
That can entame my spirits to your worship.
You foolish shepherd, wherefore do you follow her,
Like foggy south, puffing with wind and rain?
You are a thousand times a properer man
Than she a woman. 'Tis such fools as you
That makes the world full of ill-favour'd children.
'Tis not her glass, but you, that flatters her . . .
But, mistress, know yourself. Down on your knees,
And thank heaven, fasting, for a good man's love;
For I must tell you friendly in your ear:
Sell when you can; you are not for all markets. (III.v.35–60)

Another form of pastoral convention is represented by Audrey and William, who are not real rustics but country bumpkins seen through urban eyes; they are illiterate, slow-witted and not very clean. Audrey does not know the meaning of 'poetical' and this provides Touchstone with the opportunity of telling her that 'the truest poetry is the most feigning'—an ironical comment on the poetic conventions Shakespeare is exploiting in the play. Although Touchstone puts William to flight and goes through a form of marriage with Audrey, he does not intend it to be more than temporary. The simple-minded and 'foul' rustic is superior in some ways to the civilised fool. Indeed, when Touchstone attempts, by a series of quibbles, to prove that Corin is damned, that sensible and dignified shepherd gets the best of the argument.

The last kind of pastoral represented in the play is that of Rosalind and Celia, aristocrats who adopt the pastoral role. On the spur of the moment they decide to buy the farm belonging to Corin's master:

Ros.    I pray thee, if it stand with honesty
        Buy thou the cottage, pasture, and the flock,
        And thou shalt have to pay for it of us.

> *Cel.*   And we will mend thy wages. I like this place,
> And willingly would waste my time in it.

They buy the farm without even seeing it, much less calling in a
surveyor or scrutinising the accounts. We hear nothing more about
the farm. Presumably Corin continues to do all the work.

Shakespeare exploits other literary conventions. His lovers—
Rosalind, Orlando, Celia, Oliver and Phebe—would all make answer
to Marlowe's question 'Who ever loved that loved not a first sight?'
with a chorus of 'No one'. Shakespeare goes out of his way to
underline the absurdity, as when Rosalind tells Orlando of the
match between Celia and Oliver:

> Nay, 'tis true. There was never anything so sudden, but the
> fight of two rams and Caesar's thrasonical brag of 'I came,
> saw, and overcame'. For your brother and my sister, no sooner
> met but they look'd; no sooner look'd but they lov'd; no
> sooner lov'd but they sigh'd; no sooner sigh'd but they asked
> one another the reason; no sooner knew the reason but they
> sought the remedy—and in these degrees have they made a
> pair of stairs to marriage, which they will climb incontinent, or
> else be incontinent before marriage.          (V.ii.27–36)

One other romantic convention may be mentioned—the sudden
conversion of a villain. In the twinkling of an eye, Oliver is
converted from being a murderous, avaricious scoundrel with no
redeeming characteristics into a pleasant and acceptable husband
for Celia. The usurping Duke is a cruel tyrant and in Act V is about
to exterminate his brother and the other outlaws when he meets an
old religious man, and, we are told,

> After some question with him, was converted
> Both from his enterprise and from the world.

Some actors of these parts, conscious of the improbability of the
conversions, have attempted to prepare the audience by presenting
Frederick and Oliver as psychological wrecks, on the verge of
nervous breakdowns. This is surely wrong, for Shakespeare was
merely rounding off his comedy with a happy ending, the improbability being part of the fun. To force *As You Like It* into a
naturalistic mode is to maim it. In the last act there is a scene which

becomes almost operatic in its mockery of naturalism, with a quartet of wailing lovers:

*Pheb.* Good shepherd, tell this youth what 'tis to love.
*Sil.* It is to be all made of sighs and tears;
And so am I for Phebe.
*Pheb.* And I for Ganymede.
*Orl.* And I for Rosalind.
*Ros.* And I for no woman. . . .
*Sil.* It is to be all made of fantasy,
All made of passion, and all made of wishes;
All adoration, duty, and observance,
All humbleness, all patience, and impatience,
All purity, all trial, all obedience;
And so am I for Phebe.
*Pheb.* And so am I for Ganymede.
*Orl.* And so am I for Rosalind.
*Ros.* And so am I for no woman.
*Pheb.* If this be so, why blame you me to love you?
*Sil.* If this be so, why blame you me to love you?
*Orl.* If this be so, why blame you me to love you?
*Ros.* Why do you speak too 'Why blame you me to love you?'
*Orl.* To her that is not here, nor doth not hear.

(V.ii.76–101)

At this point Rosalind drops into prose and laughs at the artificiality of the scene:

Pray you, no more of this; 'tis like the howling of Irish wolves against the moon.

The finest scenes in the play are, of course, those in Arden between Orlando and Rosalind. Bernard Shaw ascribed their success to the fact that they were written in prose and there is a grain of truth in this paradox since, as we have seen, Shakespeare at this time in his career found it easier to express individualities of character in prose than in verse. Not wholly true, however, for Shaw himself complained that if you wreck the beauty of Shakespeare's lines 'by a harsh, jarring utterance, you will make your audience wince, as if you were singing Mozart out of tune' and Dorothea Baird's 'dainty, pleading narrow-lipped, little torrent of

gabble will not do for Shakespeare's Rosalind'. She resembled a
'canary trying to sing Handel'.[56]

Shaw's explanation of Rosalind's popularity need not be taken
seriously—that she speaks blank verse for only a few minutes, that
she soon gets into doublet and hose, and that like Shaw's Ann
Whitefield, she takes the initiative and does not wait to be wooed.
But Shaw was right to protest about the confusion of life and art by
those critics who describe Rosalind as 'a perfect type of woman-
hood'. To him she was 'simply an extension into five acts of the
most affectionate, fortunate, delightful five minutes in the life of a
charming woman'. This is not quite true, however, because
Rosalind is given misfortunes, as well as a wit that has never been
excelled.[57]

It is important to remember that the effect of these scenes in 1600
was rather different from that in the modern theatre: for Shakespeare did not have a Peggy Ashcroft or a Vanessa Redgrave to play
his heroine. His original audience would have seen a boy imper-
sonating a woman who was also a princess; they then saw this
princess pretending to be Ganymede, and Ganymede pretending to
be Rosalind, but in so doing guying the real Rosalind. It is
sometimes said that the chief reason why Shakespeare's heroines so
often disguised themselves as men was to simplify the task of the
actors playing the parts. This may have been true with some of the
early plays—the Induction to *The Taming of the Shrew*, Julia in
*The Two Gentlemen of Verona*—but Rosalind is far too complex
to be explained in this way. In Shakespeare's day there were a
number of different images imposed one on the other. We have a
boy pretending to be a woman, pretending to be a boy, pretending
to be a woman, satirising feminine behaviour. Rosalind, moreover,
though pretending to cure Orlando, is making certain she will fail;
for she makes him love the pretended Rosalind, and love more the
real one of which Ganymede is but the shadow.

In the scenes when Rosalind pretends to be Rosalind, Orlando is
merely a feed to her brilliant improvisations. Luckily his character
has been established early in the play. His name is that of a famous
lover, Orlando Furioso, whose story had been dramatised by
Greene;[58] and like his namesake he carves his love's name on tree
trunks. He shows both dignity and courage in his struggles with his
brother and Charles the wrestler; he saves the lives of Adam and of
Oliver; he answers Jaques's cynicism good-humouredly and sen-

sibly; iconographically he has been compared with Hercules,[59] and it is only as a lover that he is at a loss.

Most of Shakespeare's comedy is a critique of love; and in *As You Like It* different kinds of love are examined—the lust of Touchstone, the self-love of Jaques, the pride and vanity of Phebe, and the sentimental idealism of Orlando—are all found wanting. It would be a mistake, then, to regard the play as a mere pot-boiler, although it is obvious from the triumphant epilogue that it made the plot boil merrily: it is a highly sophisticated play that uses all the stalest devices of romantic fiction and popular drama so as to satisfy what Hamlet called 'the judicious'.

Perhaps the judicious of Shakespeare's day appreciated Touchstone more than we can. He never comes up to Jaques's description of him. Shaw, with pardonable exaggeration, asked, 'Who would endure such humour from anyone but Shakespeare?—an Eskimo would demand his money back if a modern author offered him such fare.'[60] The wit of Rosalind is undimmed by time; but Touchstone is dimmed. Yet Armin, who played the part, must have given such a performance that he opened Shakespeare's eyes to his potentialities and encouraged the poet to write the parts of Feste and Lear's Fool. The name Touchstone alludes to the fact that Armin had been a goldsmith—a nice private joke which is superior to any he is given to speak.

# 10
# Twelfth Night

In a performance of *Twelfth Night* at the Liverpool Playhouse some years ago the first two scenes were transposed so as to give Viola more time to don her masculine attire. The play, moreover, opened with a scene on board ship with Viola asking the Captain 'What country, friends is this?' The question could not in fact be heard because it, and the dialogue of the whole scene, was drowned by the noise of the sailors down below singing shanties. This did not greatly matter because throughout the scene a colour film was projected on the cyclorama, so that the ship appeared to be sailing down the coast of Jugoslavia, until at the end the harbour of Dubrovnik came into view. This is not the only production in which the first two scenes have been transposed, but even without the Liverpudlian aberrations, even if the play begins with the shipwrecked Viola on the coast of Illyria, the transposition is to be deplored. It is important that we should see Orsino before the Captain speaks of his love for Olivia, and before Viola proposes to take service with him. It is still more important that the play should begin and end not with words but with music, the only one of Shakespeare's plays which does.[61] The scene establishes both Orsino's sentimental love for Olivia and Olivia's equally sentimental love for her dead brother. The first words of the play should be:

> If music be the food of love, play on.
> Give me excess of it.

Orsino, it is made clear, is not in love with a woman, but with love; and the music provides an accompaniment to his self-indulgent day-dreaming. Olivia, in much the same way, rather fancies herself as a bereaved sister:

> The element itself, till seven years' heat,
> Shall not behold her face at ample view;
> But like a cloistress she will veiled walk,
> And water once a day her chamber round
> With eye-offending brine.                          (I.i.26–30)

The idea of Olivia walking once round her chamber each morning for seven years and squeezing out ritual tears for a dead brother whom she is afraid of forgetting—we are reminded that the salt in the tears is a preservative—is absurd to the audience, though not to Orsino; and its absurdity is still more apparent when we have the chance of comparing her actual behaviour with this account. Her picture of herself is quite different from the reality. She is not veiled like a nun, except when Orsino's messenger is received; we never see her shed a single tear; she enjoys the Fool; and she gets satisfaction from unveiling her face for Cesario to admire. When Geraldine McEwan played the part at Stratford-upon-Avon, she thoroughly enjoyed guying Olivia's affectations; but funny as this was, it is better to have Olivia unconscious, or only partly conscious, that she is putting on an act. We have to remember that she is still very young, and that Orsino is not really in love with her. Olivia's apparent inaccessibility is part of her charm. Orsino might almost say with the later poet:

Oh, what a stroke 'twould be! sure I should die,
Should I but hear my mistress once say 'ay'.

By the second scene of Act II we have been introduced to all the characters, including Olivia's four potential suitors, Orsino, Sebastian, Sir Andrew and Malvolio. On the appearance of Sebastian we know that Olivia's infatuation with Cesario will be happily resolved, and that Viola's love for Orsino will eventually be returned. Shakespeare, as Bertrand Evans demonstrated,[62] does not hoodwink his audience: it is the characters' ignorance of what the audience know that provides much of the irony. In Act II, scene ii Viola is given a soliloquy which neatly sums up the situation. Malvolio has just handed over Olivia's ring:

I left no ring with her; what means this lady?
Fortune forbid my outside have not charm'd her!
She made good view of me; indeed, so much
That methought her eyes had lost her tongue,
For she did speak in starts distractedly.
She loves me, sure: the cunning of her passion
Invites me in this churlish messenger.
None of my lord's ring! Why, he sent her none.
I am the man. If it be so—as 'tis—
Poor lady, she were better love a dream.
Disguise, I see thou art a wickedness
Wherein the pregnant enemy does much.
How easy is it for the proper-false
In women's waxen hearts to set their forms!
Alas, our frailty is the cause, not we!
For such as we are made of, such we be.
How will this fadge? My master loves her dearly,
And I, poor monster, fond as much on him;
And she, mistaken, seems to dote on me.
What will come of this? As I am man,
My state is desperate for my master's love;
As I am woman—now alas the day!—
What thriftless sighs shall poor Olivia breathe!
O Time, thou must untangle this, not I;
It is too hard a knot for me t'untie.          (II.ii.15–39)

The knots have been tied. In the remainder of the play we watch them being untied. The speech illustrates Viola's sympathetic humour and her lack of sentimentality and self-pity. It is characteristic of her that she should call herself 'poor monster' and show more pity for Orsino and Olivia than she does for herself.

By this point in the play all three plots have been set going. Viola has disguised herself as Cesario, fallen in love with Orsino, been sent to Olivia to plead his love and aroused that woman's love for herself. Malvolio's contemptuous words about Feste plant the seed of revenge; and Sir Andrew's hope of winning Olivia's hand, encouraged by Sir Toby, prepare the way for his reluctant challenge.

There follows the wonderfully funny scene (II.i) in which Malvolio in his night-shirt interrupts the revellers, and Maria plots her revenge with Feste and Sir Toby.[63] Sir Toby is a pleasant scoundrel, who is half-drunk for most of the play, who loves quarrelling and who gulls Sir Andrew out of his money as Iago gulls Roderigo. Sir Andrew is a simpleton, and Feste a professional Fool. They are less worthy as citizens than Olivia's steward, who is sober, industrious and reliable; and yet our sympathies in the theatre are wholly with the plotters. Some armchair critics have been led astray by Lamb's famous description of Malvolio as played by Bensley:

> Malvolio is not essentially ludicrous. He becomes comic but by accident. He is cold, austere, repelling; but dignified, consistent, and, for what appears, rather of an over-stretched morality. Maria described him as a sort of Puritan; and he might have worn his gold chain with honour in one of our old roundhead families, in the service of a Lambert, or a Lady Fairfax. But his morality and his manners are misplaced in Illyria. He is opposed to the proper *levities* of the piece, and falls in the unequal contest. Still his pride, or his gravity (call it which you will), is inherent, and native to the man, not mock or affected, which latter only are the fit objects to excite laughter. His quality is at the best unlovely, but neither buffoon nor contemptible. His bearing is lofty, a little above his station, but probably not much above his deserts. We see no reason why he should not have been brave, honourable, accomplished.[64]

According to other descriptions of Bensley's performance Lamb's memory was at fault and his interpretation of Malvolio really derived from his reading. Yet Shakespeare is careful to direct our responses. In the first scene in which he appears, he not merely criticises Feste, he criticises Olivia as well:

> I protest I take these wise men that crow so at these set kind of fools, no better than the fools' zanies.

Olivia, he implies, who has just been enjoying Feste's fooling, is acting as his stooge or feed. It is then that Olivia tells us that Malvolio is sick of self-love. This, we are meant to understand, is the central fact of his character. His self-love is apparent in the pompous description he gives of Cesario, in the way he distorts Olivia's message when she sends the ring, and in his dreams of marriage. He would not have been tricked by the forged letter if it had not seemed to be an answer to his own fantasies; this is made clear by his soliloquy just before he picks up the letter:

> Having been three months married to her, sitting in my state
> . . . Calling my officers about me, in my branch'd velvet gown,
> having come from a day-bed—where I have left Olivia
> sleeping—and then to have the humour of state; and after a
> demure travel of regard, telling them I know my place as I
> would they should do theirs, to ask for my kinsman Toby . . .
> Seven of my people, with an obedient start, make out for him. I
> frown the while, and perchance wind up my watch, or play
> with my—some rich jewel. Toby approaches, curtsies there to
> me . . . I extend my hand to him thus, quenching my familiar
> smile with an austere regard of control—saying 'Cousin Toby,
> my fortunes having cast me on your niece give me this
> prerogative of speech . . . You must amend your drunken-
> ness.'                                                    (II.v.41–68)

It is apparent that he is not in love with Olivia, but with the wealth and power marriage with her would bring. His ambitions are a nice fusion of sensuality, snobbery and the desire to interfere with the freedom of others.

We recover a little sympathy for him when he is treated as a madman and in his last speech, for the first time, he is allowed the dignity of verse. Shakespeare, as always gives the devil his due. Although Olivia admits that he has been notoriously abused, and had earlier rated his value at one half of her dowry, she makes no attempt to punish the culprits. Her last words to Malvolio may remind the audience of his withering remarks on professional fools:[65] 'Alas, poor fool, how have they baffled thee!'

Lamb's assumption that Malvolio is a puritan is based on Maria's remark that he is 'a kind of puritan', by which she means that he disapproves of harmless pleasures. She is picking up Sir Toby's question: 'Dost thou think because thou art virtuous there shall be no more cakes and ale?' But Maria soon corrects herself:[66]

> The devil a puritan he is, or anything constantly but a time-pleaser; an affection'd ass that cons state without book, and utters it by great swarths; the best persuaded of himself, so cramm'd as he thinks, with excellencies that it is his grounds of faith that all that look on him love him; and on that vice in him will my revenge find notable cause to work.     (II.iii.137–42)

Elizabethan actors and dramatists had no reason to love puritans because of their opposition to the stage; but Shakespeare's tolerance can be seen from the exchange between Sir Andrew and Sir Toby when Maria says that Malvolio is a puritan:

> *Sir And.*   If I thought that, I'ld beat him like a dog.
> *Sir Tob.*   What, for being a Puritan? Thy exquisite reason, dear knight.
> *Sir And.*   I have no exquisite reason for't; but I have reason good enough.
>
>                                                                    (II.iii.132–6)

To have no exquisite reason is, of course, a sign of irrational prejudice.

It is Feste who acts as a kind of chorus throughout the play; he is much more a touchstone than the character of that name. He sees through Malvolio's self-love and ambition; he appears to recognise that Maria intends to become Lady Belch; he satirises the element of sentimentality in Olivia's grief and in Orsino's melancholy; and, when Viola tips him, he thanks her with the words 'Now is next commodity of hair, send thee a beard'. He does not necessarily see through Viola's disguise, nor does he refer (as she quibblingly interprets) to her love for Orsino. He jokes with the other characters, laughs at them, sings for them, duns them for money, and (as Viola recognises) he is shrewd judge of character:

This fellow is wise enough to play the fool;
And to do that well craves a kind of wit.
He must observe their mood on whom he jests,
The quality of persons, and the time;
And, like the haggard, check at every feather
That comes before his eye. This is a practice
As full of labour as a wise man's art;
For folly that he wisely shows is fit;
But wise men, folly-fall'n, quite taint their wit.

(III.ii.57–65)

He has an unerring instinct for singing appropriate songs to his clients. When he sings to Orsino he asks the melancholy god to protect him, and his song fits in with the Duke's character and mood:

Come away, come away, death;
    And in sad cypress let me be laid;
Fly away, fly away, breath,
    I am slain by a fair cruel maid.        (II.iv.50–3)

As Sir Andrew chooses a love-song, because he does not care for good life, he sings 'O mistress mine', with its *carpe diem* theme:

What is love? 'Tis not hereafter,
Present mirth hath present laughter;
    What's to come is still unsure.
In delay there lies no plenty,
Then come kiss me, sweet and twenty;
    Youth's a stuff will not endure.        (II.iii.46–51)

His final song, after the rest of the cast have departed, is concerned with paradise lost, the innocence of childhood giving place to drunkenness, hangovers, and the rain that raineth every day. It is wrong to play Feste as a dying consumptive, as has sometimes been done, but despite his professional patter he is one of the most melancholy of Shakespeare's Fools, exceeded only by Lavache in *All's Well that Ends Well*.

The scene in which Feste sings before Orsino is constructed round his song. The tune is played during the initial dialogue between Orsino and Cesario and it is in this scene that she begins her education of the man she loves.[67] The conventional melancholy of the lover of the fair cruel maid is a commentary on Orsino's love for Olivia and on the more genuine, but still unreturned, love of Viola for Orsino. When she describes the tune of the old and antique song—

> It gives a very echo to the seat
> Where Love is thron'd—

Orsino recognises that Cesario must have been in love. And, for the first time in the play, he is roused to take an interest in something other than his own emotions. When he hears that Cesario's beloved is about his own age, he tells her that this is too old:

> let thy love be younger than thyself,
> Or thy affection cannot hold the bent;
> For women are as roses, whose fair flower
> Being once display'd doth fall that very hour.

(II.iv.35–8)

He recognises, again for the first time, that men's fancies

> are more giddy and unfirm,
> More longing, wavering, sooner lost and won
> Than women's are.

Ironically enough, after the song, he forgets this piece of insight; and asserts the superiority of his love to woman's:

> There is no woman's sides
> Can bide the beating of so strong a passion
> As love doth give my heart; no woman's heart
> So big to hold so much; they lack retention.
> Alas, their love may be call'd appetite.

(II.iv.92–6)

It is in answer to this piece of self-deception that Cesario tells the story of her imaginary sister[68] and so reveals the painfulness of her own position—not merely because her true love is unreturned and apparently unreturnable, but because she realises the element of sentimentality in Orsino's love for her rival.[69] But we know that Viola is too intelligent and too well-balanced to go the way of her 'sister';

> My father had a daughter lov'd a man,
> As it might be perhaps, were I a woman,

I should your lordship.
  And what's her history?
 A blank, my lord. She never told her love,
But let concealment, like a worm 'i th' bud,
Feed on her damask cheek. She pin'd in thought;
And with a green and yellow melancholy
She sat like Patience on a monument,
Smiling at grief. Was not this love indeed?
We men may say more, swear more, but indeed
Our shows are more than will; for still we prove
Much in our vows, but little in our love.

(II.iv.107–17)

Orsino is again taken out of himself sufficiently to ask if Cesario's sister had died of her love. When at the end of the play Cesario's sex is revealed, Orsino remembers this story and Cesario's confession that she would never love a woman as much as she loved him, and he proposes marriage. Just before this, however, there is a very strange episode when Orsino, suspecting that Olivia is in love with Cesario, and that this is the reason for his own lack of success, suddenly makes a ranting speech in which he proposes first to kill Olivia (as the thief in Heliodorus's story kills the woman he loves) and then changes his mind and decides to kill Cesario, whom he loves, merely to spite Olivia:

Why should I not, had I the heart to do it,
Like to the Egyptian thief at point of death,
Kill what I love?—a savage jealousy
That sometime savours nobly. But hear me this:
Since you to non-regardance cast my faith
And that I partly know the instrument
That screws me from my true place in your favour,
Live you the marble-breasted tyrant still;
But this your minion, whom I know you love,
And whom, by heaven I swear, I tender dearly,
Him will I tear out of that cruel eye
Where he sits crowned in his master's spite.
Come, boy, with me; my thoughts are ripe in mischief;
I'll sacrifice the lamb that I do love
To spite a raven's heart within a dove.

(V.ii.111–25)

It is possible to explain Orsino's melodramatic behaviour in more than one way. The overtly homosexual love of Antonio for Sebastian may suggest that Orsino is unconsciously jealous of the boy as well as of Olivia. But Viola, losing for a moment her common sense, declares:

> And I, most jocund, apt, and willingly
> To do you rest, a thousand deaths would die.

She knows that if the worst comes to the worst she can reveal her sex, and she uses the opportunity to make a declaration of the love she has hidden so long. She tells Olivia she is going

> After him I love,
> More than I love these eyes, more than my life,
> More by all mores, than e'er I shall love wife.
> If I do feign, you witnesses above,
> Punish my life for tainting of my love!

> (V.i.128–32)

It is, perhaps, unnecessary to seek for psychological explanations of this episode. Shakespeare uses it to bring about the revelation that Olivia is married and, as she supposes, to Cesario.

*Twelfth Night* is generally regarded as the crown of Shakespearian comedy, partly because it is a recapitulation of his comic method,[70] partly because the funny scenes are firmly based on character, and partly because it is the most poetical of the plays written up to this time, poetical not merely in the sense that it contains magnificent passages of poetry and two of Shakespeare's finest songs, but poetical in its total atmosphere. There are no imperfectly realised characters—with the possible exception of Fabian—and every member of the cast is given excellent opportunities. Sir Andrew Aguecheek, for example, a comparatively minor character, who has little to do in the main plot, except to challenge Viola to a duel; but every speech he has is perfectly in character, and nearly every line gets a laugh. We are told, before he appears, that he speaks 'three or four languages word for word without book'; but when Sir Toby asks: 'Pourquoi, my dear knight?', he replies 'What is "pourquoi"—do or not do?' Or, when he has been baffled by Maria's jokes, he remarks: 'Methinks sometimes I have no more wit than a Christian or an ordinary man has; but I am a great eater of beef, and I believe that does harm to my wit.' Or when Sir Toby asks him if he is good at these kickshawses, he replies; 'As any man in Illyria, whatsoever he be, under the degree of my betters; and yet I will not compare with an old man.' Or, when he is half drunk in the early hours of the morning, and Sir Toby tells him that Maria adores him, he says pathetically 'I was ador'd once too'.

The play is extraordinarily varied in its appeal. Viola is without the coruscating wit of Rosalind and Beatrice, but she can be quietly witty and ironical as she shows in her first embassy to Olivia. She retains both the admiration and the affection of the audience throughout the play. She may perhaps be described as the most lyrical of Shakespeare's heroines. Yet the scenes in which she appears would lose half their effectiveness if they were not juxta-posed with others of a more earthy character: The 'patience on a monument' scene is immediately preceded by the midnight revelling and immediately followed by Malvolio's discovery of the letter he thinks is Olivia's; and this in turn is followed by the exquisite scene in which Olivia proposes to Cesario, exquisite because of Shakes-peare's surmounting of the inherent difficulties of the situation. He retains our full sympathies for both characters, and neither loses her dignity. The recognition scene at the end, in spite of its easily parodied absurdities, is comparable to the great scene in *Iphigenia in Tauris*. The audience looks forward to the inevitable meeting of Sebastian with the sister he believes to be drowned, but this is far from detracting from its emotional impact.

*Twelfth Night*, steeped in music and poetry, is the most 'poetical' of Shakespeare's comedies. The transience of beauty, expressed more than once, and implied throughout the play, the feeling that

> women are as roses whose fair flower,
> Being once displayed, doth fall that very hour,

has many parallels in the *Sonnets*; and critics have compared[71] Keats's 'Ode on Melancholy':

> She dwells with Beauty—Beauty that must die;
>     And Joy, whose hand is ever at his lips
> Bidding adieu.

It is the most highly wrought of all Shakespeare's comedies and this is one of the reasons why Leslie Hotson's theory that it was written and rehearsed in a few days seems improbable.[72]

# IV · PROBLEM COMEDIES

The three plays considered in this section have been variously labelled as 'problem plays', 'problem comedies' and even, on a Shavian analogy, 'plays unpleasant'. Certainly the tone of the plays differs considerably from that of Shakespeare's early comedies. They are concerned mainly with sex, rather than love. The heroine of *Troilus and Cressida* sleeps with two men within the space of twenty-four hours; the hero of *All's Well that Ends Well* deserts his wife on his wedding day and commits what he thinks is adultery, and the heroine by performing the bed-trick becomes pregnant by her husband without his knowledge; the heroine of *Measure for Measure* refuses to save her brother's life by sleeping with the corrupt deputy, but cheerfully agrees to another woman taking her place. Apart from the nature of the plots, all three plays caused disquiet in the past because of their bawdy. Thersites and Pandarus harp on venereal disease and the comic relief in *Measure for Measure* is provided by bawds, pimps and lechers. The endings, moreover, are apt to leave audiences perplexed. The deserted Troilus tries vainly to avenge himself on Diomed; Helena has cornered Bertram but it is doubtful whether the play really ends well; Isabella apparently agrees to marry the Duke and Mariana is married off to the reluctant Angelo, marriages which are regarded as merely theatrical conveniences.[1]

It has been suggested on the one hand that the characteristics of the plays may be traced to Shakespeare's personal feelings resulting from the relationship with the Dark Lady of the Sonnets[2]—or some experience of which the sonnets were a dramatic projection. On the other hand, it has been argued that 'the disenchantment of the Elizabethans'[3] was widespread and that Shakespeare shared it with most of his contemporaries. Then again it has been supposed that the more realistic and satirical treatment of sex was a literary phenomenon in which Marston, Jonson and others participated,

1. Superior figures refer to notes at the end of the book (p. 207).

and that Shakespeare was complying with the fashion.⁴ There was, moreover, a war of the theatres to which Shakespeare alludes in the second act of *Hamlet* and which may have influenced *Troilus and Cressida*—notably in the sketch of Ajax in Act I, scene ii.⁵ Other critics have argued that as these three plays were written in Shakespeare's 'tragic' period, between 1600 and 1608, it is not surprising that they should share some characteristics of the tragedies. It has often been pointed out, for example, that *Hamlet* is close in spirit to *Troilus and Cressida* and that the Hecuba speeches in Act II show that the matter of Troy was still in Shakespeare's mind, as it was in the song about Helen in *All's Well that Ends Well*.⁶

There is a good deal to be said against all these explanations of the problem plays. In the first place, we do not know when they were written, some critics putting *All's Well* in Shakespeare's final period; but if we may accept the hypothesis that they were all written after *Julius Caesar* and before *Pericles*, we should remember that *Twelfth Night* belongs to the same period. Secondly, it is naïve to imagine either that a writer of tragedies has to be in a pessimistic frame of mind or that he cannot write *A Midsummer Night's Dream* in the same year as *Titus Andronicus*, *Hamlet* in the same year as *Twelfth Night*. Thirdly, although there was doubtless disenchantment at the end of Elizabeth I's reign and fear of the future, the early years of James I's reign were full of hope, especially for Shakespeare's company. Of course professional success does not guarantee personal happiness, but for many it provides a kind of substitute. Fourthly, although W. W. Lawrence's arguments⁷ about these plays have been deservedly influential we need not go all the way with him in assuming that the expectations of the audience and theatrical conventions necessarily conflicted with psychological realism.

Reacting against the view that these plays express nothing but cynicism and disgust, a large number of critics have argued that *Measure for Measure* certainly, and *All's Well that Ends Well* possibly, are plays about forgiveness.⁸ Some go further and turn *Measure for Measure* into an allegory, with Vincentio as God and Lucio as Lucifer, Elbow as the arm of the law and so on.⁹ As we shall see, there are things in *Measure for Measure* which conflict with such an interpretation. Nevertheless there are passages in these plays, as well as the general atmosphere in them and in *Hamlet*, which suggest that Shakespeare had become more conscious of the fact that he was living in a fallen world.

Most of the seven deadly sins are represented in *Troilus and Cressida*—Thersites as Envy, Diomed, Paris, Helen and Cressida as Lechery; Ajax as Pride; Achilles as Sloth at the beginning and Wrath at the end; and the omnipresent food imagery reminds us of Gluttony. One passage is of particular interest. When Troilus warns Cressida of the natural gifts and cultivated arts of the Grecian youths—hardly apparent in the Greeks we meet—he tells her that in their 'virtues'

> There lurks a still and dumb-discursive devil
> That tempts most cunningly. (IV.iv.89–90)

Although he does not doubt Cressida, he knows that no one is immune from temptation and that over-confidence often comes before a fall:

> But something may be done that we will not,
> And sometimes we are devils to ourselves,
> When we will tempt the frailty of our powers.

These lines remind us of St Paul's confession:[10]

> For I know that in mee (that is, in my flesh) dwelleth no good thing; for to wil is present with me; but I find no meanes to performe that which is good. For I doe not the good thing, which I would, but the evill, which I would not, that doe I. Now if I doe that I would not, it is no more I that doe it, but the sinne that dwelleth in me.

During the scene of Cressida's seduction, Thersites comments on the way 'the devil, lechery, with his fat rump and potato finger, tickles these two together'. This alerts us to the contrast between the bonds of heaven, tying Cressida to Troilus, and the bonds of hell, tying her to Diomed. The knot is five-finger tied and the five fingers of the devil tempting to lechery are looking, touch, foul words, kissing and copulation.[11] The first four we witness: for the fifth an assignation has been arranged.

In *Troilus and Cressida* the Christian terminology is anachronistic and, as one might expect, the plays set in the Christian era are more explicit in their references to scripture and doctrine. Hamlet, for example, associates the operations of the sexual instinct with original sin, and twice echoes the catechism.[12]

*Measure for Measure,* with its scriptural title, its parabolic undertones, and its overt concern with sin and forgiveness is the most Christian of Shakespeare's plays, and the only one to be expurgated by the Inquisition when a copy of the First Folio found its way to Spain.[13] Vincentio, on his first appearance, preaches on the test of 'Let your light so shine before men' in words partly taken from the adjacent chapter in St Mark's Gospel;[14] and for most of the play he is disguised as a friar. The world of Vienna is depraved. The sexual instinct is more dangerous than the wiles of Satan, though that cunning enemy baits his hook with a saint in order to catch a saint.[15] We need not accept the allegorical interpretation of the play, or the view that Shakespeare was fully aware of the difference between Catholic, Calvinist and Anglican views on grace,[16] or even that Shakespeare's treatment of the crucial texts on the Sermon on the Mount was ultimately more true to the spirit of Christ than that of most professional theologians;[17] but it is clear that Angelo's fall is another example of the Pauline confession—'The evill which I would not, that doe I'—and that Isabella's forgiveness of Angelo, in accordance with her earlier pleas for her brother's life, is a Christian exemplum.[18]

The theological content of *All's Well that Ends Well* has attracted less attention. In the very first scene, Parolles argues against virginity because it is made up of self-love, 'the most inhibited sin in the canon'; but the devil can cite Erasmus for his purpose[19] and Parolles contradicts his former argument when he tells Bertram, 'A young man married is a man that's marred'. The method by which he tempts his young friend is by advising him to follow his own desires. He urges him to model himself on the fashionable courtiers, 'though the devil lead the measure' and Lafen remarks that the devil is Parolles's master.

Lavatch, 'a shrewd knave and unhappy' is the most melancholy of Shakespeare's clowns and he is more like an unfrocked priest than a jester. He is always talking about damnation. He tells the wealthy Countess, his mistress, that many of the rich are damned; he confesses that he is 'driven on by the flesh'; and he alters the refrain in a ballad about Helen of Troy from 'one bad in ten' to 'one good in ten'. Helena and the Countess both belong to the saving remnant, the tenth who are saved.[20]

It has been suggested[21] that Shakespeare renamed Giletta so as to play on the contrast between Helen of Troy with his heroine. Helen of Troy was a marriage-breaker, a cause of war, a destructive force, the destroyer of a king; Helena is the healer of a king, a redemptive force, a marriage-mender and a peace-maker. One was foolish, the other intelligent; one was immoral, the other an active moral agent; one is an adultress, the other by the pretence of adultery wins back her husband; and one was the sport of fortune, while the other repudiates predestination.

Lavatch refers again to damnation when he tells Lafeu that if he wished he could serve as great a prince as him, 'The Black Prince, sir; alias, the Prince of Darkness; alias, the devil'. But he decides against it:

> I am a woodland fellow, sir, that always loved a great fire; and the master I speak of ever keeps a good fire. But, sure, he is the prince of the world; let his nobility remain in's court. I am for the house with the narrow gate, which I take to be too little for pomp to enter. Some that humble themselves may; but the many will be too chill and tender; and they'll be for the flow'ry way that leads to the broad gate and the great fire.

This recalls Macbeth's Porter's phrase, 'the primrose way to the everlasting bonfire'. It is based, of course, on two passages in St Matthew's Gospel[22] though the flowers that strew the broad way are not explicitly scriptural.

In Act IV Bertram has to listen to scathing criticisms of his character from the man who has served as his pimp:

> Count Rousillon, a foolish idle boy, but for all that very ruttish ... a dangerous and lascivious boy, who is a whale to virginity, and devours up all the fry it finds.   (IV.iii.202ff.)

What he does not hear is the frank criticism by two French Lords:

*1 Lord.* He hath perverted a young gentlewoman here in Florence, of a most chaste renown; and this night he fleshes his will in the spoil of her honour. He hath given her his monumental ring, and thinks himself made in the unchaste composition.

*2 Lord.* Now, God delay our rebellion! As we are ourselves, what things are we!

*1 Lord.* Merely our own traitors. And as in the common course of all treasons we still see them reveal

> themselves till they attain to their abhorr'd ends; so
> he that in this action contrives against his own
> nobility, in his proper stream, o'erflows himself.
> 2 *Lord.*  Is it not meant damnable in us to be trumpeters of
> our unlawful intents?
>
> (IV.iii.12ff.)

It is apparent that Bertram has been boasting of his assignation
with Diana. The Lords then discuss the news of Helena's death, and
one of them says he is heartily sorry that Bertram will be glad of it.
They do not suggest that he is exceptionally bad. It is every man,
including themselves, they are deploring. They conclude, as
Shakespeare means us to conclude, that we are all a mixture of
good and bad, the web of our life being a mingled yarn.

This is, perhaps, a sign that Shakespeare had come to have a
more sombre, or at least a more realistic, view of human nature
than he had done. There are villains in some of the earlier comedies
and sinners in all of them; but although he would have paid lip
service to the idea that all men were sinners, it is only in the
problem plays that he seems fully to have believed it. Hence the
stress in both *Measure for Measure* and *All's Well that Ends Well*
on the necessity of repentance, and the concomitant necessity of
forgiveness.


# II
# *Troilus and Cressida*

Even in Shakespeare's day, it was difficult to decide what kind of
play *Troilus and Cressida* was meant to be. In the 1609 quarto, it
was called a history on the title-page, but in his epistle the publisher
claimed that it was 'passing full of the palme comicall', none of
Shakespeare's comedies being 'more witty then this'.[23] In 1623,
after some hesitation, due partly to copyright difficulties, the
editors of the First Folio placed it at the forefront of the tragedies.
The same difficulty of classification has continued to the present
day. John Palmer, who had the advantage of seeing Edith Evans's
début as Cressida, called it a comedy; but a year later he changed
his mind and referred to it as a tragedy.[24] Oscar J. Campbell and

Alice Walker, believing it was influenced by the satirical plays of Jonson and Marston, labelled it a comical satire. Other critics, of whom I am one, have called it a tragical satire. Others again have supposed that an originally tragic play was later modified by the Pandarus epilogue.

The labels are not important except in so far as they prejudice the interpretation of character or of individual speeches. Campbell, who assumed that Troilus was satirised as an Italianate roué, interpreted his speech 'O that I thought it could be in a woman' (which expresses a doubt whether any woman can be constant to her life's end) to mean that he doubted whether any woman could 'satisfy the demands of his discriminating, if voracious sensuality'.[25] Another key speech, after Troilus has witnessed Cressida's seduction, Campbell regarded as comic. Directors, taking their cue from Campbell and Walker, have not merely made the most of the satirical scenes, they have assumed that the two debates—in the Greek camp and in Troy—should be played for laughs. Thersites and Pandarus, commentators on the war plot and the love plot, are taken to be the spokesmen for the poet; and one dramatic critic[26] headlined his review of a Stratford production: THERSITES WAS RIGHT. But Homer's account of Thersites makes it clear that he was a scurrilous railer, and this is clearly his character in Shakespeare's play. Although much of what he says is true, it is all coloured by his nasty-mindedness and malice.

Those who are determined to regard the play as a comical satire argue that the Latinised vocabulary is deliberately bombastic, or that we are meant to contrast the grandiloquent words with the sordid deeds. Those, on the other hand, who believe that the play is predominantly tragic explain the latinisms as an attempt on Shakespeare's part, perhaps imitated from Chapman's Homer,[27] to adopt a language appropriate to the Homeric characters, and they point to the Sergeant's account of the battle in the second scene of *Macbeth*, or the Dido speeches in *Hamlet*, close in time and spirit to *Troilus and Cressida*, as parallels to the language used in that play.

There are some scenes which all critics would regard as comic— for example the dialogue between Pandarus and Cressida in the second scene, or the scene in which Ajax is flattered—and there are other scenes which nearly everyone would regard as tragic (for example, the death of Hector) or predominantly serious (for example, the discussion between Ulysses and Achilles, the debate in

Troy about Helen). But there are many scenes which can be played in different ways or in which the audience's reactions are bound to be mixed. Shakespeare, indeed, often demands a mixed response. We can watch the scene between Cressida and Diomed as a black satirical comedy, with the choric comments of Thersites directing our responses. But Thersites is not aware until the end that the scene is also watched by two other characters, Troilus and Ulysses, with whom we are more likely to sympathise. Ulysses is puzzled, as well he may be, by the passionate outbursts of his guest; but to Troilus the scene he witnesses means the tragic collapse of his world. We are expected to laugh at Thersites's obscenities and, the next moment, to feel with Troilus.

Even in the two debate scenes, from which both Thersites and Pandarus, the cynical commentators, are excluded, our reactions are bound to be mixed, however much an officious director may wish to tilt our responses one way or the other. Impressively as Agamemnon and Nestor may orate, we may well feel that they are using a lot of grandiloquent words to express very simple ideas—an impression which is later supported by the account of Patroclus's parodies, in which Agamemnon's pomposity is compared to

> a strutting player whose conceit
> Lies in his hamstring

and in which his Nestor exhibits 'the faint defects of age'

> to cough and spit
> And, with a palsy-fumbling on his gorget,
> Shake in and out the rivet.

These imitations, as Ulysses is careful to explain, are slanders, but they are nevertheless recognisable from what we have seen of the originals. Ulysses's speech on degree, despite its being a tissue of commonplaces and despite the way in which the foxy orator later overturns degree, is impressive rather than hollow; for it has two important functions in the structure of the play. It illustrates the discrepancy between words and deeds which is everywhere apparent, and by its insistence on the indivisibility of order—order in the universe, in the state, and in personal relations—it prepares the way for the coming of chaos through the infidelity of Cressida.

The discrepancy between words and deeds extends also to a discrepancy between word and word. Not merely does Troilus in the first scene refuse to fight and then go off for the battlefield, he speaks scornfully of Helen, painted with the blood of both Greeks and Trojans, and in Act II passionately defends her retention because her

> youth and freshness
> Wrinkles Apollo's, and makes pale the morning.

Hector, as passionately, demonstrates that the moral laws of nature and of nations demand that Helen should be returned to Menelaus, and then, in a notorious *volte-face*, votes for her retention

> For 'tis a cause that hath no mean dependence
> Upon our joint and several dignities.

At this point we are entitled to lament the lapse of a hero or laugh at human inconsistency.

The whole point of the Cressida story, as told by Chaucer and as Shakespeare inherited it, was that Troilus was a faithful lover, Cressida a faithless one and Diomedes lecherous. Troilus can be foolish, absurdly deluded, sexually naïve; but it is difficult to see how Shakespeare could present him as an Italiante roué. Of course any poet can take a basic plot and alter the tone completely, as Nashe retold the tale of Hero and Leander,[28] but there is nothing in the love plot of *Troilus and Cressida* to suggest that Shakespeare was doing this. Indeed, at one point in the play the poet goes out of his way by the flaunting of an unnaturalistic technique to remind the audience of his following of tradition. In III.ii, just before the lovers share a bed, the three main characters in the love-plot step forward in their legendary roles of Faithful Lover, Wanton and Pander.[29] Troilus claims that he is

> true as truth's simplicity,
> And simpler than the infancy of truth

and says that in future ages he will be treated as the exemplar of faithful love:

> True swains in love shall in the world to come
> Approve their truth by Troilus; when their rhymes,
> Full of protest, of oath and big compare,
> Want similes, truth tired with iteration . . .
> Yet, after all comparisons of truth,

> As truth's authentic author to be cited,
> 'As true as Troilus' shall crown up the verse,
> And sanctify the numbers.

Cressida takes up the ritual vow:

> Prophet may you be!
> If I be false, or swerve a hair from truth,
> When time is old and hath forgot itself,
> When waterdrops have worn the stones of Troy,
> And blind oblivion swallow'd cities up,
> And mighty states characterless are grated
> To dusty nothing—yet let memory
> From false to false, among false maids in love,
> Upbraid my falsehood . . .
> Yea, let them say, to stick the heart of falsehood,
> 'As false as Cressid'.

Pandarus then rounds off the scene:

> If ever you prove false to one another, since I have taken such
> pains to bring you together, let all pitiful goers-between be
> call'd to the world's end after my name—call them all Pandars;
> let all constant men be Troiluses, all false women Cressids, and
> all brokers between Pandars. Say 'Amen'.          (III.ii.165–200)

Shakespeare would have been grotesquely incompetent at this point
in the play if he had wanted us to regard Troilus as a rake. Indeed
his speeches while he awaits the coming of Cressida read like the
fantasies of an inexperienced young man. Much has been made of
the lines where he imagines himself crossing the river Styx to a
paradise where he can

> wallow in the lily-beds
> Proposed for the deserver.

The idea that *wallow* should suggest piggery and hot lust receives a
jolt when it is realised that in the only other context where
Shakespeare uses the word it is associated with December snow and
the frosty Caucasus.[30]

Troilus's fault is not that he is a 'sexual gourmet' but that he
indulges in a fatal tendency to idealisation both with regard to
Helen and Cressida, and that he substitutes aesthetic considerations

for moral ones. As Hector tell him, anachronistically, he is

> not much
> Unlike young men, whom Aristotle thought
> Unfit to hear moral philosophy. (II.ii.165)

Yet Ulysses gives us an enthusiastic character-sketch derived from
what Aeneas has told him:

> a true knight.
> Not yet mature, yet matchless—firm of word,
> Speaking in deeds and deedless in his tongue,
> Not soon provok'd, nor being provok'd soon calm'd;
> His heart and hand both open and both free;
> For what he has he gives, what thinks he shows,
> Yet gives he not till judgment guide his bounty,
> Nor dignifies an impair thought with breath;
> Manly as Hector, but more dangerous;
> They call him Troilus, and on him erect
> A second hope as fairly built as Hector. (IV.v.96ff.)

It could be argued that Troilus does not fully deserve this eulogy on
his judgment, and it is odd to have it said that he never utters an
'impair' (i.e. unconsidered) thought. Nevertheless we are meant to
take Ulysses's speech as in some sense a choric utterance, as his
earlier speech on Cressida as a daughter of the game prepares the
way for her transformation; and Troilus does indeed emerge as the
natural leader of Troy in the last scene of the play.

The Trojan leaders are, however, deeply flawed. Although they
escape Thersites's savage debunking, it would be wrong to follow
Wilson Knight's eloquent argument that in contrast to the Greeks
they stand[31]

> for human beauty and worth, the Greek party for the bestial
> and stupid elements of man, the barren stagnancy of intellect
> divorced from action, and the criticism which exposes these
> things with jeers.

Ulysses, the one intellectual in the Greek camp, is no mere
intellectual than Hector. Nor can it be said that the Greeks stand
for intellect and the Trojans for emotion; for pride, vanity, the
pursuit of self-interest and lust (all displayed by one or more of the
Greeks) are no less emotional than sexual desire, or the worship of

honour and prestige. Wilson Knight suggests that in *Troilus and Cressida* Shakespeare's two primary values, Love and War, 'exist in a world which questions their ultimate purpose and beauty'. But what Shakespeare was doing was rather to expose the false glamour attached to sex and the royal occupation of war. Under the influence of the sexual instinct, Troilus endows Cressida, charming as she is, with moral qualities she does not possess, just as he idealises the worthless Helen. It is made clear in the debate in Troy that Helen is not worth fighting about; it is made even clearer by the one scene in which we meet the face that launched a thousand ships, a face that masks the stupidest woman in all Shakespeare's thirty-eight plays; it is made clearest of all in the exchange between Paris and Diomed, where the latter describes her as a whore:

> For every false drop in her bawdy veins
> A Grecian's life hath sunk; for every scruple
> Of her contaminated carrion weight,
> A Trojan hath been slain.                    (IV.i.71ff.)

The siege of Troy was the most famous military operation in legendary history, the origin of three of the greatest epics and of some of the greatest plays by Aeschylus, Sophocles and Euripides. Shakespeare, it is clear, was seeking for the realities behind the cosmetics of poetry, not merely in the brutal comments of Thersites but in the actions and characters of the Greek and Trojan heroes. The Trojans come off more lightly than their enemies if only because of the legend that a Trojan refugee landed in Britain, and because both Virgil and Caxton told the story from the standpoint of the defeated. Even in the *Iliad* Hector is much more sympathetic to a modern reader than his killer. Shakespeare intensifies Achilles's unpleasantness by depriving him of his genuine grievance against Agamemnon, by making the relationship between him and Patroclus more patently sexual, by making him break his solemn vow to Hecuba—the vow itself being a kind of treachery—and, above all, by turning the killing of Hector into a murder by a gang of his thugs soon after Hector has spared his life. Beside such conduct, Hector's seems venial—his voting for the continuance of the war, his chivalric treatment of the enemy in the interests of 'fair play', his refusal to heed Cassandra's warnings, and his succumbing to the temptation of some golden armour. Yet the Trojans as a whole are collectively responsible for violating the moral law, as Shakespeare makes plain. Nor was his attitude to the Trojan War essentially changed by his first opening Chapman's Homer. As we can see by the descriptions of the Greeks in the painting of the siege, which Lucrece contemplates after her rape.[32] Achilles is not described; in Ajax is to be seen 'blunt rage and rigour', Ulysses is 'sly', Pyrrhus is a brutal killer and Sinon is a hypocrite. Helen is 'the strumpet that began this stir'; Paris's lust, as in the play, is the firebrand that destroyed Troy; and Priam is blamed for his lack of wisdom in not checking his wanton son. But Lucrece believes that the Trojans as a whole ought not to have been punished for the 'private pleasure' of Paris:

> Let sin, alone committed, light alone
> Upon his head that hath transgressed so.

But by the debate in Troy on whether Helen should be handed over—which was apparently a favourite exercise in Elizabethan schools—Shakespeare emphasises that the guilt is shared by Hector, Troilus and Priam and the majority of the Trojan council.

There is another respect in which *Lucrece* is an interesting forerunner of *Troilus and Cressida*, namely in its imagery. The description of Troy, to which we have referred, is preceded by the heroine's long tirade against opportunity and Time (876–1024). Time is described as 'mis-shapen', 'carrier of grisly care', 'eater of youth', 'virtue's snare', and in a splendid phrase, 'thou ceaseless lackey to Eternity'. Some of the imagery used about Time links up with four famous passages in *Troilus and Cressida*:

> Thou grant'st no time for charitable deeds (908)

> Time's glory is to calm contending kings (939)

> To ruinate proud buildings with thy hours,
> And smear with dust their glitt'ring golden towers (944–5)

> To feed oblivion with decay of things (947)

> Let him have time a beggar's orts to crave
> And time to see one that by alms doth live
> Disdain to him disdained scraps to give. (985–7)

Ulysses's speech to Achilles on the power of Time[33] mentions 'good deeds past', the scraps which are 'alms for oblivion', the charity which, like love and friendship, is subject to 'envious and calumniating time' and the 'gilt o'er-dusted' which is no longer praised. The speech is in the very centre of the play (III.iii.145ff.) and although it is ostensibly concerned with Achilles's loss of reputation, it also reflects on the love-plot. In the previous scene, only a few lines earlier—and by a subtle trick chronologically later—the lovers have sworn eternal fidelity,

> When time is old and hath forgot itself,
> When waterdrops have worn the stones of Troy,
> And blind oblivion swallowed cities up,
> And mighty states characterless are grated
> To dusty nothing.                        (III.ii.181–5)

Between Cressida's vow and Ulysses's speech the Greeks have agreed to exchange Antenor for her and the audience knows that the lovers are to be separated. Ulysses reminds us that love is subject to time and in the scene in which Troilus parts from his beloved there are further links with Lucrece's diatribe. She too had called time injurious:[34]

> Injurious time now with a robber's haste
> Crams his rich thievery up, he knows not how.

Here, too, we have the same linkage of Time with a wallet. Troilus continues with the cooking imagery characteristic of the play and of *Lucrece,* which contains 25 drawn from that field:

> As many farewells as be stars in heaven,
> With distinct breath and consign'd kisses to them,
> He fumbles up into a loose adieu,
> And *scants* us with a single *famish'd* kiss,
> *Distasted* with the *salt* of broken tears.        (IV.iv.43–7)

As Whiter pointed out[35] the last line was suggested by the idea of broken meats. The kitchen imagery is repeated (as Whiter again pointed out) in Troilus's speech after he has witnessed Cressida's seduction by Diomed:

> The fractions of her faith, orts of her love,
> The fragments, scraps, the bits and greasy relics
> Of her o'er-eaten faith, are bound to Diomed.

> (V.ii.156–8)

Both *orts* and *scraps* echo the *Lucrece* passage.

Most of the food images in *Lucrece* associate sexual desire with feeding, and its satisfaction with surfeiting. Tarquin considers that 'the profit of excess/Is but to surfeit'; his lust is compared to a lion's 'sharp hunger'; he is described after his crime as 'surfeit-taking'—

> His taste delicious, in digestion souring,
> Devours his will, that liv'd by foul devouring;—

and, we are told a few lines later that

> Drunken Desire must vomit his receipt,
> Ere he can see his own abomination.

The link between the time and cooking imagery is that time is not merely a devourer, but also a bloody tyrant; and the ravisher is not merely a devourer of innocence, but a tyrant as well.

It has often been pointed out that in the *Sonnets* Shakespeare seems to have been poignantly aware of the 'irreparable outrages' of Time.[36] Time is the implacable enemy of youth and beauty, of fame, and even of love. In the early sonnets the poet argues that marriage, by perpetuating the beauty of the beloved, is the one sure way of making war 'upon this bloody tyrant, Time'. Later in the sequence the poet declares that his eternal lines will immortalise the beloved—so he answers the question:

> how shall summer's honey breath hold out
> Against the wrackful siege of battering days,
> When rocks impregnable are not so stout,
> Nor gates of steel so strong, but Time decays?    (LXV)

He protests that he himself will remain constant despite Time with his scythe. He proclaims in the most confident of the sonnets that

> Love's not Time's fool, though rosy lips and cheeks
> Within his bending sickle's compass come;    (CXVI)

but he is agonisingly aware, as Troilus is half aware, that he cannot rely on the constancy of others. Although he believed that his own love would not alter when it alteration found, love is often 'converted from the thing it was'. Here in the *Sonnets*, then, whether they are fact or fiction, or a blending of both, we have a foretaste of the love-plot of *Troilus and Cressida*—an obsessive concern with the destructive power of time and a realisation of the vulnerability of constancy. Inconstancy was, of course, one of the themes of *The Two Gentlemen of Verona*, and it is touched on more light-heartedly in *A Midsummer Night's Dream*. In *Troilus and Cressida* it is treated as black comedy indeed.

Apart from the imagery linking the two plots—and there are more food images in the war scenes than in the love scenes—and apart from the exposure of glamour and idealisation of sordid realities—the plots are linked together in various ways. The immediate cause of Cressida's infidelity is the separation caused by the war, in which personal relations are ruthlessly sacrified to national policy. Yet the death of many warriors on both sides, the imminent destruction of Troy and the enslavement of the survivors can all be traced to the precisely opposite cause—the sacrifice of the public good to private desire—just as in the Greek camp the private desires and jealousies of the leaders—and the treachery of Achilles—prolong the siege.

We have seen the relevance of the Ulysses's speech on Time to the action of the play and that it was necessary for Shakespeare to make Ulysses build up the idea of the indivisibility of order for the destruction of that order by the frailty of one woman to have so devasting an effect on Troilus. Other scenes which have been condemned as 'undramatic' are equally necessary for the full expression of the ideas behind the play. The debate about the proposal to return Helen to Menelaus does not merely reveal the moral weakness of the Trojan cause and Hector's tragic flaw, it is also a discussion about the nature of values, aesthetic and moral, subjective and objective, about the distinction between true ideals and idealisations.

Hector begins the debate by stating that Helen does not belong to them, and even if she had belonged to them she would not be worth the cost of keeping her. Troilus retorts that the royal prerogative of Priam should not be confined by fears and reasons; and when Helenus reproves him Troilus retaliates *ad hominem* by accusing his brother of cowardice. Hector again asserts that Helen is not worth keeping. Troilus retorts that value is entirely subjective: 'What's aught but as 'tis valued?' Hector denies this:

> But value dwells not in particular will:
> It holds his estimate and dignity
> As well wherein 'tis precious of itself
> As in the prizer. 'Tis mad idolatry

> To make the service greater than the god;
> And the will dotes that is attributive
> To what infectiously itself affects,
> Without some image of th'affected merit. (II.ii.53ff.)

Both with regard to Helen (about whom the debate is concerned) and, as we soon discover, with regard to Cressida, Troilus is guilty of mad idolatry.

The later argument of Troilus and Paris—that by retaining Helen they wipe off the guilt of the rape, which they had all applauded— is scornfully repudiated by Hector, who points out that the

> moral laws
> Of nature and of nations speak aloud
> To have her back return'd. Thus to persist
> In doing wrong extenuates not wrong
> But makes it much more heavy (184ff.)

Hector is the only one of the debaters who sees clearly what ought to be done, and he alone votes against his conscience. He reveals at the end of the scene that he has sent a challenge to the Greeks, so that his powerful arguments are irrelevant to his actions, but the discrepancy between thought and action is, as we have seen, very relevant to the theme of the play.

Another scene of related interest is also concerned with value. Ulysses, in trying to persuade Achilles to leave his sulking, warns him that his great deeds will be forgotten if he rests on his laurels; but, before this speech on the power of time, Ulysses purports to quote from the book he is reading:

> A strange fellow here
> Writes me that man—how dearly ever parted,
> How much in having, or without or in—
> Cannot make boast to have that which he hath,
> Nor feels not what he owes, but by reflection;
> As when his virtues shining upon others
> Heat them and they retort that heat again
> To the first giver. (III.iii.95ff.)

A parallel is often cited from the first scene of *Measure for Measure* where the Duke tells Angelo,

> Heaven doth with us as we with torches do,

> Not light them for themselves; for if our virtues
> Did not go forth of us, 'twere all alike
> As if we had them not.                    (I.i.33ff.)

This in turn is based on the scriptural[37] 'Let your light so shine
before men, that they may see your good works'. But Ulysses does
not mean that we should exercise our virtues for the sake of others,
but that we have no value in ourselves and only know our worth by
the opinion of others. Whereas Troilus claims that value depends
on individual belief or prejudice, and Hector thinks it is objectively
in the thing or person assessed, Ulysses argues that it depends
entirely on the opinion of others. Achilles does not quite follow
Ulysses's point. He substitutes the mirror image for that of refrac-
tion:

> This is not strange, Ulysses.
> The beauty that is borne here in the face
> The bearer knows not, but commends itself
> To other's eyes; nor doth the eye itself—
> That most pure spirit of sense—behold itself,
> Not going from itself; but eye to eye opposed
> Salutes each other with each other's form;
> For speculation turns not to itself
> Till it hath travell'd, and is mirror'd there
> Where it may see itself.                    (III.iii.102ff.)

There is no need to suppose that Shakespeare derived this idea from
Plato. He could have thought of it for himself, or remembered
similar ideas in Cicero, in Erasmus, or in *Nosce Teipsum.* (Sir John
Davies, indeed, uses the term 'spirit of sense'.) Ulysses reverts to his
author's drift,

> Who, in his circumstance, expressly proves
> That no man is the lord of anything,
> Though in and of him there be much consisting
> Till he communicate his parts to others;
> Nor doth he of himself know them for aught
> Till he behold them formed in th'applause
> Where th'are extended; who, like an arch, reverb'rate
> The voice again.                    (114ff.)

The cynicism of this, compared with the moral imperative of the

*Measure for Measure* passage, is made apparent when Ulysses goes on immediately to discuss Ajax, admittedly worthless, but now renowned. Achilles does not know that the Greeks who pretend to admire Ajax continue to despise him, so that the glory reflected on him is worthless——and this fact really disproves Ulysses's line of argument.

In her brilliant essay ' "Opinion" and "Value" in *Troilus and Cressida*', Winifred Nowottny argues[38] that Ulysses

> who desires stability in society and conceives of that stability as dependent upon the fixity of social values, moves amid the fleeting mirror-images of opinion, images so unfixed that he himself sets up as a manipulator of their shadow-play.

This is surely true; but one is more doubtful, in view of Hector's strictures, to accept her view that Shakespeare sides with Troilus, the spokesman for poetic truth:

> Whereas Ulysses uses Degree as a protection against Chaos . . . Troilus wrests out of the actual experience of Chaos the new perception of the oppugnancy of real and indestructible entities . . . Troilus finds that poetic value may be contradicted by reason and fact, but its existence is not thereby cancelled or negated. Poetic value survives, because it can create in the teeth of fact. It is the only conception in the play which can survive, since in the world of the play every conception is challenged by fact.

As I argued a year before Mrs Nowottny's article appeared,[39] Shakespeare appears to be much more critical of Troilus than she allows; nor do I think that Troilus's belief in the truth of the imagination survives his disillusionment because Cressida's unfaithfulness seems to upset order in the microcosm and the macrocosm. In the last scenes of the play Troilus has become a realist.

Shakespeare, I believe, was more detached than some critics have allowed. Even Una Ellis-Fermor argued[40] that the content of the poet's thought is 'an implacable assertion of chaos as the ultimate fact of being', though the 'idea of chaos, of disjunction, of ultimate formlessness and negation, has by a supreme act of artistic mastery been given form'. We may agree about the artistic mastery, but not that Shakespeare was asserting that life was meaningless. He was asserting something much more limited, something defined by the world of the play. He was saying that men engage in war in support of unworthy causes; that they are deluded by the sexual instinct to fix their affections on unworthy objects; that they sometimes act in defiance of what they know to be right; that they are usually motivated by self-interest. But he was not saying that absolute values are illusions or that all women are Cressids, for Troilus himself, at the very moment of disillusionment, dissociates himself from such a position. The violation of order and the betrayal of values does not imply that all values are illusions—quite the contrary indeed.

One of the reasons why *Troilus and Cressida* has been interpreted in so many different ways is that we are continually made to change our point of view. In nearly all the other plays we look at the action through the eyes of one or two closely related characters. We see *Hamlet* through Hamlet's eyes, never through those of Claudius; *King Lear* through Lear's eyes—or Cordelia's, or Kent's—but never through the eyes of Goneril; *The Tempest* through Prospero's eyes. It is true that another point of view is often given, and a character such as Horatio or Enobarbus may sometimes act as a chorus. But in *Troilus and Cressida* the point of view is continually changing. At one moment we watch events through the eyes of Troilus, and the war seems futile. In a later scene we see the events through the eyes of Hector, and Troilus in advocating the retention of Helen seems to be a romantic young fool. In the Greek camp we see everything from Ulysses's point of view; and then, a little later, however much we despise and dislike Thersites, we became infected with his views on the situation:

> Lechery, lechery; still wars and lechery; nothing else holds
> fashion: a burning devil take them!          (V.ii.196–7)

It is this shifting of emphasis which makes the play so difficult to grasp as a unity; but although Tillyard complains[41] that Shakespeare failed to fuse his heterogeneous materials into a unity, I believe the unity is there. Yet we distort the play if we make any one character to be Shakespeare's mouthpiece. The worldly standards of Ulysses are not Shakespeare's, though Shakespeare apparently shared, until the end of the sixteenth century, some of his views on Order. In general Ulysses appears more of a Baconian than a Shakespearian in his attitude. Others have argued that Shakespeare speaks mainly through the mouth of Thersites, though Thersites was renowned for his knavish railing in all Shakespeare's sources, including the *Iliad,* and also in Heywood's play about the Trojan war, written afterwards. Shakespeare could enjoy writing his curses, as we can enjoy hearing them, without sharing the bitterness of his creature. Others, again, suppose that Hector is Shakespeare's real spokesman, though perhaps his attitude to the character was not unlike his attitude to Hotspur.

Tillyard thinks that Shakespeare was 'exploiting a range of feelings more critical and sophisticated than elemental and unfeignedly passionate', that he plays 'with the fire of tragedy without getting burnt', and that 'he meant to leave us guessing'. We may agree with him that the play provides 'a powerful if astringent delight', but doubt whether it is necessary to make all these qualifications. It is quite possible to be critical and sophisticated at the same time as one is elemental and unfeignedly passionate. This, surely, is what the metaphysical poets accomplish when they are at their best; and if we are to place *Troilus and Cressida* it is not with the banned satirists, or even with the satirical plays of Marston and Jonson, it is rather as Shakespeare's excursion into the metaphysical mode. The most remarkable thing about the play is perhaps the way in which the poet managed to fuse thought and feeling, to unify an extraordinary mass of materials, and to counter the sense of chaos and disruption, not so much by the sense of order implicit in the artistic form, as by his establishment of the values denied or corrupted in the action. Cressida does not stain our mothers. In reading most of Anouilh's plays we feel that the sordid compromises of adult life make suicide the only proper solution for an idealist. But although *Troilus and Cressida* is a kind of *pièce noire*, we should never be in danger, after seeing it performed, of thinking that it gives Shakespeare's verdict on life, at any rate his permanent verdict. Cressida did not cancel out Rosalind and Viola or make it impossible for him to create Desdemona or Cordelia. He did not 'square the general sex by Cressida's rule'.

The play, from one point of view, in its exposure of 'idealism', might be regarded as the quintessence of Ibsenism as interpreted by Shaw. From another point of view, as we have seen, it is a dramatic statement of the power of Time. From a third point of view it shows how 'we are devils to ourselves': the world and the flesh make the best the victims of the worst. We may admit that the fusing of these

themes required extraordinary imaginative power—a power which
Shakespeare on the threshold of the tragic period amply demonstrated. The real problem about the play is the failure of most critics
to appreciate it.

## 12

# *All's Well that Ends Well*

When the play which Joseph Price in his admirable book calls *The
Unfortunate Comedy*[42] was revived at Stratford in 1955, T. C.
Worsley exclaimed:[43]

> What a ridiculous, badly written, ill-constructed play *All's
> Well that Ends Well* is! ... Only piety keeps it in the
> repertoire, and that piety is surely misplaced ... No audience
> of sensible people would solemnly tolerate such rubbish.

Worsley is not one of those bard-hating critics who welcome the
opportunity of expressing the dislike and boredom they experience
with all Shakespeare's plays by attacking one of his weakest; and
his views probably reflected the views of most of the audience.
Stratford tried again in 1959 with a production of the play by
Tyrone Guthrie. He had the advantage of a magnificent performance by Dame Edith Evans as the Countess and a very good
performance by Zoe Caldwell as Helena. In spite of which Guthrie
did not trust the play. He put it into modern dress, which was
generally satisfactory, but he dressed one of the armies as Desert
Rats and introduced a new scene in which a general tried to address
the troops through a microphone. More seriously, he depicted the
chaste Diana (as her name implies) as a Cockney tart and her
mother as the keeper of a brothel. This made nonsense of the last
scene of the play. Nevertheless the play was a great success; and it
proved, if proof were needed, that whatever flaws it may possess, it
is still a good acting play, which does not need directorial cosmetics, even if we are sceptical about the appropriateness of its title.

   At the end of the play, when Bertram has capitulated to the wife
he had despised, the King, not cured of his match-making, proposes
to let Diana choose a husband, and he declares somewhat uncer-
tainly:

> All yet seems well, and if it end so meet,
> The bitter past, more welcome is the sweet.

To some critics the title is supremely cynical. How can the marriage of Bertram and Helena be anything but disastrous? Helena is too clever by half, and far too good for the snobbish, lecherous liar Bertram has proved to be. The sexual instinct, we are told, has driven a charming and virtuous girl to pursue and capture a worthless prize. She will eventually realise Bertram's shoddy character and he will never forget his humiliation at her hands.

Historical critics, such as W. W. Lawrence,[44] point out that readers of Boccaccio and Elizabethan audiences would admire the cleverness of the heroine in performing the apparently impossible task of becoming pregnant by a husband who had sworn not to consummate the marriage, and they would not probe into the psychology of either husband or wife. The difficulty of such an interpretation is that Shakespeare blackened the character of Bertram, who is more snobbish than Beltramo, insufferably rude to his bride and the bosom companion of the disreputable Parolles. Above all, Shakespeare makes Bertram's fellow officers highly critical of his morals and exposes him in the last scene as a cowardly liar. Boccaccio's characters are puppets: Shakespeare's very success in investing the characters with reality is apt to be a source of embarrassment. Moreover Bertram's speech of repentance is so feeble that readers have suspected that the poet had lost faith in the validity of his title:

> If she, my liege, can make me know this clearly
> I'll love her dearly, ever, ever dearly.

A poet dramatising Boccaccio's tale had three alternatives. He could concentrate on the cleverness of the heroine in achieving the impossible; he could examine in depth the psychology of the protagonists and show how the hero is finally cornered by a Shavian heroine—Helena was much admired by Shaw—and leave the audience in doubt whether the marriage could be satisfactory; or he could attempt to show that Helena succeeds in educating her husband, and that the marriage, against all odds, may well succeed. I think it can be shown that psychological realism is not incompatible with a potentially happy marriage.

It has often been observed[45] that the older generation is depicted sympathetically in the play, and the young are regarded as something of a disappointment—a view which must have been particularly common in the early years of the seventeenth century.[46] The Countess, 'the finest old woman's part ever written'[47] according to Shaw, obviously feels that Bertram is inferior to his father; Lafeu, who is portrayed with warmth and sympathy, is scornful of the younger generation; and when Bertram arrives at Court, the King says his father 'Might be a copy to these younger times'. Among his qualities, not shared by his son, are politeness and humility.

Helena is, of course, a notable exception to the prevailing decadence. She is loved and admired by all the sympathetic characters and even to Lavatch, the gloomy fool, she is a herb of grace.[48] She is used by Shakespeare as the exemplar of his central theme that 'virtue is the true nobility'.[49] She is not rich (as Giletta in Boccaccio's tale) and she is not given a train of suitors; but she is beautiful, virtuous, pious, self-reliant and touchingly vulnerable in her love.

A 'lady not born of any noble blood, but beautified with noble conditions, ought far to be preferred before her whose birth is noble and renowned', but whose behaviour is unnoble.[50] The King is the spokesman for these irreproachable sentiments. When Bertram refuses to accept Helena as his bride because she is a poor physician's daughter, the King replies:

> Tis only title thou disdain'st in her, the which
> I can build up. Strange is it that our bloods,
> Of colour, weight, and heat, poured all together,
> Would quite confound distinction, yet stand off
> In differences so mighty. If she be
> All that is virtuous—save what thou dislik'st,
> A poor physician's daughter—thou dislik'st
> Of virtue for the name; but do not so.

Then the King continues in rhymed couplets which solemnly enforce the moral:

> From lowest place when virtuous things proceed,
> The place is dignified by th' doer's deed;
> Where great additions swell's, and virtue none,
> It is a dropsied honour. Good alone
> Is good without a name. Vileness is so;

The property by what it is should go,
Not by the title. She is young, wise, fair;
In these to nature she's immediate heir;
And these breed honour. That is honour's scorn
Which challenges itself as honour's born
And is not like the sire. Honours thrive
When rather from our acts we them derive
Than our fore-goers. The mere word's a slave,
Debauch'd on every tomb, on every grave
A lying trophy; and as oft is dumb
Where dust and damn'd oblivion is the tomb
Of honour'd bones indeed. What should be said?
If thou canst like this creature as a maid,
I can create the rest. Virtue and she
Is her own dower; honour and wealth from me.

(II.iii.115ff.)

The contrast between true nobility and the false nobility of birth
is displayed throughout the play. Some, such as the Countess and
Lafeu, are as noble in character as they are in birth. One character,
Parolles, is ignoble in both respects. Bertram is noble in birth but
ignoble in character; and yet Helena, who is clear-sighted in every
other way, thinks of him as 'a bright particular star' in whose
'bright radiance and collateral light', she must be comforted, 'Not
in his sphere'.

Helena, unlike Bertram, knows that Parolles is a liar, a fool and a
coward, but her love of Bertram embraces the braggart, and she
cheerfully discusses her virginity with him despite his obscenity. It
enables us to get a glimpse of her sexual longing as well as of her
chastity and she is wistfully aware of the rewards her love might
offer in a speech which to Parolles is merely a prophecy of
Bertram's sexual adventures at Court.[51] In Helena's soliloquy
which follows, she makes it clear that she is not going to sit like
Patience on a monument; she is going to try to find a remedy:

Our remedies oft in ourselves do lie,
Which we ascribe to heaven. The fated sky
Gives us free scope; only doth backward pull
Our slow designs when we ourselves are dull.          (I.i.202)

The Countess makes her confess her love—in what one is

tempted to call one of Shakespeare's most exquisite scenes—and Helena says:

> I know I love in vain, strive against hope,
> Yet in this captious and intenable sieve
> I still pour in the waters of my love
> And lack not to lose still. Thus, Indian-like,
> Religious in mine error, I adore
> The sun that looks upon his worshipper
> But knows of him no more.                        (I.iii.192ff.)

In the same speech, where she refers to the Countess's experience of love, Helena, by her fusion of Diana and Venus, reinforces the point of the earlier discussion on virginity. The Countess sends her to Paris with her leave, her love, and her blessing.

At first the King refuses to let Helena try her cure, but he is won over partly by her father's fame, partly by her willingness to be tortured to death if she should fail, but mostly by the incantation of her rhymed verse.[52] She relies on prayer—'the greatest Grace lending grace'—more than on medicine; and she appears in this scene, not as a young girl desperately in love, but as one divinely inspired. Here again her virginity is important. The miraculous nature of the cure is emphasised by Lafeu's denial at the beginning of II.iii that the age of miracles is past, and by his description of it as 'A showing of a heavenly effect in an earthly actor'.

Although some sympathy is aroused for Bertram by the reluctance of all the courtiers lined up for Helena's inspection—to Lafeu's indignation, who thinks they should all be castrated—the scene is a ritual in rhymed verse, and linked in style with Helena's persuasion of the King; and, in choosing Bertram, she professes to be his servant:

> I dare not say I take you; but I give
> Me and my service ever whilst I live
> Into your guiding power.

Moreover she waives her claim to Bertram when she realises his reluctance; and he forfeits the sympathy of the audience by the rudeness of his rejection, by his choice of war in preference 'To the dark house and the detested wife', and by his refusal ever to consummate the marriage. The Countess's indignation for his 'misprizing of a maid too virtuous For the contempt of empire'; her declaration that Helena 'deserves a lord That twenty such rude boys might tend upon' and that Bertram's sword can never win again the honour he has lost guide the responses of the audience. Helena utters no word of blame. She determines to go into exile so that Bertram can return home:

> I will be gone,
> My being here it is that holds thee hence.
> Shall I stay here to do't? No, no, although
> The air of paradise did fan the house,
> And angels offic'd all.                    (III.ii.121–5)

She prays for his safety and blames herself for endangering his life.

On arriving in Florence she is lucky enough to meet the girl Bertram is trying to seduce; but since she is not seeking her husband, as in Boccaccio's tale, but is going on a pilgrimage, we are meant to understand that it is providential, rather than lucky, that she is able to take Diana's place at the assignation. It is made clear that Bertram's ring is an heirloom that should only be given to his wife and that although he thinks it dishonourable to wed a beautiful and virtuous woman below him in rank, he nevertheless seduces a woman of a still lower class under promise of marriage. Helena comments wryly on the way Bertram was able to take delight in her body in the belief that it was Diana's:

> O strange men!
> That can such sweet use make of what they hate,
> When saucy trusting of the cozen'd thoughts
> Defiles the pitchy night.                    (IV.iv.21ff.)

It provides the psychological justification for the bed-trick—the element of imagination or self-deception in sexual love.

Helena has little to do in the remainder of the play, but after she is reported dead she wins golden opinions from the Countess, the Clown, the King and even from Bertram, who (Lafeu tells us)

> lost a wife
> Whose beauty did astonish the survey
> Of richest eyes, whose words all ears took captive;
> Whose dear perfection hearts that scorned to serve
> Humbly called mistress.                    (V.iii.15ff.)

But although Helena is present only in the last thirty-five lines of the final scene, she is a 'triumphant general who has mapped the strategy from the rear' and 'she steps forward just in time to accept unconditional surrender'.[53] Whether or no the title of the play can be accepted as a straightforward comment on the ending, with Bertram's acknowledgement of his wife, depends on our acceptance of his education and reformation, the second miracle that the play presents to us.

Shakespeare makes it clear from what even his friends say that Bertram is disgracefully proud of his birth, that he is a poor judge of character, that his one redeeming characteristic is personal bravery, and that he is insolent and cruel to his wife. The deficiencies of his character are brought out by his friendship with Parolles, who flatters him and his vices, and acts as his pimp. Other characters see through him at once. Lafeu warns Bertram that 'there is no kernel in this light nut'; Diana immediately characterises him as a vile rascal; his fellow-soldiers expose him as a coward and a traitor who not merely reveals military secrets, but makes slanderous statements about Bertram and other officers. Parolles's exposure is also an exposure of Bertram; and his fellow-soldiers, while admiring the latter's bravery, are clearly shocked by his morals. They deplore his attempt to seduce the chaste Diana and by his callousness in keeping his assignation with Diana on the day he hears of his wife's death. What they do not know is that he had promised to marry Diana, without the slightest intention of keeping his word.

The exposure of Parolles is the first step in Bertram's re-education and we are told he is upset by a letter from his mother, reproving him for his treatment of Helena. He returns home with some reputation as a soldier, but with an unenviable reputation as a seducer of virgins. As a French lord charitably puts it:

> The web of our life is of a mingled yarn, good and ill together. Our virtues would be proud if our faults whipt them not; and our crimes would despair if they were not cherished by our virtues . . . The great dignity that his valour hath here acquired for him shall at home be encountered with a shame as ample.                                                    (IV.iii.66–9)

When Bertram returns to Rousillon, he thinks that he is freed from the fetters of what he regards as a misalliance, and he assumes that he has seen the last of Diana. A marriage is arranged with

Lafeu's daughter and he alleges that a prior attachment to her was his main objection to marrying Helena:

> Thence it came
> That she whom all men prais'd, and whom myself,
> Since I have lost, have lov'd, was in mine eye
> The dust that did offend it.

It is clear that the King has not wholly forgiven Bertram's treatment of Helena:

> love that comes too late,
> Like a remorseful pardon slowly carried,
> To the great sender turns a sour offence,
> Crying 'That's good that's gone'. (V.iii.52–60)

Still, the Countess urges the King to regard Bertram's offence as 'Natural rebellion done i' th' blaze of youth', and Lafeu is reconciled to him, as he seems to have turned over a new leaf.

At this point his ordeal begins. The King recognises the ring Bertram gives Lafeu as a token for his daughter, as the one he had given Helena. He claims that it was thrown to him from a casement in Florence, but he is forthwith arrested on suspicion of murdering his wife. Then Diana's letter is read, claiming Bertram as a husband. He retorts that she was a common prostitute, but she proves him a liar by showing the ancestral ring Bertram thought he had given her. Diana, in Barbara Everett's phrase,[54] 'has pursued Bertram like a prim and pretty member of the Eumenides', driving him from lie to lie. Even the Parolles he now despises is brought in to expose him. Accused of murder, a self-confessed adulterer and liar, Bertram's 'fame is shrewdly gored'. The man who thought Helena was too far beneath him is despised by everyone. At this point the pregnant Helena enters, and all is explained. Obviously she might have spared Bertram an unpleasant ordeal, without having Diana as an accomplice by pointing to the ring on his finger—a symbol of the King's power. She does not spare Bertram, partly because Shakespeare wanted a more prolonged and exciting scene, and partly because Helena knows that her husband's corruption can only be cured by such torture. As Bertrand Evans says,[55] Bertram has been

> scratched deep by the longest and stealthiest nails in Shakes-

peare. Yet the scratches are benign, for against the great odds
of a corrupt world they have cured his corruption.

So we may hope. It is worth remembering that all Bertram's worst
traits were added by Shakespeare—his friendship with Parolles, his
rejoicing at the death of his wife, his promise of marriage to the girl
in Florence, the parting with the ancestral heirloom, his smirching
of the girl's character. The blacker his character, the greater the
miracle of his redemption.

Some of the dissatisfaction with the ending of the play is that
there are less than thirty lines between the final entrance of Helena
and the end of the play, and of these Bertram is given less than
three. He takes only half a line to acknowledge Helena as his wife,
when he replies to her 'The name and not the thing' with the words
'Both, both, O pardon!' Otherwise he is given a perfunctory couplet
in the conditional mood. But what we miss in reading can be
provided by a good performance. We can only guess what is
passing through Bertram's mind as his hidden sin and shame are
brought to light, and then he thinks he will be executed for a
murder he did not actually commit. His relief when he sees that she
is alive will be obvious; but a good actor will convey by a look, a
gesture, a pause, his genuine repentance as the Count in *The
Marriage of Figaro*, when he is exposed, is given only two words to
sing, '*Contessa, perdona!*' The reconciliation is helped by Helena's
visible pregnancy and of Bertram's memory of the night when he
made sweet use of the woman he thought he hated. All is not yet
well, because this is only the beginning of Helena and Bertram's
marriage; but the audience can hope that Bertram will find in his
wife what she had prophesied when she thought marriage with him
was an impossible dream:

> There shall your master have a thousand loves,
> A mother, and a mistress, and a friend,
> A phoenix, captain, and an enemy,
> A guide, a goddess, and a sovereign,
> A counsellor, a traitress, and a dear;
> His humble ambition, proud humility,
> His jarring concord, and his discord dulcet,
> His faith, his sweet disaster; with a world
> Of pretty, fond, adoptious christendoms
> That blinking Cupid gossips.                    (I.i.154–63)

# 13
# *Measure for Measure*

Until the present century *Measure for Measure* had few admirers. 'Beyond any competition, the most offensive play in the English language', wrote one critic, and Coleridge confessed that it was the only one of Shakespeare's plays he disliked. Even as late as the 1930s a lady wrote to *The Gloucestershire Echo* to complain:[56]

> My sense of decency and cleanliness are outraged ... The coarse and crude language of the characters, their unhygienic habits, and the light way they spoke of women and sex, disgusted me, who am no prude.

In 1935 it was said that the play insulted 'the respectability of Melton Mowbray people'; two years later the Vicar of Buxton objected to a performance in the town; and in 1970 the Joint Matriculation Board received complaints for including it in the Advanced Level syllabus. By this time, however, such complaints wore an old-fashioned air: all responsible critics now agreed, with different reservations, and with widely differing interpretations, that the play was masterly. The change was due partly to increasing frankness and to the relevance of the play to an increasingly permissive society, but it was also due to a realisation that the play is about forgiveness, that the author was not shown by the play to be disillusioned and disgusted with life, and that it is absurd to find in it 'the lowest depths of Jacobean cynicism'.[57]

Those critics who admire the play nevertheless disagree among themselves. Some argue that Shakespeare began the play as an impressive tragi-comedy, written in some of his greatest verse, with the main characters superbly delineated and the painful situation of Isabella, the temptation of Angelo and the fears of Claudio all poignantly displayed. Then, it is said, at the moment when Isabella rejects Claudio's plea and the eavesdropping Duke intervenes, we are precipitated into a different sort of play, an amusing comedy of intrigue, written mainly in prose, in which the characters become puppets manipulated by the Duke. So inferior, it is claimed, is the second half of the play, that some think that Shakespeare must have had a collaborator—possibly Middleton, whose early play, *Phoenix*, is about a ruler who disguises himself to discover the abuses of the city.

Although there is no evidence that Shakespeare had a collaborator, it is true that the tone of the play changes after line 151 of Act III, scene i. Most of the scenes thereafter are written in prose, and what verse there is is much less impressive than that of the scenes in which Isabella pleads for her brother's life and in which Claudio pleads with her to accept Angelo's monstrous offer. Tillyard argues particularly that the last long scene, whether witnessed in the theatre or read in the study is a failure:[58]

> Its main effect is that of labour. Shakespeare took trouble; he complicated enormously; he brought a vast amount of dramatic matter together. The actors know it is a big scene and they try to make it go. Perhaps their efforts just succeed; but then the success will be a tribute more to their efforts than to the scene itself.

Unfortunately for Tillyard's argument, in each of the half dozen productions I have seen this last act has been an immense success. (The only exception, a recent production at Stratford-upon-Avon in which the Duke was supposed to be the hated actor-manager of the company, and in which he was let down from the skies as a *Deus ex machina*, cannot be blamed on Shakespeare.)

It is true that most of the best poetry is in the first half of the play and that there is comparatively little memorable poetry in the last act, but a reader may not realise the effectiveness of that act unless he makes allowances for the dramatic use of silences. Angelo has very little to say but the audience can watch his face during the torture he experiences; Isabella and Claudio say nothing to each other, but silence is the perfectest herald of joy; Isabella does not reply to the Duke's proposal of marriage, but whether she accepts or refuses words are unnecessary; and, above all, it requires three appeals by Mariana before Isabella kneels to the Duke to beg for Angelo's life. In Peter Brook's production there was a long pause after Mariana's third appeal; and Kenneth Tynan argued[59] that Shakespeare's final scene had been enormously improved by the (superior?) genius of Peter Brook.

Into this dreadful act [Brook] inserts half a dozen long pauses, working up a new miracle of tension which Shakespeare knew nothing about. The thirty-five seconds of dead silence which elapse before Isabella decides to make her plea for Angelo's life were a long, prickly moment of doubt which had every heart in the theatre throbbing.

Tynan's mistake was to suppose that such a long pause had not been Shakespeare's intention. What Brook had really done was to recover that intention, as a good director should.

The deterioration of the last acts of the play from the point of view of a reader may be admitted, but not from the point of view of an audience. The two halves of the play are less disparate than the two halves of *The Winter's Tale*, that much admired diptych. Nevertheless, it may well be argued that the solution to the problem posed in the first acts of *Measure for Measure* is something of an evasion.

One line of criticism, stemming from Walter Pater, and including such diverse figures as G. Wilson Knight, R. W. Chambers, Muriel Bradbrook and Roy Battenhouse, interprets the play as a religious or morality play, parabolic or allegorical.[60] Knight compared Vincentio to the man in the parable who took a journey into a far country. Professor Bradbrook pointed out affinities with morality plays, and suggested that the play might be named *The Contention between Justice and Mercy, or False Authority unmasked by Truth and Humility*. Professor Battenhouse went further still and claimed that the whole play is an allegory of the Atonement—Vincentio being God, Isabella 'devoted to God', Claudio 'lame one', Elbow the arm of the law and Lucio Lucifer. Less tendentiously, R. W. Chambers in his British Academy Lecture in 1937, pointed out that the play was performed, perhaps for the first time, on the feast of St Stephen, that its theme is Christian forgiveness, and that the Duke tests Isabella by seeing whether she can forgive the man who has wronged her, actually withholding from her the knowledge that Claudio has not been executed.

When we come to examine these 'Christian' interpretations of the play we find that the critics differ radically among themselves. Chambers and Knight agree against Battenhouse and Bradbrook that the play is not allegorical, but whereas Chambers thinks of Isabella as a saintly creature whose anger against Claudio is successfully designed to shame him into a proper frame of mind,

Knight argues that she has failed in her ordeal:[61]

> Is her fall any less than Angelo's? Deeper, I think. With whom
> is Isabel angry? Not only with her brother. Ever since Angelo's
> suggestion she has been afraid. Now Claudio has forced the
> responsibility of choice on her. She cannot sacrifice herself . . .
> She has been stung—lanced on a spot of her soul. She knows
> now that it is not all saintliness, she sees her own soul and sees
> it as something small, frightened, despicable, too frail to dream
> of such a sacrifice. Though she does not admit it, she is
> infuriated, not with Claudio, but herself. Saints should not
> speak like this.

Even Traversi, much more sympathetic to Isabella, declares that
although the dilemma—between her duty as sister and Sister—is
beyond any perfect solution, she 'shows no understanding of the
natural root of Claudio's sin'.[62]

We should remember than in none of Shakespeare's possible
sources is the heroine a novice about to enter the sisterhood of St.
Clare. There can be little doubt that the poet made the alteration
deliberately. Any ordinary virtuous woman would at least consider
acceding to Angelo's blackmail—Isabella, as conceived by Shakespeare, could not. In addition to having an innate horror of sexual
vice—though not, as some think, of sex itself—Isabella's religious
convictions and training would make her regard death of a beloved
brother less of an evil than the attempt to redeem him by
committing a mortal sin, regarded by Claudio as the least but by
her as the greatest. It should, moreover, be stressed that the
notorious couplet in which she expresses her decision—

> Then Isabel live chaste, and brother die!
> More than our brother is our chastity—            (II.iv.184–5)

should not be regarded as priggish and self-regarding. They are a
nice example of Shakespeare's habit of informing the audience by a
gnomic couplet of the essence of the situation.

Isabella genuinely believes—and her belief would be shared by
some at least of the original audience—that

> Better it were a brother died at once,
> Than that a sister by redeeming him
> Should die for ever.                              (II.iv.106–8)

Nor is there any reason to doubt her assertion to Claudio:

> O were it but my life,
> I'ld throw it down for your deliverance
> As frankly as a pin. (III.i.105–7)

These two sentences chime with what she had told Angelo:

> were I under the terms of death,
> Th'impression of keen whips I'd wear as rubies,
> And strip myself to death as to a bed
> That longing have been sick for, ere I'd yield
> My body up to shame. (II.iv.100–4)

There is nothing in these speeches which supports Wilson Knight's remarks about the fearfulness and meanness of spirit of Isabella. Besides being fervently religious and anxious for severer restrictions than the sisterhood means to impose on her, she is also one willing and anxious for self-sacrifice, and one who is (one is tempted to say) charged with sublimated sensuousness. Claudio recognises— and this is the first thing we hear of Isabella—that

> in her youth
> There is a prone and speechless dialect
> Such as move men. (I.ii.175–7)

Sir Arthur Quiller-Couch was foolish to speak of there being something rancid in her chastity,[63] and so was the critic who said that her humanity was pitiless, her virtue self-indulgent, unimaginative and self-absorbed. And yet one cannot but feel that R. W. Chambers was a little disingenuous in his discussion of the scene between Isabella and her brother, when he justifies her violent outburst by saying it was an agonised outcry which brings Claudio to his senses as cold reasoning would not have done.[64] This is what she actually says:

> O you beast!
> O faithless coward! O dishonest wretch!
> Wilt thou be made a man out of my vice?
> Is't not a kind of incest to take life
> From thine own sister's shame? What should I think?
> Heaven shield my mother play'd my father fair!

For such a warped slip of wilderness
Ne'er issued from his blood. Take my defiance!
Die, perish. Might but my bending down
Reprieve thee from thy fate, it should proceed;
I'll pray a thousand prayers for thy death,
No word to save thee. . . .
                              O fie, fie, fie!
Thy sin's not accidental, but a trade.
Mercy to thee would prove itself a bawd;
'Tis best that thou diest quickly.

*Claud.*                      O, hear me, Isabella.

                                        (III.i.138–52)

In the first place we should note that R. W. Chambers is wrong to
say that Isabella's outburst has the effect he describes. Claudio is
still pleading for his life when the Duke intervenes, and his change
of heart is due to his being told that Angelo had no intention of
seducing Isabella. Secondly, it is not Isabella's anger which is so
disturbing to an audience, but rather her complete lack of sympathy
with her brother's wish to live and the extraordinary way in which
she blackens her mother's reputation and refers to mercy—on
which she had eloquently spoken to Angelo—as a bawd.

Some critics, who have accepted part of the allegorical interpretation of the play and have allowed that the Duke in some sense
stands for God, have argued that Shakespeare was satirising the
idea of the providential government of the universe.[65] Vincentio, it
is said, is a self-important busy-body, full of dubious schemes, cruel
with regard to Isabella, when he conceals the fact that Claudio has
not been executed, lying to Claudio about Angelo's intentions, and
pardoning everyone except Lucio, the one person who had person-
ally offended him.

At one point in the play the Duke is compared to God. Angelo,
when he sees the unmasking of the Friar-Duke, exclaims:

                  O my dread lord,
I should be guiltier than my guiltiness
To think I can be undiscernible,
When I perceive your grace, like power divine,
Hath look'd upon my passes.                    (V.i.364–8)

The Duke is like God in one respect—his apparent omniscience.

Angelo, of course, is not equating him with God. Critics have rightly pointed out that to a Jacobean audience, and especially to James I himself, a ruler was God's deputy; and that the good ruler would symbolise some characteristics of the deity.[66] It may be that it is only in this respect that we should allow Vincentio's allegorical significance.

It has been argued that morality techniques and allegory do not blend successfully with the unusually naturalistic methods of characterisation used by Shakespeare in the first two acts of the play.[67] When we have watched the agony and fall of Angelo, the tragic dilemma of Isabella and Claudio's terror of death, we cannot easily let them fade into abstractions. I think this is to misunderstand Shakespeare's methods. His allegorising is never more than intermittent. The biblical title and echoes from the gospels may have prepared a church-going, homily-instructed audience for such moments as Angelo's words about the Duke, for hearing a theological undertone in the Duke's marriage to Isabella, and in suspecting now and again that Lucio is another name for Lucifer.

It has been argued with equal force that the psychological realism conflicts with the theatrical trickery of the second half of the play. We are led to expect a serious working out of the problems involved in the situation and are given instead a series of evasions—entertaining and bustling scenes which are nevertheless disappointing. In particular we are asked to swallow the bed-trick, impossible in itself, and which a Friar should not propose nor a novice accept.

We saw in connection with *All's Well that Ends Well* that the bed-trick can be defended. In *Measure for Measure* it is thematically necessary for Angelo to be caught in the same sin for which he has sentenced Claudio. Just as Claudio and Juliet were a betrothed couple who postponed marriage—but not sexual relations—so as not to lose a dowry, so Angelo, once engaged to Mariana, but repudiating her because of a dispute about her dowry, is tricked into sleeping with her. His fault is, of course, much worse than Claudio's, because of his shabby blackening of Mariana's character, his blackmail of Isabella, and his failure to keep his side of the bargain.

Mariana's substitution for Isabella is not the only one in the play.[68] The plot is set in motion by the fact the Duke chooses Angelo as his substitute. The Duke himself acts as a substitute as

prison visitor and as Juliet's confessor. Mistress Overdone acts as a
substitute mother for Lucio's bastard by Kate Keepdown. But the
most peculiar substitutions, so peculiar that Shakespeare deliberately calls our attention to them, are the two heads designed to be
substituted for Claudio's on the block. The first is Barnardine, a
drunken murderer with no redeeming characteristics. He is created
for the sole purpose of providing a head which can be sent to
Angelo as Claudio's. He is

> A man that apprehends death no more dreadfully but as a
> drunken sleep; careless, reckless, and fearless of what's past,
> present, or to come; insensible of mortality, and desperately
> mortal.                                                    (IV.ii.135–8)

The Duke forthwith orders his execution and a few seconds later
changes his mind

> A creature unprepar'd, unmeet for death,
> And to transport him in the mind he is
> Were damnable.                                             (IV.iii.63–5)

Some critics supposed that it was Shakespeare, rather than the
Duke, who could not bear to have the rogue killed. This surely is
less likely than the poet's wish to call our attention as forcibly as
possible to the theme of substitution. The Provost reveals that
Ragozine, a notorious pirate, has just died of a fever, and that
(unlike Barnardine) he closely resembles Claudio. As we haven't
seen the pirate, and as he is conveniently dead already, he cannot
charm us into wishing for his reprieve. The Duke exclaims, as well
he might,

> O, tis an accident that heaven provides.

It is, in fact, a coincidence manufactured not by the deity but by the
dramatist; and if, as has been suggested,[69] Shakespeare himself
played the part of the Duke, the line would bring down the house.
    It has been observed that in one of Isabella's speeches to Angelo,
she points out that all men are sinners:

> Why, all the souls that were were forfeit once
> And He that might the vantage best have took
> Found out the remedy.                                      (II.ii.74–6)

This divine substitution is the climax of this particular theme. It is a
long way from the substitution of a dead pirate's head for that of a

drunken murderer; but the bed-trick performed by the loving and forgiving Mariana expresses in carnal terms something of the same idea of sacrifice.

Another theme, of more central importance, is what the Duke calls in his opening speech, the properties of government, particularly with regard to law—whether leniency or severity is the best policy, to what extent sins and crimes should be made to coincide, how may the teaching of Christ be reconciled with the exercise of government and law, what are the qualities to be looked for in a good ruler. Considered from the realistic point of view—and at times we are encouraged to do this—the deplorable state of Vienna is directly due to the Duke's policy of not enforcing the 'strict statutes and most biting laws' during a period of fourteen years: the laws are ignored and 'liberty plucks justice by the nose'. Friar Thomas quite properly asks him why he has left it to Angelo to enforce the law; and the Duke replies that he wants to avoid the inevitable unpopularity. He confesses, too, that he wants to test Angelo, to see whether power will change his purpose—but this remark is not part of the realistic motivation but merely a hint to the audience of what is to follow.

Later in the play[70] the Duke is given a curious soliloquy on the qualities of a good ruler, contrasted with Angelo's failure:

> He who the sword of heaven will bear
> Should be as holy as severe;
> Pattern in himself to know,
> Grace to stand, and virtue go.          (III.i.243–67)

Finally, in the last scene of the play, the Duke is seen dispensing justice. At first, still in disguise, he claims to have seen

>                    corruption boil and bubble
> Till it o'errun the stew. Laws for all faults,
> But faults so countenanc'd that the strong statutes
> Stand like the forfeits in a barber's shop
> As much in mock as mark.                (316–20)

This presumably refers to the time before Angelo's sterner regime. When the Duke is revealed in his proper person, he makes a whole series of decisions, some of which he retracts. 1. He orders Angelo to marry Mariana. 2. He orders the execution of Angelo. 3. He discharges the Provost. 4. He pardons Barnardine. 5. He pardons

Claudio. 6. He pardons Angelo. 7. He sentences Lucio to be whipped and hanged after marrying Kate Keepdown. 8. He remits Lucio's other forfeits but insists on the marriage.

It is usually said that the Duke has decided in general that leniency is better than severity, but that he is unduly harsh with Lucio because he has been slandered and cannot forgive. I doubt whether either half of this sentence is true. The Duke is not lenient because he believes that leniency is the right policy but because we have come to the last scene of a comedy where pardon is the price of a happy ending; and Lucio is made to marry his whore in fulfilment of his promise, so that the play ends with four marriages. The audience has enjoyed Lucio's company, but they recognise that in the moral scale he is lower than Angelo. He has some feeling for Claudio—and perhaps his friendship makes us feel that Claudio too is a bit of a rake—and his speech to Isabella about Juliet's pregnancy is splendid, but his malicious inventions about the Duke and his evidence against Pompey and Mistress Overdone show him to be an entertaining scoundrel. The Duke has two soliloquies on the way rulers are slandered, and when he finally sentences Lucio he justifies the forced marriage by saying 'Slandering a prince deserves it'. King James, who was probably a member of the original audience, would certainly have approved; and, however much we have laughed with Lucio, his slander of the Duke makes us expect his exposure and punishment. It is worth noting that after listening to Lucio's slanders, the Duke gets Escalus to give a more objective account of his character and he is glad to hear himself described as 'a gentleman of all temperance'.

On the level of political theory, Vincentio is not held up to us as a model ruler; but on the level of plot, he is the stage-manager, the puppet-master, who ensures that all will end satisfactorily; and in the way he allows people freedom to sin at the same time as he controls their destinies he may be thought to symbolise the apparent difficulty of reconciling free will and predestination, which the compilers of the Thirty-Nine Articles found so perplexing.

Escalus, who is firm but merciful, who recognises the extent of human frailty and the limitations of justice, is the most sympathetic character, and the one Shakespeare sets up as an exemplar. But several other characters contribute to the debate. When Escalus warns Angelo that under certain circumstances he might commit the same offence as Claudio, Angelo accepts the possibility, but adds:

> When I, that censure him, to do so offend,
> Let mine own judgement pattern out my death
> And nothing come in partial.                    (II.i.29–31)

Not unnaturally Pompey asks if Escalus means 'to geld and splay all the youth of the city' and Lucio tells the Duke that it would be a good thing if Angelo showed 'a little more lenity to lechery'. But the most impassioned and most profound discussion of justice occurs in the first encounter between Angelo and Isabella, with the judge arguing that to condemn the crime but not the criminal would reduce him to a cipher, and that punishment is a deterrent, while Isabella pleads for mercy, points out that we are all sinners in the sight of God, that Angelo should ask himself if he is not guilty in his heart, even though he has not acted his thought, that people in power are liable to become tyrants, and that

>            man, proud man,
> Dress'd in a little brief authority,
> Most ignorant of what he's most assured,
> His glassy essence, like an angry ape
> Plays such fantastic tricks before high heaven
> As makes the angels weep.                       (II.ii.117ff.)

We are faced with the impossibility of achieving justice in a fallen world, but a dramatist can make all end well by the invention of the accidents that heaven does not always provide.

It is, of course, sexual instinct which is the anarchic force that makes corruption boil and bubble in Vienna. It is against a background of Mistress Overdone's profession that the bottled-up austerity of Angelo must be judged. The wry jests on the effects of the pox, the inhabitants of the prison enumerated by Pompey, 'all great doers in our trade', show a society in which the comparatively innocent Claudio and Juliet fall foul of the revived law—though Juliet's replies to the 'Friar' reveal that she is the most saintly character in the play.

There are other paradoxes. Angelo, who has never been in love and never been troubled by the rebellion of his codpiece, lusts after a woman as puritanical as himself, so that he exclaims:

> O cunning enemy that, to catch a saint
> With saints dost bait thy hook.                        (II.ii.180–1)

The gnomic line spoken by Escalus earlier,

> Some rise by sin, and some by virtue fall,

is exemplified in both halves by the fate of Angelo. It is his 'virtue', his lack of temptation by the sins of the flesh because he is guilty of the prime sin of the spirit, which makes him a prey to his violent passion for a novice. On the other hand, it is his sin which makes his redemption possible. In blackmailing a woman into committing fornication he thinks he has committed mortal sin; But this brings him to a full realisation that he is a miserable sinner and Mariana's love and forgiveness make it possible to hope that in his marriage he will become

> much more the better
> For being a little bad—

less proud, less censorious, more aware of his faults.

The exposure of Angelo in the final scene is due more to his own sense of guilt than to any actual proof; but it resembles the final scene of *All's Well that Ends Well*. In both cases a woman claims she has been seduced by a man, and the man erroneously believes himself guilty. But whereas Bertram tries to wriggle out of the situation, and of the suspicion of murder, by lie after lie, Angelo says nothing for more than 150 lines, and after the admission that he knew Mariana in the past, he is silent again for another 85 lines. A good actor can make these silences speak more eloquently than words.

*Measure for Measure* is a complex play and no simple interpretation corresponds to our experience of it, even when directors have tried to simplify matters by cuts or alterations.[71] However much the Duke is made to be a symbol of divinity, the audience will be delighted by Lucio's outrageous slanders; and however much our sympathies are directed to Claudio and Lucio and away from Isabella and the old fantastical Duke of dark corners, there are passages and whole scenes where our sympathies will be switched.

What I have been suggesting is that the conflicting impressions we get from scene to scene, the alternation of theatrical fantasy and psychological realism of satirical comedy and religious allegory, bewildering as it may seem to be, lends its peculiar flavour to what may be regarded as the profoundest of Shakespeare's comedies. It is hardly too much to say that what used to be regarded as defects are the means by which Shakespeare achieves his effects.[72]

# V · TRAGI-COMEDIES

The Victorians made one major discovery about Shakespeare. By a combination of external and internal evidence, they found out in what order the plays were written. The external evidence included records of performances at court, and the dates of publication of nearly half the plays. The internal evidence included topical references, echoes of published books and the metrical characteristics of the plays.

Once the approximate order of the plays was settled, it became possible for the first time to write an account of Shakespeare's *development*, impossible for Dr Johnson or Coleridge. It even became possible, but dangerous, to link the known facts of Shakespeare's life with the content of the plays. At its worst this sort of identification of the poet with his writings could lead to extreme sentimentality. One Victorian critic described[1] how Shakespeare retired to Stratford, and

> there peace came to him, Miranda and Perdita in their lovely freshness and charm greeted him, and he was laid by his quiet Avon side.

Dowden likewise compared[2] Shakespeare to

> a ship, beaten and storm-tossed, but yet entering harbour with sails full set, to anchor in peace.

The circumnavigator of the soul (as Sir Edmund Chambers put it) got safely home after his arduous voyage. He had attained an 'ultimate mood of grave serenity'. To which Strachey retorted[3] that Shakespeare, far from being serene, was bored

> bored with people, bored with real life, bored with drama, bored in fact with everything except poetry and poetical dreams.

---

1. Superior figures refer to notes at the end of the book (p. 210).

More recently Professor Charlton propounded[4] a curious mixture of Dowdenian serenity and Stracheian boredom. The benignity of the Romances, he said,

> must not sentimentalise our judgment into a false appraisement of their dramatic worth. Poetically they are of great price. As glimpses, too, of the ingrained charitableness, the temperamental gentleness, the serene and benevolent tolerance of Shakespeare the mortal, they are even beyond all aesthetic price ... But in no sense are they an answer nor even a substantial makeweight to the great tragedies. Shakespeare's vision of the depths of man's suffering, of the essential tragedy of his lot, remains as his deepest insight into human destiny.
>
> Yet though the tragedies abide as Shakespeare's firmest grasp of ultimate truth, unaltered and unanswered by these last plays, there is nevertheless a pleasant recompense, if but a very partial mitigation in these romances. They are an old man's consolation for the inescapable harshness of man's portion, a compensation which pleases the more, because with coming of age something of the terror of the things the dramatist in his strength has hitherto seen has been blunted by the weakening of his power of imaginative vision ... There can scarcely be a shadow of doubt that in the Romances, Shakespeare the dramatist is declining in dramatic power.

We may pass over the idea that Shakespeare was an old man at the age of 44 (when he wrote *Pericles*). But is it not absurd to think that we can have poetry as great as ever, poetry 'even beyond all aesthetic price' when there was a decline in dramatic power, a weakening of imaginative vision, and the kind of escapist art implied by the phrase 'an old man's consolation for the inescapable harshness of man's lot'? That is not the way great poetry is written, and a false picture of reality cannot be beyond all aesthetic price.

The plays Shakespeare wrote between 1608 and 1613 are obviously very different in kind from the plays written in the previous six years. Between 1604 and 1607 nearly all the plays had been tragic. Suddenly in 1608 there was a change. All the plays which follow, though containing tragic elements, are not ultimately tragic. Pericles for fifteen years believes his wife is dead, but is reunited to her in the end. Posthumus thinks that Imogen has been murdered by his orders, but finds her again in the last act. Leontes thinks that he has lost his wife, his son and his daughter, but after fifteen years he regains his wife and daughter, and obtains a son-in-law in place of his dead son. In *Henry VIII* Queen Katherine dies, but Queen Anne gives birth to Princess Elizabeth. Even in *The Two Noble Kinsmen*, though Arcite dies, Palamon marries the heroine and lives happily ever after.

The difference between the great tragedies and the 'romances' has been explained in several different ways. We may dismiss, for lack of evidence, the theory that Shakespeare had a nervous breakdown from which he recovered under the care of Dr Hall. Until recently the favourite explanation was the influence of the popular plays of Beaumont and Fletcher. Shakespeare, we are told, had 'a keen eye for theatrical success'[5] and was quite prepared to follow the fashion. *Philaster* was performed by his company and he started to write *Cymbeline* in the same style, in which the excitement aroused by individual scenes was more important than the probability of plots or the consistency of the characters. Shakespeare, we are assured, had a wife and family to support and the biggest house in his native town; he could not afford the luxury of art for art's sake; every day he watched anxiously the graph of the theatre's takings; and, of course, he had to think of his fellow-actors whose livelihood depended on his pen.

It is true that there are strong resemblances between *Philaster* and *Cymbeline*, but we do not know the exact date of either. All Fletcher's plays are filled with echoes of Shakespeare's earlier work and many of the characteristics of the romances may be derived not from Fletcher but from Shakespeare himself. Perhaps the two dramatists read each other's plays scene by scene as they were written. The question of priority does not greatly matter since 'Shakespeare used for the culminating expression of his faith in reality that form which its inventors had devised as a means of escape'.[6]

Another explanation is that the plays were written for performance at the Blackfriars Theatre, rather than at the Globe. There the more affluent audience demanded a different kind of play, with more spectacle than the public theatre could accommodate, and incorporating some elements of the court masque. But most of the plays were also performed at the Globe (where Forman saw *Cymbeline* and *The Winter's Tale*) and the masque elements are not the most striking parts of the plays.

The last explanation which has been advanced for the characteristics of the plays of the last period is that a number of old plays had been revived with unexpected success, and that a number of dramatists, including Heywood, Day and Shakespeare, began to write a more sophisticated form of the old romantic dramas—a series of episodic scenes in which after many adventures all turns out happily. *Pericles* certainly has this form. But the other three romances are carefully plotted, *The Tempest* being the most structurally perfect of all Shakespeare's plays.

None of the various explanations is wholly satisfactory, they are not mutually exclusive, and Shakespeare's plays, however much they resemble their alleged models in superficialities, are essentially quite different, and different one from the other. Nevertheless it may be as well to detail the similarities.

1. In all the plays there are wanderings, in most of them voyages.
2. All the plays end with reunions—of husband and wife, father and child, brother and brother, brother and sister, mother and daughter.
3. In all the plays (except *Pericles*) there is forgiveness and reconciliation, cemented by marriage.
4. All the plays exhibit the intrusion of the divine into human affairs—Diana, Jupiter, Apollo, Mars and Venus, Ceres and Juno (in the masque in *The Tempest*). We are made to feel, as we do not in previous plays, that the action is under the control of providence.[7]
5. All the plays have an extraordinary mixture of genres and what I have called the apotheosis of anachronism.

All these characteristics together differentiate the plays of Shakespeare's last period from the tragi-comedies of Beaumont and Fletcher, the primitive romances of the pre-Shakespearian stage, and the plays of Heywood and Day. One is therefore driven to suppose that Shakespeare chose to write his tragi-comedies partly because, after eight years of tragic writing he wished (in Keats's phrase) to devote himself to other sensations; and partly because he was obsessed with ideas of reconciliation and forgiveness.[8]

Perhaps these plays are best regarded as tragi-comedies—a genre described by Guarini as a mixture of tragedy and comedy; taking from the former great persons, a plot which is verisimilar, but not true, tempered passions, 'the delight, not the sadness, the danger not the death'; and from the latter modest amusement, 'a feigned complication, a happy reversal, and above all, the comic order'. John Fletcher in his preface to *The Faithful Shepherdess*, though indebted to Guarini, has a rather different emphasis:

> A tragie-comedy is not so called in respect of mirth and killing, but in respect it wants deaths, which is inough to make it no tragedie, yet brings some neere it, which is inough to make it no comedie, which must be a representation of familiar people, with such kinde of trouble as no life be questiond.

The descriptions could partially fit some of Shakespeare's early comedies—*Much Ado about Nothing, The Merchant of Venice, Measure for Measure*—and they could certainly be applied to the plays of the final period. It is true that there are deaths in three of them; but no one worries about the fate of Antiochus, Antigonus or Cloten, even if we grieve briefly for that of Mamillius. In other respects Shakespeare seems closer to Guarini than to Fletcher, for his characters are great persons rather than familiar people; but like Fletcher he allows a god to be introduced, and some of his characters are 'mean'.

# 14
# *Pericles*

Dryden asserted[9] that *Pericles* was one of Shakespeare's earliest plays and he has been supported by more recent critics who have pointed out resemblances between its plot and that of *The Comedy of Errors*. In both plays fathers are separated from their wives and children, to recover them in the end after journeying in the eastern Mediterranean; in both the wives are discovered in a religious order. But those who believe that Dryden was right presumably allow that the last three acts could not have been written in their present form at the beginning of Shakespeare's career; and even the first two acts, cruder as they are, are totally different in style from *The Comedy of Errors*—a difference that could be explained by the process by which the text got into print.

Plays like *Mucedorus* had been revived with some success and

Shakespeare, we must assume, was asked to revise *Pericles* for the stage. It was a 'strange eventful history', an episodic story both naïve and absurd, in which the hero undergoes a series of adventures—falling in love, guessing a riddle, fleeing for his life, relieving the people of Tharsus, being shipwrecked, winning a tournament and a princess, losing her in childbirth, believing his daughter has died and so on.

Ben Jonson referred to *Pericles*, in a moment of pique, as 'a mouldy tale'—a hit, presumably, not merely at the antiquity of the Apollonius story, but as its naïvety. It consists of a series of events linked together only by the fact that they illustrate the operations of fortune in the life of the hero. There is no integral connection between Apollonius's wooing of the daughter of Antiochus and the later episodes of his marriage, the loss of his wife and daughter, and his final reunion with them. Apollonius happens to meet his bride when he leaves Tyre for fear of the wrath of Antiochus. Even if Shakespeare had dramatised only the second part of the story—the separation of his hero from his wife and daughter and his ultimate reunion with them—he would not have been able to imbue it with the kind of significance to be found in *Cymbeline* or *The Winter's Tale*. Posthumus loses his wife, and Leontes his wife and children, through their own fault; and they earn the restoration of their lost ones by their penitence. The misfortunes which befall Pericles can hardly be said to be due to his own sins, though it has been suggested that he was paying for his inability to recognise until too late the evil hidden beneath the fair exterior of Antiochus's daughter. It is possible, however, that an attempt by Shakespeare to impose significance on his material has been blurred by the corruption of the text, and that Thaisa's time in the temple of Diana was in expiation of the sin of taking the name of the goddess in vain.[10] But the trials which Pericles and his family undergo are also a means of testing them, their final happiness exemplifying the scriptural text 'Whom the Lord loveth, He chasteneth'.

In fact the play is more sophisticated than it appears. The episodic technique, more appropriate to a narrative than to a drama, is excused by the use of Gower. Although the Gower choruses would not satisfy a modern student of Middle English, they do suggest, with remarkable skill, the general atmosphere of Gower's garrulous masterpiece. His rudimentary art, with its monotonous octosyllabic lines, its neutral diction, its rare imagery, and its pervasive moralising, appealed to the simple curiosity of its readers. They asked 'What happened next?' The causal relationship between one incident and the next and the psychology of the characters were equally unimportant. Incident followed after incident, with a running commentary designed to point the appropriate morals. Shakespeare has caught the manner to perfection, even though he cannot refrain from an occasional touch of better poetry. He doubtless recalled Chaucer's epithet for Gower—'moral'— when he penned the last lines of the play:

> In Antiochus and his daughter you have heard
> Of monstrous lust the due and just reward:
> In Pericles, his queen, and daughter, seen,
> Although assail'd with fortune fierce and keen,
> Virtue preserv'd from fell destruction's blast,
> Led on by heaven, and crown'd with joy at last.
> In Helicanus may you well descry
> A figure of truth, of faith, of loyalty;
> In reverend Cerimon there well appears
> The worth that learned charity aye wears . . .

The naïvety of Gower's chorus provides a suitable framework for the play. Shakespeare was asking his audience to listen to the story in an unsophisticated frame of mind, forgetting for the time being the kind of intelligent response they would make to *King Lear* or *Twelfth Night*, and adopting rather the simpler and relaxed attitude suitable to a play like *Mucedorus* or *The Rare Triumphs of Love and Fortune*.

When all allowances have been made for textual corruption, it is apparent that both character and incident in *Pericles* have been deliberately simplified. The characters are either very good or very evil. Only with Lysimachus is there any doubt. He has to be fundamentally decent to enable him to marry Marina; but he has to be something of a rake to enable him to be a prospective client in the brothel. Most of Shakespeare's audience would not have worried about this; and they would cheerfully assume that he had been converted, as even Boult is converted, by Marina's purity. But Shakespeare himself seems to have had a twinge of uneasiness on the matter and he throws in a hint at the end of the brothel-scene that Lysimachus, like Duke Vincentio in *Measure for Measure* or a modern social scientist, was making a study of the red-light district for reputable motives:

> Had I brought hither a corrupted mind
> Thy speech had altered it . . .
> For me, be you thoughten
> That I came with no ill intent; for to me
> The very doors and windows savour vilely.     (IV.vi.103–9)

These lines are difficult to reconcile with the way Lysimachus is greeted by the Bawd as an old customer, and we have to assume either that Lysimachus is whitewashing himself to Marina or that Shakespeare belatedly realised that Lysimachus as he had depicted him was not a suitable husband for her.

Not merely is the characterisation simplified: we have the feeling, as Eliot pointed out as true of all Shakespeare's final plays, that the characters are 'the work of a writer who has finally seen through the dramatic action of men into a spiritual action which transcends it'.[11] Fate manipulates the characters of *Pericles* for the purpose of arousing in them—and hence in the audience—the joy of the man in the parable, who finds that which is lost.

Shakespeare's mature style first becomes apparent in Act III with the birth of Marina, the burial of Thaisa at sea and her restoration by the medical skill of Cerimon. In this scene we have the first use of the jewel imagery which is used to effectively in the last act.

> Behold,
> Her eyelids, cases to those heavenly jewels
> Which Pericles hath lost, begin to part
> Their fringes of bright gold; the diamonds
> Of a most praised water do appear,
> To make the world twice rich.          (III.ii.103–8)

So Pericles is reminded of Thaisa when he sees his daughter in the ship:

> Her eyes as jewel-like
> And cased as richly.

In this recognition scene Pericles uses an image which recalls Cesario's description of her imaginary sister who 'sat like Patience on a monument, Smiling at grief', but so refined and intensified that they provide a wonderful evocation of the central theme of the play:

If thine considered prove the thousandth part
Of my endurance, thou art a man, and I
Have suffered like a girl. Yet thou dost look
Like Patience gazing on kings' graves, and smiling
Extremity out of act.

(V.i.134–8)

These lines suggest all that Marina has undergone—the loss of her mother and nurse, so that the world seems to her 'a lasting storm, Whirring' her from her friends, her treatment by Dionyza, her attempted murder, her kidnapping by pirates and the attempts on her chastity in the brothel. The lines also suggest both her royal birth and her courage and patience in adversity. But they do not merely depict the emblematic figure of Marina, they also crystallise the theme of the play. Pericles sees in his daughter's face the signs of tribulation patiently endured. She has had more to bear than the common lot of humanity, the deaths of those we love, which Pericles had borne less patiently. The father and daughter are drawn together by mutual sympathy and by the unconscious ties of blood. Death is smiled out of act. And this, as it turns out, is precisely what happens: the two loved ones are restored to Pericles, and the whole family is reunited. The theme of restoration after sorrows and bereavement, this particular scene, and the figure of Marina are all embodied in this image.

Yet the play, as a whole, is unsatisfactory. Even if a better text had been preserved, we should probably have to admit that Shakespeare did not fully succeed in converting his crude original into a vehicle for his new vision. The misfortunes that befall Pericles are accidental. The restoration of wife and child seem to be due to the blind working of fate, rather than to the inscrutable workings of Providence. A joy deferred may be sweeter to the mind; but a sixteen-year deferment seems too much of a good thing. Why does Thaisa make no attempt to discover her husband? Why does Pericles leave his daughter with the wicked Dionyza? Why should Marina be chosen to cure her father's melancholy? But one does not dream of asking such questions, for the events are distanced by Gower's commentary. It is the moral of the story which is important, not the characters; and the characters exist only as emblematic figures. Dionyza is Seeming, Antiochus is Lechery, Marina is Chastity; and Pericles himself is a kind of Everyman, whose voyages symbolise the changes and chances of this mortal life.

In the plays that followed Shakespeare set out to eliminate accidents—though some accidents remain—and to infuse the restoration theme with ethical meaning. The new meaning becomes much more complex than that represented by Gower's platitudes, on incest—

> Bad child! worse father! to entice his own
> To evil should be done by none.—

on hypocrisy—

> No visor does become black villany
> So well as soft and tender flattery—

and on Pericles and his family—

> Although assailed with fortune fierce and keen,
> Virtue preserved from fell destruction's blast,
> Led on by heaven, and crowned with joy at last.

This is too easy. In the later plays, therefore, Shakespeare replaced the workings of an arbitrary providence by the operations of sin and repentance. Hermione and Perdita are restored to Leontes only after he has suffered remorse and penitence for sixteen years; Imogen is restored to Posthumus only when he has earned her forgiveness; and in *The Tempest* the whole action of the play is controlled by the wronged and forgiving Prospero.

# 15
# *Cymbeline*

Recent critics have stressed the significance of *Cymbeline* for a Jacobean audience.[12] The birth of Christ in the twenty-third year of that monarch's reign, and the era of peace which followed, linked the end of *Antony and Cleopatra* and the peace of Augustus with the peace policy of James I. The play, although dubiously historical, could be regarded as linking the Roman plays with the English Histories.[13] Moreover it has been pointed out that 'blessed' Milford Haven would be remembered as the port where Richmond landed, subsequently to defeat Richard III at Bosworth and to found the Tudor dynasty. Richmond was James I's great-grandfather. James claimed that he fulfilled Merlin's prophecy of the union of Britain, the first to do so since Brute, Aeneas's grandson, whose wife's name was Inogene.

Such allegorical correspondences are necessarily selective and intermittent; and, in any case, such topicality the play may have had for its original audience should not be thought to excuse its dramatic shortcomings, if shortcomings they be.

Victorian poets fell in love with Imogen and Tennyson asked for a copy of the play to be buried with him for her sake. But one character, however desirable, does not turn a bad play into a good one; and most critics, however reluctantly, have tended to concur with Dr Johnson's magisterial dismissal of the play:[14]

> To remark the folly of the fiction, the absurdity of the conduct, the confusion of the names and manners of different times, and the impossibility of the events in any system of life, were to waste criticism upon unresisting imbecility, upon faults too evident for detection, and too gross for aggravation.

Granville-Barker, though not going so far in his condemnation, confessed that in this play the poet was a wearied artist.[15] Certainly it is a strange mixture of history, fiction and fantasy. Sometimes it appears to be the age of Augustus, at others we are in Boccaccio's world, at others again in the never-never land of the pastoral. Shakespeare was indebted to three old plays, to Heliodorus and to an analogue of the Snow-White story. It has been argued that he, like Fletcher, ruthlessly sacrifices character to immediate theatrical sensation. The most notorious example of this is the scene where Imogen awakens from her drugged sleep beside the headless body of Cloten, which she thinks is that of her husband. The audience is asked to believe in the wonder-drug, that Cloten would wish to rape Imogen in her husband's clothes, that in ancient Wales they did not inter corpses, and that Imogen would mistake Cloten's body for her husband's. Yet all these points, formidable as they are, do not conflict with the integrity of the characters. Imogen has said that Posthumus's meanest garment is dearer to her than her boorish suitor, and it is psychologically plausible for him to conceive the idea of raping her while dressed in his rival's clothes. Even her mistake about the identity of the corpse can be explained as a symbolic reminder of the Cloten-like behaviour of Posthumus. At least we can say that Shakespeare's ingenious preparation for this scene does not support the view that *Cymbeline* was the work of a wearied artist; nor does the masterly verse.[16]

But why, one must ask, did Shakespeare give us such a queer jumble of places and conventions? Why do we move from the Rome of Augustus to Boccaccio's Italy, from pastoral to pseudo-history, from fairy-tale to classical mythology, from *Decameron* to Donne. Was Shakespeare juxtaposing 'planes of reality'[17] to jolt us from our expectation that the play would be a reasonably faithful reflection of real life? Was it his reply to well-meaning critics who pointed out the absurdity of Othello believing that his wife had committed adultery a thousand times when they had arrived in Cyprus less than a week before? At least, he seems to be saying, don't confuse art and life.

That he was as skilful as ever can be seen not merely from the cool way he yokes together heterogeneous materials, and from the quality of the verse, but also from the expertness of individual scenes. In the wager scene, for example, he makes the hero bet on his wife's chastity in such a way that when the scene is performed we are made to feel that if he had refused the wager it would have suggested a lack of faith in his wife. Or consider the marvellous scene when Iachimo emerges from the trunk. His speech conveys, despite its evil purpose, a sensuous appreciation of Imogen's beauty, which almost makes one think he values it more than Posthumus does:

> Cytherea,
> How bravely thou becomest thy bed, freshly,
> And whiter than the sheets! That I might touch!
> But kiss, one kiss! Rubies unparagon'd,
> How dearly they do't! 'Tis her breathing that
> Perfumes the chamber thus: the flame o' the taper
> Bows toward her, and would under-peep her lids,
> To see the enclosed lights, now canopied
> Under these windows, white and azure laced
> With blue of heaven's own tinct.                    (II.ii.14–23)

Shakespeare's craftsmanship is seen at its most ingenious in the last scene of the play. Bernard Shaw, who wrote a new fifth act for performance at Stratford-upon-Avon, complained that Shakespeare's last act was[18]

> a tedious string of unsurprising denouements sugared with insincere sentimentality after a ludicrous stage battle. With one exception [Imogen], the characters have vanished and left nothing but dolls being moved about like glass balls in the game of solitaire, until they are all properly rearranged.

Shaw therefore advised directors to substitute his own fifth act; but he had the grace to admit that Shakespeare's version, if played in full, was superior to his own. The point of this distinction was brought home to me by Sir Donald Wolfit's production, which had the same cuts as Henry Irving's fifty years before. As a result of the cuts, the last scene was unintentionally funny. When played in full, the twenty revelations in the space of some 500 lines do not seem absurd. When Imogen embraces her husband with the words:

> Why did you throw your wedded lady from you?
> Think that you are upon a rock; and now
> Throw me again             (V.v.261–3)

Posthumus replies:

>       Hang there, like fruit, my soul,
> Till the tree die!

Equally powerful is the hero's forgiveness of the repentant villain:

>       Kneel not to me,
> The power that I have on you is to spare you,
> The malice towards you to forgive you. Live,
> And deal with others better.      (V.v.417–20)

As we reach the end of the play we realise that everything has been arranged—and arranged with superb artistry—so that this ritual of recognition and forgiveness can be enacted. Without the fall, the suffering and the repentance of the hero, he would not have experienced the joy of reconciliation and forgiveness. As a background to this ritual is the restoration of the King's sons, the general pardon of the prisoners, the peace with Rome.

    It may be objected that no one doubts Shakespeare's theatrical effectiveness, but that we expect more than that from his mature work—expertise is not incompatible with decadence and exhaustion. Bertrand Evans, who is full of admiration for Shakespeare's

artistry, complains[19] that Jupiter's appearance has no direct conse-
quence. He is simply there to reassure the audience that all will be
well and so 'enables us to watch the tortuous denouement with
minds free from anxiety. From this point of view it is an artistic
master stroke.' But, he adds, 'it is also an artistic fraud' in that all
the elements for a happy ending are already present. The *Deus ex
machina* normally intervenes to prevent a tragedy, to 'elucidate a
situation', to bring about a happy ending. But although Jupiter does
none of these things, we should not write him off as an artistic
fraud. Nor, indeed, is it true that we watch the last scene with
minds free from anxiety; it would not be as moving and dramatic as
it is, if they were. All we have been promised is that Imogen and
Posthumus will be reunited.

Another complaint on which something should be said is that
Posthumus has behaved so atrociously that the audience finds it
difficult to forgive him. Whereas sixteen years of remorse qualify
Leontes for our sympathy, Imogen forgives her husband within the
same number of weeks. The whole of the last act of the play is
devoted to the repentance of Posthumus.

Shakespeare could rely, perhaps, on the melodramatic convention that the calumniator of female innocence is always believed.
But Iachimo's 'proof' is convincing enough in the theatre: it
convinces Philario as well as the hero. Posthumus in his fury and
disillusionment goes further than Troilus, who had refused to
square the general sex by Cressid's rule. He declares that all men
are bastards and that his own mother, who seemed 'the Dian of that
time' was unchaste.[20] Nevertheless, when he hears from Pisanio
that Imogen has been slain he immediately repents, recognising that
even unfaithful wives are often morally superior to their husbands:

> If each of you should take this course, how many
> Must murder wives much better than themselves
> For wrying but a little.

He wishes that the gods had punished him for his own sins and
saved the 'mistress of Britain', the 'noble' Imogen to repent. He
determines to die in battle as a punishment for his sin against her:

> For thee, O Imogen, even for whom my life
> Is every breath a death, and thus, unknown,
> Pitied nor hated, to the face of peril
> Myself I'll dedicate.                                    (V.i.26–9)

He has forgiven Imogen while he still believes her guilty of what he describes as 'a little fault'. This conversion, extraordinary by Elizabethan standards,[21] should go far to reinstate Posthumus in the eyes of even a modern audience. Nor is this all. In the battle he exhibits outstanding bravery and afterwards resumes his Roman dress in the hope that Cymbeline will order the execution of his prisoners. In prison, he prays for death—

> For Imogen's dear life, take mine; and though
> 'Tis not so dear, yet 'tis a life—

and then communes with her spirit in silence. At this point the ghosts declare that Posthumus, as Imogen's choice of him proves, is a man without a peer in Britain, they complain that the gods have treated him badly, and appeal to Jupiter to relent. This vision and Jupiter's promise complete Posthumus's rehabilitation; he has become worthy of Imogen. He shows his worthiness in the final scene by pardoning Iachimo and reproaching himself as a credulous fool, a murderer and a villain

> That all th' abhorred things o' th' earth amend
> By being worse than they.

By such means Shakespeare convinces us that Posthumus may properly be rewarded by the gods who cross those they love. But he is absent from the stage for the whole of Acts III and IV. It is Imogen who dominates the play.

The portrait of Imogen is indeed the best answer to those who profess to believe that Shakespeare's powers of characterisation had declined. It is true that Bernard Shaw told Ellen Terry that Shakespeare had confused two different characters in the part—[22]

> a real woman divined by Shakespeare without his knowing it clearly, a natural aristocrat, with a high temper and perfect courage ... and an idiotic paragon of virtue produced by Shakespeare's views of what a woman ought to be, a person who sews and cooks and reads improving books until midnight ... and is in a chronic state of suspicion of improper behaviour on the part of other people (especially her husband) with abandoned females.

To which one can only retort that natural aristocrats in Shakespeare's day knew how to sew. Ovid's *Metamorphoses*, the book

Imogen was reading till she fell asleep, could hardly be regarded as an improving book. The tale of Philomel, which she was perusing, is a horror story of rape, mutilation and murder. Nor is it fair to say that she was in a chronic state of suspicion about her husband's fidelity. She immediately rejects Iachimo's slanders and comes to believe them only when she learns that he has ordered Pisanio to murder her:

> Iachimo,
> Thou didst accuse him of incontinency;
> Thou then look'dst like a villain; now, methinks,
> Thy favour's good enough. Some jay of Italy,
> Whose mother was her painting, hath betrayed him.

In its context, the accusation reads like a pathetic attempt by Imogen to explain Posthumus's conduct.[23]

Shakespeare convinces us of her forgiveness of Posthumus and does it without shutting her up for fifteen years as he does Hermione. He gives her an extraordinary vitality by the nature of the verse she has to speak, impetuous, spontaneous, generous, life-enhancing, what Cymbeline calls 'the tune of Imogen'. She is created not merely by her own words but through the idea we get of her from the words and actions of others—the hatred of the Queen, the lust of Cloten, the love of her brothers, the loyalty of Pisanio, the affection of Lucius, and Iachimo's immediate realisation that she is unique, the Arabian bird.

It should also be said that the mourning for 'Fidele' and the exquisite elegy spoken over her supposed grave contribute to our admiration for her, as though a perfect poem had been incarnated in her.

We have had some wonderful Imogens during the past thirty years. In spite of Ellen Terry's charm and her great generosity of spirit, Irving's production was not a good setting for her performance. Another Victorian actress, Helen Faucit, by all accounts a splendid Hermione, seems not to have understood Imogen. She decided[24] that 'this delicately nurtured creature' would not long survive her terrible ordeal. Her happiness came too late. More revealing than this sentimental idea of the character is Helen Faucit's account of her disagreement with Macready about her dress as Fidele:

which I had ordered to be made with a tunic that descended to the ankles. On going to the theatre at the last rehearsal, he told me, with many apologies and much concern, that he had given directions to have my dress altered. He had taken the liberty of doing this, he said, without consulting me, because, although he could understand the reasons which had weighed with me in ordering the dress to be made as I had done, he was sure I would forgive him when he explained to me that such a dress would not tell the story, and that one half the audience—all, in fact, who did not know the play—would not discover that it was a disguise, but would suppose Imogen to be still in woman's attire. Remonstrance was too late, and, with many tears, I had to yield, and add to my own terror to that of Imogen when first entering the cave. I managed, however, to devise a kind of compromise, by swathing myself in the 'franklin housewife's riding-cloak', which I kept about me as I went into the cave; and this I caused to be wrapped round me afterwards when the brothers carry in Imogen.

This Imogen, one is tempted to say, would at least justify Posthumus's complaint:

Me of my lawful pleasure she restrain'd
And pray'd me oft forbearance.

He goes on to say that he was sexually aroused by her rosy pudency. One would like to think that Shakespeare did not share these views.

# 16
# *The Winter's Tale*

When Dr Simon Forman saw a performance of *The Winter's Tale* in 1611, he made no mention in his notes of the revivification of Hermione, though he gives a reasonably accurate account of the rest of the play.[25]

Observe there how Leontes, the King of Sicilia was overcome with jealousy of his wife with the King of Bohemia his friend that came to see him, and how he contrived his death and would have had his cup-bearer to have poisoned (him). Who

gave the King of Bohemia warning thereof and fled with him to
Bohemia. Remember also how he sent to the Oracle of Apollo
and the answer of Apollo that she was guiltless . . . and how
except the child was found again that was lost the King should
die without issue, for the child was carried into Bohemia and
there laid on a forest and brought up by a shepherd. And the
King of Bohemia his son married that wench, and how they
fled into Sicilia to Leontes, and the shepherd having showed
the letter of the nobleman by whom Leontes was sent away
that child and the jewels found about her, she was known to be
Leontes' daughter . . .

Remember also the rogue that came in all tottered like coll
pixci and how he feigned him sick and to have been robbed of
all that he has, and how he cosened the poor man of all his
money, and after came to the sheep-sheer with a pedlar's pack
and their cosened them again of all their money; and how he
changed apparel with the King of Bohemia his son, and then
how he turned courtier etc. Beware of trusting feigned beggars
or fawning fellows.

It has been argued,[26] therefore, that when Forman saw the play,
Hermione was not restored to life, and that in this version
Shakespeare followed his source more closely than in the play as we
have it. In *Pandosto: or the Triumph of Time* Bellaria (Hermione)
does actually die; and years later Pandosto (Leontes) falls in love
with his daughter, Fawnia. When he learns that his love for her is
incestuous, he commits suicide. As Forman does not mention such a
conclusion to the play, Shakespeare presumably deviated from
Greene's story in this respect; and as Forman is inaccurate in his
account of *Macbeth*, he may be equally so in his omission of
Hermione's resurrection.

*The Winter's Tale* may be regarded as a compound of *Pericles*
and *Cymbeline*. Shakespeare took the apparent death of the wife,
the loss of the daughter and the reuniting of the family after a lapse
of years; and to avoid the earlier impression of an arbitrary
providence loading the hero with undeserved misfortune, Shakespeare added the jealousy theme from *Cymbeline*. In *Othello* and
*Cymbeline* jealousy had been aroused in a not naturally jealous
man by the machinations of a villain. In *The Winter's Tale* the
jealousy is self-generated.

Some critics have argued[27] that Leontes is jealous from the start of the play and that he is testing his suspicions when Polixenes is being pressed to prolong his visit. This is not Shakespeare's intention as can be seen from his abandonment of the motivation provided by Greene—the fact that Bellaria keeps on visiting her guest's bedroom.

Nevertheless it should be remembered that when Hermione enters with Leontes and Polixenes, she is visibly pregnant; and Polixenes, in his first speech, says:

> Nine changes of the wat'rry star hath been
> The shepherd's note since we have left our throne
> Without a burden.

As William Matchett has remarked,[28] Shakespeare has filled this speech with 'the diction of conception, fertility and gratitude'. The audience is bound to associate the nine-month period with Hermione's pregnancy, and to suspect, while Leontes is still unsuspicious, that Polixenes is the father of Hermione's unborn child. So we can hardly blame Leontes.

Shakespeare wonderfully suggests the operation of jealousy, not merely by the pouring out of foul images but by an extraordinary dislocation of syntax. These speeches contrast with Polixenes's description of his boyish friendship with Leontes, when they were unaware of the Fall and of original sin, 'the hereditary imposition'—not merely a prelapsarian but a pre-sexual state:

> We were as twinn'd lambs, that did frisk i' th' sun,
> And bleat the one at th' other: What we chang'd
> Was innocence for innocence; we knew not
> The doctrine of ill-doing, no nor dream'd
> That any did. Had we pursu'd that life,
> And our weak spirits ne'er been higher rear'd
> With stronger blood, we should have answer'd heaven
> Boldly 'Not guilty', the imposition clear'd
> Hereditary ours.                                        (I.ii.67–75)

Although, in some sense, the world of Bohemia seems to recreate this pastoral innocence, there is no suggestion there, as there is here, that sex is the serpent that leads to banishment from Eden.

The pattern of reconciliation and restoration resembles that of the other tragi-comedies, but there are three notable differences.

First, some of the evil done cannot be put right: Mamillius is dead,
even if Leontes obtains a son-in-law who will take his place as ruler
of Sicilia. Secondly, until the death of Antigonus the play is wholly
tragic, with only the ambiguous oracle holding out hope for the
future. Thirdly, and most significantly, the audience is kept in the
dark. We know, unlike Pericles, that Marina and Thaisa are alive;
that Pisanio has spared Imogen; that the doctor has substituted a
harmless drug for the poison of the royal vivisectress; but we do not
know that Paulina is lying:

> O Lords,
> When I have said, cry woe: the Queen, the Queen,
> The sweet'st, dear'st creature's dead: and vengeance for't
> Not dropp'd down yet . . .
>
> I say she's dead: I'll swear't. If word, nor oath
> Prevail not, go and see: if you can bring
> Tincture, or lustre in his lip, her eye
> Heat outwardly, or breath within, I'll serve you
> As I would do the Gods.                          (III.ii.196–204)

Leontes asks Paulina to take him to the dead bodies of Hermione
and Mamillius—'One grave shall be for both'. In the last scene
Leontes says of his wife:

> I saw her
> (As I thought) dead: and have (in vain) said many
> A prayer upon her grave.

In between these passages there are many references to Hermione's
death. More significant is Antigonus's account of his vision of the
ghost of Hermione: he says to the babe on the coast of Bohemia:

> thy Mother
> Appear'ed to me last night: for ne'er was dream
> So like a waking. To me comes a creature,
> Sometimes her head on one side, some another,
> I never saw a vessel of like sorrow,
> So filled, and so becoming: in pure white robes
> Like very sanctity she did approach
> My cabin where I lay: thrice bow'd before me
> And (gasping to begin some speech) her eyes
> Became two spouts; the fury spent, anon

Did this break from her. 'Good Antigonus,
Since Fate (against thy better disposition)
Hath made thy person for the thrower-out
Of my poor babe, according to thine oath,
Places remote enough are in Bohemia;
There weep, and leave it crying: and for the babe
Is counted lost for ever, Perdita
I prithee call't: for this ungentle business
Put on thee by my Lord, thou ne'er shalt see
Thy wife Paulina more'. And so, with shrieks,
She melted into air. Affrighted much
I did collect myself, and thought
This was so, and no slumber. Dreams are toys,
Yet for this once, yea superstitiously,
I will be squar'd by this. I do believe
Hermione hath suffer'd death. (III.iii.17–42)

The vision behaves as a ghost, chooses a name for her daughter, and prophecies Antigonus's death. I think there can be no doubt that even if Shakespeare did not intend Hermione to be dead at this point in the play, he intended us to think so. For this he has been taken to task by Professor B. Evans.[29] Shakespeare does not normally deceive his audience.

Why, then does he depart from his ordinary principles of dramaturgy and leave us to suppose that Hermione is dead and buried?

A number of critics have argued that Shakespeare was writing a kind of immortality 'myth'; and if Hermione's 'resurrection' was to convey that kind of impression, the audience must share the belief of Leontes and Antigonus that she had actually died. Professor Bryant, for example, says that the play makes the 'hardest possible sense' from the Christian point of view. The characters, as Paulina says, are 'precious winners all' because 'they have been granted grace to see the resurrection'.[30] But, as Leslie Bethell pointed out,[31] it is not a genuine resurrection; at most it could be regarded as a symbol of resurrection for Shakespeare calls attention to Hermione's wrinkles and to Paulina's daily visits to the house where she was hidden. As Adrien Bonjour suggests[32]

The reanimation of Hermione's statue may thus be considered as a symbol of the redeeming power of true repentance which may win again a long lost love and atone for the disastrous consequences of a past crime.

For a long time arm-chair critics regarded the statue scene as a failure. Charlotte Lennox, for example, spoke of the scene as 'a mean and absurd contrivance':[33]

> for can it be imagined that Hermione, a virtuous and affectionate wife, would conceal herself during sixteen years in a solitary house, though she was sensible that her repentant husband was all that time consuming away with grief and remorse for her death: and what reason could she have for chosing to live in such a miserable confinement when she might have been happy in the possession of her husband's affection and have shared his throne? How ridiculous also in a great Queen, on so interesting an occasion, to submit to such buffoonery as standing on a pedestal, motionless, her eyes fixed, and at last to be conjured down by a magical command of Paulina.

*Pandosto*, she concludes, had nothing 'so low and improbable' and, although 'paltry', was greatly superior to the play.

A German critic, Heinrich Bulthaupt (1889) makes a similar complaint. He finds it incredible that the Hermione of the first part of the play would consent to 'this farce of a statue' and he declares that every charm 'is put to flight by the ever-recurring dense, rationalist preparation of the scene':

> Instead of using some means full of the miraculous, Shakespeare lets Paulina play Providence. Thus the scaffolding creaks in all its joints; human passion and grandeur are inconceivably mingled with the affectation of a comedian. Our tragic sympathy, our moral indignation has been quickened,—but she, whom we commiserated, trifles away our sympathy with a living statue which she represents, and the man, for whom we wished the heaviest punishment, garners the fairest harvest of indulgent fate. A plot which should have been treated only as a tragedy, is, without intrinsic justification, conducted to a superficial end of reconciliation.

It is significant that the complaints were made by readers rather than spectators. Spectators, even when they saw only eighteenth-century adaptations, did not share the disapproval of many of the critics. Mrs Inchbald, who foolishly included Garrick's adaptation in her collection of the *British Theatre*, admitted that when Mrs Siddons played Hermione, the statue scene was 'far more grand in exhibition than the reader will possibly behold in idea'; and Thomas Campbell, the poet, replying to Mrs Lennox remarked dryly: 'Mrs Lennox says, that the statue scene is low and ridiculous. I am sure Mrs Siddons used to make it appear to us in a different light.' Campbell had the advantage of being Mrs Siddons's biographer; and in describing her performance he said:

> Mrs Siddons looked the statue, even to literal illusion; and, whilst the drapery hid her lower limbs, it showed a beauty of head, neck, shoulders and arms, that Praciteles might have studied. This statue scene has hardly its parallel for enchantment even in Shakespeare's theatre. The star of his genius was at its zenith when he composed it; but it was only a Siddons that could do justice to its romantic perfection. The heart of everyone who saw her when she burst from the semblance of sculpture into motion, and embraced her daughter, Perdita, must throb and glow at the recollection.

There are more detailed accounts of performances of the statue scene by Macready and Helen Faucit in 1847. Helen Faucit herself gave a full account of the performance in her book *On Some of Shakespeare's Female Characters* and there are long reviews in contemporary newspapers. Helen Faucit's performance was described as 'the finest combination of Grecian sculpture, Italian painting and British acting, that has in our day been seen on the stage'. Another reviewer said 'It was the most entrancing thing we ever remember to have seen—actually suspending the blood, and taking the breath away. It was something supernatural almost.' Hermione has a long period in which she does not speak, and in the space of 160 lines she had only one short speech, addressed not to Leontes but to Perdita. In Euripides's play, when Herakles brings back Alcestis from the grave, she remains completely silent for the rest of the play; and although there is no evidence that Shakespeare had read *Alcestis*, he seems to have shared Euripides's dramatic tact in this particular. But it is nevertheless difficult for the actress playing Hermione. It is a great strain on the nerves and muscles, as Helen Faucit observed, to stand motionless for so long, when even a movement of the eyelashes would destroy the illusion. Helen Faucit was helped by the fact that her arm was resting on a pedestal. But when music sounded, and she turned her head to let her eyes rest on Leontes, this had 'a startling, magnetic effect upon all'. She moved down the steps from the dais and paused at a short distance from Leontes. 'At first he stood speechless, as if turned to stone; his face with an awestruck look upon it.' When Paulina says 'Nay, present your hand', Leontes advanced, hesitantly, and touched the hand held out to him. Then he cried, 'O, she's warm!' These words were deleted from many acting versions, for fear they should raise a laugh, but the tone in which they were spoken impressed critics of both Macready and Gielgud. Helen Faucit had been warned, at one of the rehearsals, to be prepared for something extraordinary—but it was not until the first performance before an audience that she realised the point of the warning. Macready's joy at finding Hermione alive seemed uncontrollable. 'Now he was prostrate at her feet, then enfolding her in his arms.' The veil covering her head and neck fell off. Her hair came unbound and fell over her shoulders and Macready kissed and caressed it. The change in Macready was so sudden and overwhelming, that Helen Faucit cried out. Macready whispered to her 'Don't be frightened, my child! don't be frightened! Control yourself.' As this went on, the audience were tumultuously applauding, with a sound like a storm of hail. When Perdita and Florizel knelt at her feet, Hermione looked, she was told, 'like Niobe, all tears'.

I have described this performance at some length to show that, however much the scene might be criticised in the study, it created a tremendous effect in the theatre; so much so, that at one performance, at Edinburgh, when Hermione descended from her pedestal, 'the audience simultaneously rose from their seats, as if drawn out of them by surprise and reverential awe at the presence of one who bore more of heaven than of earth about her'. As one Scottish critic said: 'When she descended from her pedestal, with a slow and gliding motion, and wearing the look of a being consecrated by long years of prayer and sorrow and seclusion, it seemed to us as if we looked upon a being almost too pure to be gazed on with unveiled eyes'; and an Irish critic said

> We think not then of the symmetry of form, the perfection of outline, so far beyond the rarest achievement of art. For the

spirit which breathes from the face, where grief has long grown
calm, and suffering brightened into a heavenly pity, in the pure
world of thought—the spirit which bears within it so much of
heaven, with all that is best of earth, alone possesses our every
faculty.

These critics, in some ways typically Victorian, express themselves in a rather sentimental way; but they illustrate the impact of
the scene on the spectators, and they show that Shakespeare had
triumphantly overcome the improbabilities of his fable.

Glynne Wickham has shown that the 'statue' of Hermione would
have resembled the painted effigies on Elizabethan and Jacobean
tombs and would have been a familiar sight to Shakespeare's
original audience. Music is used to create the right atmosphere of
the scene, and the poet avoids any 'noble' speeches by Hermione—she does not speak to Leontes, any more than Alcestis
speaks to her husband when she returns from the grave.

The actors, therefore, taught the critics that the statue scene
could be overwhelmingly effective in performance. So indeed, could
they have demonstrated the effectiveness of the penultimate scene.

If Shakespeare (as Johnson said) was merely saving himself
trouble by reporting, instead of representing, the discovery of
Perdita's birth, we could cheerfully throw him to the wolves. Nor
can we seriously defend him on the grounds that the play would
otherwise be too full of powerful scenes. But it may nevertheless be
true that if he had dramatised the recognition of Perdita as
powerfully as he did the restoration of Hermione, the emphasis of
the play would be changed. Hermione has been absent from the
stage for the best part of three acts, and another long scene with
Perdita would have made it more difficult to restore Hermione, not
merely to life, but as the central character of the play. A mere
resurrection would be child's play compared with this feat of
dramaturgy.

But the assumption of literary critics that the scene is ineffective
on the stage is quite unfounded. My own experience is confirmed
by that of Nevill Coghill and Arthur Colby Sprague, and by Peter
Brook's famous production in 1951. Nor was Bethell right when he
suggested that in the affected prose of the courtiers, Shakespeare
was satirising court jargon, as he had done with Osric in the last act
of *Hamlet*. He was in fact using the Arcadian style, and though we

may smile at some of the conceits, the general effect is not comic. As Coghill said,[34] the courtiers are

> over the edge of tears in the happy excitement and feel a noble, indeed a partly miraculous joy, for the oracle has been fulfilled; so far as they can they temper their tears with their wit. What could be a more delightful mixture of drollery and tenderness.

Princess Elizabeth was betrothed to the ruler of Bohemia when *The Winter's Tale* was first performed, and everyone in the audience would know that that country was without a sea-coast. Shakespeare deliberately departed from his source in transposing the two countries, thus warning his audience that his Bohemia was an imaginary place.[35] There are other wildly improbable things in the play—that Perdita should be deposited on the coast of her future husband's country, that Antigonus should be conveniently eaten by the bear, an event which is intentionally funny as described by the Clown. The late S. L. Bethell rightly pointed out[36] that Shakespeare kept on calling attention to the absurdities of out-moded conventions, and he argued that by reminding the audience that they were watching a play he was using a Brechtian alienation technique. But the continual reminder that the action is 'like an old tale' has, perhaps, precisely the opposite effect: by it Shakespeare undermines our incredulity.

Many critics have called attention to the mythical overtones of the play. Leontes has been compared to the Fisher King of *The Waste Land*. Both Perdita and Hermione, like Proserpine, are lost and found. Shakespeare knew the story in his favourite Ovid and perhaps in Claudian's poem.[37] Proserpine is the Spring goddess and her story is recalled when Perdita distributes the flowers at the feast

> O Proserpina,
> For the flowers now, that, frighted, thou let'st fall
> From Dis's waggon: daffodils,
> That come before the swallow dares, and take
> The winds of March with beauty: violets (dim,
> But sweeter than the lids of Juno's eyes,
> Or Cytherea's breath); pale primroses,
> That die unmarried, ere they can behold
> Bright Phoebus in his strength (a malady

> Most incident to maids); bold oxlips, and
> The crown-imperial: lilies of all kinds,
> (The flower-de-luce being one). O, these I lack,
> To make you garlands of: and my sweet friend,
> To strew him o'er and o'er.                    (IV.iv.116–29)

Florizel in his first speech had said that Perdita, dressed as a goddess, was no shepherdess, 'but Flora Peering in April's front'. Flora is the Roman equivalent of the Queen of the May. Perdita, therefore, symbolises the spring, and like Proserpine she had been taken from her mother. All through her speeches there is a contrast between spring and winter, and between love and death. She mentions the flowers of the spring, the virgin branches of the maidens, the flowers which Proserpine let fall; and, in contrast to this, she refers to the blasts of January, the god of the underworld and the maids who die unmarried. Love and Death are brought together in the lines:

> No, like a bank, for love to lie and play on,
> Not like a corse; or, if; not to be buried,
> But quick, and in mine arms.                    (IV.iv.130–2)

In this scene we have a boy, acting the part of a girl, who is supposed to be a shepherdess but who is in fact a lost princess, who is playing the part of Flora and speaking of the spring goddess. This five-fold complication makes it impossible for the audience to relax into a sentimental admiration for a simple pastoral.

When the lovers arrive in Sicily, Perdita is described in extravagant terms, as one who

> Would she begin a sect, might quench the zeal
> Of all professors else, make proselytes
> Of who she but bid follow.                    (V.i.107–9)

Leontes goes further and addresses her as 'Goddess', welcome 'as is the spring to the earth'. It is almost as though Perdita had become the part she played, her return to Sicilia—to which place Proserpine also returned—marking the end of the winter of sterility.

The fault of most pastoral plays is sentimentality, not entirely avoided by Tasso and Guarini and their English imitators. Shakespeare avoids this fault, in the pastoral scenes in both *Cymbeline* and *The Winter's Tale* by juxtaposing them with scenes of a more realistic kind. The exquisite love-scenes give us the vision of a regenerated mankind, a picture of ideal spontaneity, of humanity made perfect by becoming itself:

> What you do,
> Still betters what is done. When you speak, sweet,
> I'ld have you do it ever: when you sing,
> I'ld have you buy, and sell so: so give almes,
> Pray so: and for the ordering of your affayres,
> To sing them too. When you do dance, I wish you
> A wave o' th' sea, that you might ever do
> Nothing but that: move still, still so:
> And own no other function. Each your doing,
> (So singular, in each particular)
> Crowns what you are doing in the present deeds,
> That all your actes, are queens.          (IV.iv.135–46)

This, one might say, is Shakespeare's answer to the corruption of man's heart, the hereditary imposition; the answer, one might say, to his own tragedies. He is saying, as Shelley was to put it,[38] that love redeems from decay the visitations of the divinity. But the scene would seem unreal without the threat to the happiness of the lovers from Florizel's irate father, without the earthiness and gullibility of the rustics, and, above all, without the presence of the confidence-trickster, Autolycus.

Morally speaking, Autolycus is a scoundrel. He steals from one of his victims by exploiting the parable of the good Samaritan. Nor do his songs ignore the seamy side of life, though this fact may be concealed from some readers by their ignorance of the slang terms. In 'When daffodils begin to peer' a doxy is a gangster's Moll, an aunt is a whore.

The oracle read at Hermione's trial, the name of Perdita, and the humorous report of the death of Antigonus all imply that the tragic events will have a happier sequel. The sequel is introduced by the appearance of Time, who apologises ironically for the crime of sliding over sixteen years and thus replies to the ghost of Sidney. Shakespeare at the end of his career was seeking an appropriate form, one in which both the tragedy and the reconciliation were dramatised to the full. The instant repentance of Proteus, Angelo and Bertram may satisfy playgoers but the murderous jealousy of Posthumus and Leontes requires months or years for its atonement.

If one rewrites *The Winter's Tale*, as Garrick did,[39] so that Leontes's sin was committed sixteen years before the start of the play, its impact is sadly reduced. The form Shakespeare evolved enabled him to reproduce something of the effect of the Greek romances which so greatly influenced Elizabethan fiction.

The sub-title of *Pandosto* is 'The Triumph of Time', with the motto *Temporis filia veritas*. As Shakespeare makes clear, Time 'makes and unfolds error'. Time is both the destroyer and the revealer; but, as Professor Inga-Stina Ewbank pointed out,[40] 'the simple identification of time as either Revealer or Destroyer has been obliterated'. Hermione's restoration conquers time; 'she is a living proof that "Love's not Time's fool" ', so that 'time has at last in its triumph brought about its own defeat'. Professor Ewbank stresses:

> This does not efface the human suffering that has gone before, however, and that weighs so heavily on the play right till the very end. Rather than a myth of immortality, then, this play is a probing into the human condition and . . . it looks at what time means and does to man.

It will be apparent how necessary it was for Shakespeare to violate the unity of time, if these complex feelings about the human condition were to be conveyed to the audience. The spectators at the revelation of Perdita's parentage 'looked as they had heard of a world ransomed or one destroyed'; and Paulina invokes Hermione on her pedestal:

> Bequeath to death your dumbness, for from him
> Dear life redeems you.

The characters at the end of the play are redeemed from the flux of time, from the world of error, confusion and sin.

# 17
# *The Tempest*

Henry James, in his own final period, when all his great novels were written, contributed an introduction to an edition of *The Tempest*, and some of his remarks will serve as a useful starting-point for what I want to say about the play. James argues that for the first and only time in his career Shakespeare could write as he wished:[41]

> Such a masterpiece puts before me the very act of the momentous conjunction taking place for the poet, at a given hour, between his charged inspiration and his clarified experience: or, as I should perhaps better express it, between his human curiosity and his aesthetic passion. Then (if he happens to have been, all his career, more or less the slave of the former) he yields, by way of a change, to the impulse of allowing the latter, for a magnificent moment, the upper hand.

Henry James's experiences in the theatre had been uniformly disastrous; and this was not merely because his mind was too subtle and delicate for the taste of actors and audience, but because he tried (in an absurdly ineffective way) to provide what was wanted. He could not really imagine a poet to whom the theatre was far from being an environment which cramped and warped his imagination, but was indeed a necessary stimulus to his highest powers. Shakespeare became a great poet by conquering the medium to which he submitted. It is therefore absurd to pretend that in *Hamlet* or *King Lear* Shakespeare was working against the grain; or to imagine that in *The Tempest* he was, for the first time, writing to please himself.

*The Tempest* is a natural sequel to the other plays discussed in this section. The sea is an important symbol of separation and estrangement, as in *Pericles* and *The Winter's Tale*; as in the latter a children's marriage cements the reconciliation of the parents; and as in *Cymbeline* and *The Winter's Tale* there is betrayal and forgiveness. But in place of sexual jealousy we have a more universal form of evil—the naked pursuit of self-interest; the hero, instead of being the sinner, is a more or less innocent victim; and instead of a choric Gower or Time to bridge the gulf of the years, we have treachery set in the past, and the action limited to the actual time of performance. Time, with Shakespeare's humorous connivance, had defied the unity of time; now the poet demonstrates that it was not through incompetence that he has gone against Sidney's advice.[42] The unity of place is provided by the island; the unity of time is provided by the account of the past in the second scene of the play; and the unity of action is caused by Prospero's total control the situation—a control which is also the poet's.

There are, perhaps, losses as well as gains. *The Tempest* is generally thought to be less exciting in the theatre than either *Cymbeline* or *The Winter's Tale*, because we know all the time what is going to happen. Prospero, it is clear, brings his enemies to the island for the express purpose of marrying his daughter to the son of one of them. There is some justification for the remark of the French critic that Shakespeare at last succeeded in preserving the unities of place and time by eliminating action altogether.

It is a play that demands suitable music and elaborate scenic effects. It is the only one of Shakespeare's plays in which spectacle is important; but the spectacle is subordinated to the poetry which is as great as ever. Henry James speaks of the way Shakespeare sinks 'as deep as we like, but what he sinks into, beyond all else, is the lucid stillness of his style'. James continues:[43]

> The resources of such a style, the provision of images, emblems, energies of every sort, laid up in advance, affects us as the storehouse of a king before a famine or a siege—which not only, by its scale, braves depletion or exhaustion, but bursts, through mere excess of quantity or presence, out of all doors and windows. It renders the poverties and obscurities of our world, as I say, in the dazzling terms of a richer and better.

Spectacle and poetry together do not add up to drama. Shakespeare also presents us with action. We know what the end will be, but we do not know how the end will be reached. Although Ferdinand is destined to marry Miranda and Prospero will forgive his enemies, we see enacted in the course of the play the actual drama of forgiveness. The act of forgiveness is not merely the conclusion of a sixteen-year process—it is also an epitome and re-enactment of that process in a couple of hours. For although, before the initial tempest, Prospero has forgiven his enemies, when he actually has them in his power he has once again to overcome the desire for vengeance. Nor does the fact that Prospero preordains the action of the play mean that it is without dramatic tension, that it is mere ritual; though the element of ritual is, I think, important.

From the theatrical point of view, the most difficult part of the play is the second scene of Act I in which Prospero has three interviews with Miranda, Ariel and Caliban, by which the audience is informed of the events of the past twelve years—the original conspiracy of Antonio and Alonzo to depose Prospero, the miraculous escape to the enchanted island, Prospero's education of Miranda, Ariel's refusal to obey Sycorax and her punishment of him, his rescue by means of Prospero's art, the initial friendly relations with Caliban cut short by his attempt to rape Miranda and the storm raised by Prospero to wreck his enemies on the island. All this is conveyed in some 350 lines.

The scene would be as boring as the retrospective accounts in some classical dramas if it were treated as simple narrative for the information of the audience. But it can be made legitimately exciting. First, there is the initial tension between Miranda and her father, her indignation with Caliban (if one accepts the Folio attribution of one speech)[44] and her spirited defence of Ferdinand. This prevents her from being the colourless, odourless, tasteless creature, whose sweet insipidity is a substitute for character, as she is sometimes played. Secondly, it is important that Prospero should be played not calm of mind, all passion spent, but one who has brooded for twelve years on his brother's treachery, the memory of which still rankles. He is an angry old man, whose rage is precipitated by his memories of the past. He is moreover one who neglected his duties as a ruler and thereby opened the door to his brother's treachery, so that his violent speeches about Antonio are animated partly by a desire to excuse himself. Caliban, obviously, has to be restrained; but Prospero is also enraged by Ariel's request for liberty before the agreed date. No doubt the violence of his threats are used as a substitute for punishment; but the violence seems oddly excessive when one considers how tenderly he loves Ariel, his diligence, his bird, his fine, quaint, tricksy and delicate spirit. The whole of the second scene, in which he like Miranda looks into the dark backward and abysm of time and summons up remembrance of things past, is not emotion recollected in tranquillity, but treachery recollected in anger.

It should also be remembered that the original treachery of the three men of sin is repeated on an even more evil level when Antonio tempts Sebastian to murder Alonzo and Gonzalo. More evil and, in effect, pointless; for, as far as they know, they are stranded on the island without hope of rescue. It seems almost to be evil for evil's sake, or evil out of habit, rather than evil for the sake of achieving power. This second conspiracy is parodied by a third, that of Caliban and his associates, which nearly succeeds because of

Prospero's absent-mindedness. In the concluding scene of the play the three conspiracies are linked together when Prospero introduces Caliban and his confederates to Antonio and his.

In the end Prospero forgives all his enemies, but it may be worth while to detail the steps by which he is brought to this. The actual moment of forgiveness is clearly marked. It occurs in the dialogue with Ariel at the beginning of Act V and to appreciate its significance we must consider what Ariel is. Shakespeare probably took the name (which admirably suits an airy spirit) from the twenty-ninth chapter of Isaiah, in which there is also mention of a spirit of divination, and some passages which recall the way Ariel flamed amazement in the King's ship and exhibited a devouring grace in playing the harpy. The importance of this chapter has been pointed out by Robert Graves, and more recently by Ann Pasternak Slater.[45] But even though the name of Ariel has biblical associations—one may say that Isaiah is his godparent—what Shakespeare reveals of his history gives a totally different impression. Sycorax, Caliban's mother, imprisoned Ariel in a cloven pine for a dozen years because he was a spirit 'too delicate/To act her earthy and abhorr'd commands'. On the death of Sycorax, Ariel would have remained for ever in the pine-tree if Prospero had not arrived on the island, heard his groans and released him by means of his art. This was twelve years before the opening of the play; and the two twelve-year periods have caused speculation among the critics who have wondered if the twenty-four years had a private meaning for the poet. (For example, it is suggested that twelve years before he wrote *The Tempest* was the beginning of the tragic period, and twelve years before that he arrived from Stratford to be imprisoned in the theatre.)[46] At least we can say that Ariel, at some moments, represents the poetic imagination, and his desire for freedom is said to reflect Shakespeare's wish to retire, though about this we may well have doubts.

In Act V Ariel, who has carried out Prospero's commands, tells him that his charm

> so strongly works
> That if you now beheld them, your affections
> Would become tender . . .
> Mine would, sir, were I human.

Prospero replies, in what are perhaps the key lines of the play:

And mine shall.
Hast thou, which art but air, a touch, a feeling
Of their afflictions, and shall not myself,
One of their kind, that relish all as sharply
Passion as they, be kindlier moved than thou art?
Though with their high wrongs I am struck to the quick,
Yet, with my nobler reason, 'gainst my fury
Do I take part; the rarer action is
In virtue than in vengeance; they being penitent,
The sole drift of my purpose doth extend
Not a frown further. Go, release them, Ariel.      (V.i.17–30)

It has been pointed out[47] only recently that these lines are a very close echo of a passage in Florio's translation of Montaigne's essays. It is the beginning of the essay on Cruelty (II.11).

Methinks *Vertue* is another manner of thing, and *much more noble* than the inclinations unto Goodnesse, which in us are engendered ... He that through a naturall facilitie and genuine mildnesse should neglect or contemne injuries received, should no doubt performe *a rare action*, and worthy commendation: but he who being *toucht and stung to the quicke* with any wrong or offence received, should arme himself with *reason against* this *furiously* blind desire of *revenge*, and in the end after a great conflict yield himselfe master over it, should doubtlesse *doe much more* The first should doe well, the other vertuously: the one action might be termed Goodnesse, the other *Vertue*.

Ariel, being a spirit, is not able to feel with the sufferers; but he knows that if he were human, he would. He is what may be called 'conscienceless imagination'. Shakespeare makes Prospero forgive his enemies at the prompting of Ariel. The implication is that forgiveness is prompted by the imagination because only by imagination are we able to put ourselves in the place of others. As Shelley put it: 'The great instrument of moral good is the imagination and poetry administers to the effect by acting upon the cause.'[48]

Notice, however, that neither the virtuous behaviour described by Montaigne, nor Prospero's own decision to forgive, can really be regarded as Christian. Prospero refrains from vengeance; he does not whole-heartedly forgive. The advice of Seneca was to pardon all offences where there was any sign of repentance or hope of amendment, to revenge oneself by refraining from revenge.[49]

> A good man executeth his offices without confusion or fear, and in such sort will perform those things that are worthy a good man, that he will do nothing that is unworthy a man . . . It is the part of a great mind to despise injuries: it is a contumelious kind of revenge, that he thought him unworthy to revenge himself on . . . That man is great and noble, that after the manner of a mighty wild beast, listeneth securely the barking of lesser dogs . . . A man that is truly valiant, and that knoweth his own worth, revengeth not an injury, because he feeleth it not . . . How far more worthy a thing is it to despise all injuries and contumelies, as if the mind were impregnable. Revenge is a confession of pain. The mind is not great which is animated by injury.

So Prospero forgives because it is the rarer action, not because it is a Christian duty.

Shakespeare keeps three surprises up his sleeve. Alonso, we know, has already repented, after Ariel, in the guise of a harpy, had denounced the three men of sin. In its context—the murderous plotting of Antonio and Sebastian, the presumed drowning of Alonso's son, the vanishing of the enchanted banquet—the effect of the speech is tremendous:

> You are three men of sin, whom destiny,
> That hath to instrument this lower world
> And what is in't, the never-surfeited sea
> Hath caused to belch up, yea, and on this island
> Where man doth not inhabit, you 'mongst men
> Being most unfit to live. I have made you mad
> And even with such like valour men hang and drown
> Their proper selves. You fools! I and my fellows
> Are ministers of fate . . . But remember
> (For that's my business to you) that you three
> From Milan did supplant good Prospero;
> Exposed unto the sea (which have requit it)
> Him and his innocent child: for which foul deed,
> The powers delaying, not forgetting, have

Incensed the seas and shores, yea all the creatures
Against your peace . . . Thee of thy son, Alonso,
They have bereft; and do pronounce by me,
Lingering perdition (worse than any death
Can be at once) shall step by step attend
You and your ways; whose wraths to guard you from—
Which here, in this most desolate isle, else falls
Upon your heads—is nothing but heart's sorrow,
And a clear life ensuing.                                        (III.iii.53–82)

The men of sin feel themselves paralysed by guilt and fear; they are
reminded of their isolation on a desert isle; they are called mad and
warned that only penitence can avert the lingering perdition which
seems already to have afflicted them.[50] They rush out in a mad
stampede.

'They being penitent' says Prospero, he will forgive them. But
what if they are not? Gonzalo knows that their desperation is
caused by the consciousness of guilt. Alonso believes that he has
been punished by the death of his son and heir. Ariel later describes
them as 'all three distracted'. In the final scene Prospero cordially
forgives the penitent Alonso; he realises that Sebastian is suffering
from the inward pinches of conscience and he too, though more
reluctantly, is forgiven. But Antonio shows no signs of repentance;
Prospero despises him and hates him—to call him brother, he says,
would infect his mouth[51]—but he does not expose his treachery to
Alonso, nor does he avenge himself. Presumably Prospero's knowledge of his brother is some sort of safeguard about his future
conduct. So Prospero does not demand repentance after all.

The next surprise comes with regard to Caliban. Perhaps it is
necessary to say that Caliban is not a portrait of the Elizabethan
groundlings, Miranda being Shakespeare's poetry they sought to
violate. Nor is he Shakespeare's portrait of the proletariat and the
democracy threatened in the early years of the seventeenth century.
Nor is he even Shakespeare's satirical comment on the rise of
imperialism, the noble savage dispossessed by the ignoble white
men, Stephano and Trinculo. (When I first came to Liverpool there
was a docker called George Garrett who wrote a powerful essay in
praise of Caliban entitled 'That Four-flusher Prospero'[52]—but
Prospero cannot objectively be regarded as an exploiter.) Nor can I
even bring myself to agree with the Freudians who as long ago as

1914 described Caliban as a phallic demon. More plausibly Caliban can be taken to represent the animal nature of man, as the ordinary sensual man, as the mystery of iniquity, as Original Sin.

It is obvious that he is at moments a primitive savage,[53] at moments he represents the flesh, but he is given a love of music and a vein of poetry which sets him above the dregs of civilisation, Stephano and Trinculo and the three men of sin. Prospero, because of his attempted rape of Miranda, describes him as a born devil—his father was a devil—one on whose nature nurture will never stick, a thing of darkness, Prospero's greatest educational failure. But, to the surprise of his master, he decides to be wise hereafter and seek for grace.

The last surprise comes in the epilogue. It has often been noted that from one point of view *The Tempest* can be regarded as a dramatisation of the activity of the dramatist. Shakespeare must have been conscious of parallels between his own situation and that of Prospero. When the great magician says farewell to his art and retires to Milan, it is difficult to believe that the thought did not cross Shakespeare's mind that he too was making his last bow as actor and dramatist. It is true, as everyone knows, that the speech is adapted from Ovid; but (it has been pointed out) Shakespeare in his tragedies could be said to have bedimmed

> The noontide sun, call'd forth the mutinous winds,
> And 'twixt the green sea and the azur'd vault
> Set roaring war: the strong-bas'd promontory
> Have I made shake, and by the spurs pluck'd up
> The pine and cedar; graves, at my command,
> Have wak'd their sleepers, op'd, and let 'em forth
> By my so potent art.                                (V.i.42ff.)

Auden in his verse commentary on *The Tempest* (*The Sea and the Mirror*) seemed to assume that Shakespeare was writing about his own retirement; and Rilke in his poem 'Ariel' also treated Prospero as a persona of the poet himself:[54]

> Now he terrifies me,
> This man who's duke again.—The way he draws
> The wire into his head, and hangs himself
> Beside the other puppets, and henceforth
> Asks mercy of the play! What epilogue

Of achieved mastery! Putting off, standing there
With only one's own strength: 'which is most faint.'

Rilke is referring to the very curious epilogue. This begins with a
conventional appeal for applause:

> release me from my bands,
> With the help of your good hands.

But it ends with a solemn appeal for the prayers of the audience.
Partly, I think, Shakespeare is saying farewell to the people he
had served so well, and on whose response his plays ultimately
depended. But partly, he is drawing the moral of the play. Auden
said in an early essay that the greatest art is that which teaches
people to unlearn hatred and to learn love; and this is precisely the
function of *The Tempest*:

> Now I want
> Spirits to enforce, art to enchant;
> And my ending is despair,
> Unless I be relieved by prayer;
> Which pierces so, that it assaults
> Mercy itself, and frees all faults.
> As you from crimes would pardoned be,
> Let your indulgence set me free.

This is the third surprise to which reference was made. The proud,
disdainful forgiveness of Prospero is linked in the Epilogue to a
humble Christian prayer for forgiveness—forgiveness for Prospero,
for the actor who plays the part, and for the poet himself.

It has often been noticed that Prospero plays the double role of
dramatist and protagonist. All the other characters are his puppets,
unknowingly acting out his wishes, but he himself is the leading
character in the play he stages. It is therefore appropriate that at the
moment when the spirit-actors and the whole spectacle created by
Prospero for the betrothed couple vanish into thin air, Prospero
should draw a parallel between the transitory nature of human life
and the pageant beheld by the audience on the stage and in the
theatre.

The vanishing of the spirits (Enid Welsford has suggested)[55] was
done by the use of gauze curtains as in the dissolving scenes of court
masques, curtains 'which being drawn one over another to resem-

ble flying mists, gave to the scene an appearance of gradual
dissolution'. When the actors and the scenery were totally concealed, the process was reversed, and when the last curtain was
withdrawn nothing was left behind. Shakespeare was doubtless
drawing on memories of the Bible:[56]

> And all the host of heaven shall be dissolved, and the heavens
> shall bee folden like a booke . . . The heavens shall passe away
> with a noyse, and the elements shall melt with heate, and the
> earth with the works that are therein, shall be burnt up.

He was also remembering Renaissance commonplaces about muta-
bility, such as the mutability cantos at the end of *The Faerie
Queene*, and passages in Alexander's dreary Senecan play, in which
Darius's glory is said to be [57]

> A meere illusion made to mock the sight,
> Whose best was but the shaddowe of a dreame
>
> .    .    .
>
> Let greatnesse of her glassie scepters vaunt;
> Not sceptours, no, but reeds, soone bruis'd, sone broken:
> And let this worldlie pompe our wits enchant.
> All fades, and scarcelie leaues behinde a token.
> Those golden Pallaces, those gorgeous halles,
> With fourniture superfluouslie faire:
> Those statelie Courts, those sky-encountring walles
> Evanishe all like vapours in the aire.

From these and doubtless from other passages Shakespeare distilled
Prospero's lines:

> Our revels now are ended. These our actors,
> As I foretold you, were all spirits, and
> Are melted into air . . . into thin air;
> And like the baseless fabric of this vision,
> The cloud-capped towers, the gorgeous palaces,
> The solemn temples, the great globe itself,
> Yea, all which it inherit, shall dissolve,
> And, like this insubstantial pageant faded,
> Leave not a rack behind. We are such stuff
> As dreams are made on, and our little life
> Is rounded with a sleep.                              (IV.i.148)

We are the fabric on which dreams are woven, as on a tapestry, the dreams, perhaps, of the creator. Our life ends with the sleep of death, and we are insubstantial as the characters in a play—and as the characters of a play within the play, performed by spirits—and, as Theseus reminds us 'the best of this kind are but shadows', and as the haunted Thane of Cawdor proclaims:

> Life's but a walking shadow, a poor player
> That struts and frets his hour upon the stage.

The implication is that characters in a play possess as much reality as 'real' people. (This is one of Pirandello's obsessive themes. Are the six characters in search of an author more or less real than the actors who attempt to impersonate them?)

Prospero's speech links the spirit-actors in the masque with Ferdinand and Miranda whose parts, one may say, have been written for them by Prospero; and the audience on the stage is a paradigm of the audience off the stage—of ourselves. Prospero in the world of the play acts as Providence; and he is the protagonist of the action he has himself willed. In the same way Shakespeare creates the plays in which he himself performs; but just as Prospero learns from Ariel in the course of the action, so Shakespeare's plays are the means by which his own experience becomes fully conscious. The poet's characters—Falstaff and Hamlet, Lear and Cleopatra—created (or recreated) Shakespeare.

The audience, like Miranda and Ferdinand, have been watching the masque; but as we know from the motto of the Globe Theatre,[58] and from Jaques's variations on it in *As You Like It*, the spectators are themselves actors on the stage of the world. The drama itself, as Elizabethans often mentioned, is an image of life, the dramatist, as well as the actor, holding a mirror up to nature; and as actors on the stage of the world we are taking part in a kind of divine drama. Similar ideas were expressed by Calderón in *Life's a Dream* and *The Theatre of the World*, and Frances Yates in a recent book has argued[59] that the evidence

> all points to the Theatre of the World as the 'Idea' of the Globe Theatre. To the cosmic meanings of the ancient theatre, with its plan based on the triangulations within the zodiac, was added the religious meanings of the theatre as temple, and the related religious and cosmic meanings of the Renaissance

church. The Globe Theatre was a magical theatre, a cosmic theatre, a religious theatre, an actors' theatre, designed to give fullest support to the voices and the gestures of the players as they enacted the drama of the life of man within the Theatre of the World ... His theatre would have been for Shakespeare the pattern of the universe, the idea of the Macrocosm, the world stage on which the Microcosm acted his parts.

Frances Yates, in another book, has argued much less convincingly that Prospero is a portrait of Dr John Dee, who was suspected of dabbling in the black art and who urged King James to have him examined so that the could clear his name. He, like Prospero, dealt only in white magic. Although we must reject the idea that Prospero is a portrait of Dee, it is important to recognise that his art was quite unlike that of Oberon or Puck. *The Tempest* is much closer to real life. As Kittredge pointed out[60] Prospero was to a Jacobean audience

> no mere figure of impossible romance, tricked out with sorcerer's robe and book of spells to tickle their fancy for the marvellous.

His art was an accepted method of controlling the forces of nature, no more impossible than nuclear physics would be to a modern audience.

There was, of course, another way by which Shakespeare gave the play a topical relevance. Just before he wrote it news had arrived of the shipwreck in the Bermudas of the ships chartered by the Virginia Company. Shakespeare could have heard the details from his old acquaintance, William Strachey,[61] or from one of the Digges family.[62] Leonard contributed verses to the First Folio and his step-father was the overseer of Shakespeare's will. Leonard's brother, Sir Dudley, was a member of the Council of the Virginia Company, and his sister married Sir Antony Palmer, another member of the Council. There is no doubt that Shakespeare made use of the accounts of the shipwreck and his picture of Prospero's island owes a good deal to these. Moreover he obtained details from a number of travel books, from one of which he got the name of Caliban's god, Setebos,[63] and it is well known that he had been reading Montaigne's essay on the cannibals—which provided him with a name for his native and the basis for Gonzalo's commonwealth.

It is usually referred to as Gonzalo's ideal commonwealth, but as the villains point out, and as Gonzalo himself is aware, it is merely a pipe-dream, prompted by tales of the New World.

> I'th'commonwealth I would by contraries
> Execute all things; for no kind of traffic
> Would I admit; no name of magistrate;
> Letters should not be known; riches, poverty,
> And use of service, none; contract, succession,
> Bourn, bound of land, tilth, vineyard, none;
> No use of metal, corn, or wine, or oil;
> No occupation; all men idle, all;
> And women too, but innocent and pure;
> No sovereignty . . .
> All things in common nature should produce
> Without sweat or endeavour. Treason, felony,
> Sword, pike, knife, gun, or need of any engine,
> Would I not have; but nature should bring forth,
> Of its own kind, all foison, all abundance,
> To feed my innocent people.                    (II.i.15off.)

This return to Eden is, of course, impossible. Dreams of the state withering away sometimes lead to the opposite; and most Utopias are not serious blueprints for a future society, they are rather criticisms of existing society. Caliban is Shakespeare's answer to Gonzalo; but the island, if not the world in miniature, poses (as *Measure for Measure* had done) problems of government. In several previous plays Shakespeare had depicted good men who were unsuccessful monarchs. In *The Tempest* he shows us a philosopher-prince who loses his throne by treachery and regains it by his art, learning in his second period of rule to avoid the mistakes of his first—or so we are led to hope.

As in the other tragi-comedies of Shakespeare's final period, people are given second chances. Thaisa is resurrected, Marina escapes death at the hands of the pirates, Imogen revives after her funeral, Hermione comes down from her pedestal, Perdita is restored to her parents, the rotten carcase of a butt which the rats had instinctively quit, brings Miranda and Prospero safely to the island. These departures from our normal expectations have some-times been regarded as signs of the decline of Shakespeare's poetic powers, as though he were too tired to face reality, or too anxious to fit in with the latest fashions to continue to write tragedy. In a word, he was guilty of sentimentality.

It is true that the world of these plays appears to be providentially governed—and this is underlined by the numerous theophanies,[64] Diana in *Pericles*, Jupiter in *Cymbeline*, the oracle of Apollo in *The Winter's Tale*, and (if only in the masque), Juno and Ceres in *The Tempest*. But we should note that the happy endings do not actually require divine intervention—they require the repentance of Leontes and Leonatus, the patience of Hermione and Prospero. It is, moreover, untrue to pretend that Shakespeare now evades the problem of evil. One has only to think of Sebastian and Antonio, of Caliban and Stephano—all of whom could be taken to illustrate the mystery of iniquity. Nor is there anything sentimental about Prospero. He is stern with Ariel (whom he loves) as well as with Caliban. He makes Ferdinand a slave so as to arouse Miranda's pity for him; and even those who think Prospero is a self-portrait of Shakespeare are somewhat perturbed by his repeated warnings to Ferdinand not to forestall the marriage ceremony:

> If thou dost break her virgin-knot before
> All sanctimonious ceremonies may
> With full and holy rite be ministred,
> No sweet aspersion shall the heavens let fall
> To make this contract grow.          (IV.i.15–19)

Ferdinand protests the purity of his love; but later on Prospero again warns him not to give dalliance too much the rein.

> The strongest oaths are straw
> To th'fire i'th' blood.

What is more, the theme of the masque with which Prospero entertains the lovers—and with which Shakespeare tactlessly entertains Princess Elizabeth and her betrothed—is the importance of pre-nuptial chastity. Shakespeare's views may have been influenced by the decline of morals at the court of James I; but it has been suggested that Prospero's love for his dear one, his loved darling, who outstrips all praise, reflects an unconscious jealousy of Ferdinand. [Barbara Melchiori has written[65] of the obsession with incest in Shakespeare's final period—in the first act of *Pericles*, in Greene's *Pandosto*, and in Leontes' first reactions to Perdita before he knows her identity.]

*The Tempest* is far from being a sentimental day-dream. Prospero's austerity and sternness are a natural result of his brooding for twelve years on the treachery which deprived him of his kingdom and which nearly cost him his life and that of his beloved child. Yet, like the other wronged characters in the last plays, Prospero overcomes his natural desire for vengeance. As Spinoza said:[66]

> He who wishes to avenge his injuries by returning hate for hate cannot fail to be unhappy. He, on the other hand, who endeavours to combat hatred with love, finds in this struggle both joy and security . . . He has less need than any one of Fortune's aid.

Prospero forgives; but there is nothing in the play to suggest that forgiveness came easily to him, or that the play is without extreme tension.

I have suggested that Shakespeare was concerned with problems of government, with the tensions between power and virtue. It is striking that all the characters are involved in this problem in one way or another—Antonio and Sebastian plotting against Alonso; Alonso suffering from pangs of guilt for his former action; Caliban plotting with Stephano and Trinculo against Prospero; Ariel yearning for freedom; Prospero himself looking forward to handing over his power to his son-in-law; and even the young lovers use images of freedom and slavery. Ferdinand tells Miranda:

> Full many a Lady
> I have ey'd with best regard, and many a time
> Th' harmony of their tongues hath into bondage
> Brought my too diligent ear.
> The very instant that I saw you, did
> My heart fly to your service; there resides
> To make me slave to it, and for your sake
> As I this patient log-man.                              (III.i.39ff.)

Miranda echoes the same idea:

> To be your fellow
> You may deny me, but I'll be your servant
> Whether you will or no.

Ferdinand replies:

> My Mistress (dearest)
And I thus humble ever.

Miranda asks:

> My husband, then?

and Ferdinand replies:

> Ay, with a heart as willing
As bondage e'er of freedom.

Both Ferdinand and Miranda find liberty in bondage to each other because they realise (in the words of the prayer) that 'Love's service is perfect freedom'.

Caliban and his fellow-conspirators, on the other hand, hope to obtain freedom by murder:

> Ban, ban, Ca-Calyban
Has a new master, get a new man.
Freedom, hey-day, hey-day, freedom.

But, of course, the hope of freedom without responsibility is an illusion; and Caliban found himself more enslaved by Trinculo and Stephano than ever he had been by Prospero. A generation later, after Milton had lived through the English Revolution, he was bitterly disillusioned by the results; and he told his fellow-countrymen that they could not really be free so long as they were enslaved by their passions:[67]

> Know that to be free is the same thing as to be pious, wise, temperate, just, frugal, abstinent, magnanimous and brave; so to be the opposite of all these is to be a slave ... You, therefore, who wish to retain your freedom, learn wisdom; or, at least, stop being fools. If you think slavery an intolerable evil, learn obedience to reason and learn how to govern your selves; and at last say farewell to your dissensions, your jealousies, your superstitions, and your lusts.

Shakespeare would have expressed it rather differently. He would have been less puritanical and put less stress on abstinence and frugality, and more on love and forgiveness. Like Keats, he was certain of nothing but the holiness of the heart's affections and the truth of the imagination.

It has been suggested that Auden's poem about *The Tempest* is concerned with the power and the limitations of art; and I want in conclusion to consider the play from this point of view. It would be generally accepted that it belongs to the frontier between ethics and aesthetics, between the real world and the imagined world of art. What Shakespeare appears to be doing, not merely in *The Tempest* but in *Cymbeline* and *The Winter's Tale*, is creating an imaginary world, so as to 'raise and erect the mind, by submitting the shows of things to the desires of the mind'. It is not escapist art, the desires of Shakespeare's mind are closely linked with a realisation of the conditions of their fulfilment. No doubt there will always be sin and suffering and art provides no armour against fate; but in what Henry James called 'the luminous paradise of art',[68] all losses are restored and sorrows end. Here in a mirror we see the necessity of forgiveness. What else is Prospero's magic but the power of poetry?

Prospero and Miranda arrive at the island, escaping miraculously from the treacherous world of Milan, the infant Miranda infused with a fortitude from heaven, preserving her father (as he claims). Years later the magical storm brings the sinners to the island, but now power has been transferred to their victim. A few hours later the whole party embarks for the return voyage to Milan—a return to the real world, but with some sort of guarantee that things will be better than they were—that both Naples and Milan will be governed well because of what the characters have learnt.

# 18
# *The Two Noble Kinsmen*

A number of critics have denied that Shakespeare had any hand in *The Two Noble Kinsmen*; one critic, Paul Bertram, thought that Shakespeare wrote it all;[69] but I still adhere to the view that the original title-page was right in crediting the play to Shakespeare and Fletcher. This was the view of Pope, Coleridge, Tennyson and Swinburne, with Shelley the only poet who denied Shakespeare's responsibility for some scenes. In the present chapter the joint authorship of the play will be assumed.

*The Two Noble Kinsmen* begins where *A Midsummer Night's Dream* ends—with the marriage of Theseus and Hippolyta.

Eighteen years or more separate the two plays, and the stage
had changed a good deal in the interval. The only entertainment
provided for Duke Theseus on his wedding day is a performance by
some not very talented actors of the tragedy of Pyramus and
Thisbe. The opening stage-direction in *The Two Noble Kinsmen*
illustrates the difference:

> Enter Hymen with a Torch burning; a Boy in a white Robe,
> singing and strewing Flowers; after Hymen, a Nimph, encom-
> past in her Tresses, bearing a wheaten Garland; then Theseus,
> between two other Nimphs with wheaten Chaplets on their
> heades; then Hipolita, the Bride, led by Pirithous, and another
> holding a Garland over her head (*her Tresses likewise hang-
> ing*). After her, Emilia, holding up her Train. (*Artesius and
> Attendants.*)

Immediately after the singing of the very beautiful bridal
song—'Roses their sharp spines being gone'—which Dowden and
others ascribe to Fletcher, the ceremonies are interrupted by the
appearance of

> three Queenes, in Blacke, with vailes staind, with imperiall
> Crownes. The first Queene fals downe at the foote of Theseus;
> The second fals downe at the foote of Hypolita; The third
> before Emilia.

The pleading of the three queens whose husbands lie unburied at
the order of Creon is much more effective than it is in the source,
*The Knight's Tale* of Chaucer, where instead of three queens
speaking antiphonally we have a whole procession of women with
a single spokeswoman. Chaucer's Theseus, moreover, is already
married to Hippolyta, and he needs no persuading to make war on
Creon. In the play the ceremony is not yet over, and Theseus,
though ready to set out on a campaign, wants at first to finish his
wedding. He is persuaded by his bride and Emilia to postpone the
ceremony until after his campaign. The only characteristic which
distinguishes Theseus from any heroic figure is that he is continually revoking his firm decisions at the wish of his women-folk. He
carries a stage further what has often been observed in the
characters of Shakespeare's final period—a tendency to flattening
and conventionality which we do not get in the comedies and
tragedies written between 1597 and 1607.

But, in fact, this first scene does not require profound or subtle characterisation. It requires only an eloquent treatment of the initial situation—the mourning queens interrupting the wedding —and it would be inappropriate for the characters to be individualised. Within this convention the whole scene is written with masterly ease and assurance. Shakespeare has developed one stage further the elaborate syntax and subtle rhythms to be found in *Cymbeline* and *The Winter's Tale*, so that we almost forget we are listening to verse.

Emilia is one of the most prominent characters in the first scene. In the second we are introduced to the prospective rivals for her love. Here Shakespeare is less successful than he had been in the first scene, where characterisation is of secondary importance, for the twin heroes are as indistinguishable as Tweedledum and Tweedledee. Although the verse remains skilful, the general impression of the scene is one of perfunctoriness.

The third scene is designed to amplify the character of Emilia by a comparison of the masculine friendship of Theseus and Pirithous with Emilia's love for the dead Flavina. Her conviction that she will never love a man as much as she loved the child prepares the way for her inability to choose between Palamon and Arcite. The speech is important also because friendship and loyalty constitute one of the main themes of the play.

The fourth scene is concerned with Theseus's victory and the taking prisoner of the desperately wounded friends. The fifth scene, dealing with the funeral of the three kings, provides another opportunity for music and pageantry, appreciated by the patrons of the Blackfriars Theatre. It is not certain whether these two short scenes are Shakespeare's, but they round off the theme of the unburied kings, and they are in keeping with the rest of the act.

The play, up to this point, has obviously been well planned and well written. Theodore Spencer, in his valuable article on the play, while admitting the superb rhetoric of parts of the first and third scenes, complained that the writing was tired, the muscles behind it slack and old.[70] It seems to me, on the contrary, that there is no sign of tiredness or flabbiness in the actual writing. Only in the characterisation does there seem to be a definite falling off—a process that had begun with *Pericles*—though we may say with Mr Eliot that Shakespeare in his final plays was seeing through the actions of men into a spiritual action which transcended them.

In addition to the friendship theme which I have mentioned, Shakespeare states two other themes in the first act of the play—the power of fortune and the inscrutable workings of the Gods. Fortune is referred to many times. When Theseus first beheld the young bride of King Capaneus, Fortune, at her 'Dimpled her cheek with smiles'; and looking on her in her widowed state he observes:

> O greife and time
> Fearefull consumers, you will all devoure.

In the second scene we are told that the villainy of Creon

> almost puts
> Faith in a feavour, and deïfies alone
> Voluble chance.

Fortune, it appears, becomes a goddess, only through man's frailty. But at the end of the scene Arcite submits all to the event, 'that never-erring Arbitratour'; and he tells Palamon:

> Let us follow
> The Becking of our chance.

In the third scene Hippolyta wishes Theseus power 'To dare ill-dealing Fortune'; and at the end of the scene she prays not *to* Fortune, but for his fortunes.

The references to the gods are equally significant, and they are plainly designed to prepare the way for the great invocations of Mars, Venus and Diana which were the climax of Chaucer's tale. In Act II, which is almost certainly Fletcher's work, and again in the parts of Acts III and IV which appear to be his, there is a sudden cessation of significant references to fortune and the gods.

It is usually said that the thirteen Fletcher scenes in the middle of the play, though manifestly inferior poetically to Shakespeare's, display his usual sense of the theatre. Certainly some individual scenes are effective, but some of them are much less effective than one might have expected. The underplot of the jailer's daughter is bungled and we are not shown the scene between the girl and Palamon. The mad speeches do not convince one. This is not how mad people speak; it is not even a literary correlative of such speech: it is a sentimental substitute for it.

It is usually said that the jailer's daughter is a crude imitation of Ophelia, but apart from the fact that both girls are crossed in love and sing snatches of song, and both play with flowers by a stream, there is really very little resemblance. Fletcher's fault is not that of plagiarism. Nor, I think, should we complain (as the older critics inevitably did) of the lack of maidenly modesty in a girl so much in love that she wants Palamon without a wedding-ring, or of the alleged indecency when the doctor advises her young man to pretend to be Palamon and to lie with her as a means of curing her madness. What we can reasonably complain of, apart from the monotony I have just mentioned, and Fletcher's avoidance of a scene between Palamon and the girl, are the artificiality and unreality of the mad speeches, the way in which the madness is used to arouse laughter, and the disparity between the speaker of courtly prose in Act II and the girl in Act V who has one 'poor petticoat and two coarse smocks'.

Every reader will notice the transformation of Palamon and Arcite in Act II. Instead of being the disillusioned social critics of Act I—haunted, as Theodore Spencer put it, by the ghost of Timon; haunted at least by the ghosts of contemporary commentators and satirists—they appear as elegant, sentimental figures who have obviously never brooded on social questions. Thebes, no longer decadent, is described as noble. It is true that in one of Palamon's speeches he speaks of the court of Creon,

> Where sin is Iustice, lust and ignorance
> The vertues of the great ones;

and declares that

> all those pleasures
> That woe the wils of men to vanity
> I see through now.

But the implication is that he has been brought to this state of mind since his imprisonment. Another obvious discrepancy is to be found in Act III, scene iii, where Palamon and Arcite rally each other on their previous love-affairs. This conflicts with Palamon's prayer to Venus, in which, with obvious sincerity, he contrasts his chaste conduct with that of libertines.

There is a sudden drop in poetic quality in the prison scene. The rhythm becomes flabbier, the language and imagery more conventional. In place of vivid metaphors we get rather tired similes. Despite which the scene is theatrically effective.

At the beginning of Act III Shakespeare's hand is once more apparent in the opening soliloquy of Arcite:

> O Queene *Emilia*,
> Fresher than May, sweeter
> Than her gold buttons on the bowes, or all
> Th'enamelld knackes o' the Meade or garden! yea,
> We challenge too the bancke of any Nymph,
> That makes the streame seeme flowers; thou, O Iewell
> O' th wood, o' th world, hast likewise blest a place
> With thy sole presence!

Not only was Fletcher incapable of producing what Murry called 'this unearthly melody of a shattered blank-verse rhythm', and what Theodore Spencer beautifully described as 'the caught breath, the broken wonder, the magical invocation . . . trembling through a shattered rhythm into words', but the lines are manifestly written by the author of similar passages in *Pericles, Cymbeline* and *The Winter's Tale*. The jewel image is taken up in the last speech of the play when Theseus refers to Emilia as 'your stolen jewel'.

Shakespeare may have written a few more speeches in this scene, but nearly all critics are agreed that it soon drops into typical Fletcherian cadences and sentimentality:

> brave soules in shades,
> That have dyde manly, which will seeke of me
> Some newes from earth, they shall get none but this,
> That thou art brave and noble.                    (III.i.85–8)

The best of Fletcher's scenes is that which follows the interruption of the duel by Theseus; but effective too, in its preposterous way, is the scene in Act IV, in which Emilia compares the portraits of Palamon and Arcite. Her oscillation between the two suitors is a means of preserving suspense.

Shakespeare seems to have contributed the whole of the fifth act except the second scene and the first eighteen lines of the first. The invocations of Mars, Venus and Diana were the climax of Chaucer's tale, as they are of the play; and Shakespeare, without any verbal borrowing, takes the general argument of two of his speeches from Chaucer. Arcite's invocation of Mars is perhaps coloured by Elizabethan views on the social function of war. So Arcite addresses Mars as

> thou grand decider
> Of dusty and old tytles, that healst with blood
> The earth when it is sicke, and cur'st the world
> O' the pluresie of people.                               (V.i.69–72)

The surge and thunder of Shakespeare's final style is better illustrated by the beginning of the speech:

> Thou mighty one, that with thy power hast turnd
> Greene Neptune into purple; whose Approach
> Comets prewarne; whose havocke in vast Feild
> Vnearthed skulls proclaime; whose breath blowes downe
> The teeming Ceres foyzon; who dost plucke
> With hand armypotent from forth blew clowdes
> The masond Turrets; that both mak'st and break'st
> The stony girthes of cities; me thy puple
> Yongest follower of thy Drom, instruct this day
> With military skill; that to thy lawde
> I may advance my streamer, and by thee
> Be stil'd the Lord o' th' day.                           (V.i.55–66)

Shakespeare's use of words was still as vigorous as ever, and so too was his habit of pictorialising his ideas. City walls are presented as 'stony girths'; and the idea that walls are built as a protection in war, and destroyed in the course of war, is condensed into the deliberately harsh phrase 'mak'st and break'st'. The destruction of castles or towers is presented in a hyperbolical picture of Mars plucking them from among the clouds. Some words—*unearthed, prewarn* and *masond*—Shakespeare had not used at all; and *armypotent* had previously been used in deliberately bombastic passages.

The speech is beautifully contrasted with the slow movement of Emilia's address to Diana, with its long roll of epithets and cold imagery:

> O sacred, shadowie, cold, and constant Queene,
> Abandoner of Revells, mute, contemplative,
> Sweet, solitary, white, as chaste and pure
> As winde fand snow.                                      (V.i.143–6)

It is noteworthy that the impression of purity is maintained by the use not only of such epithets and images as the ones I have just quoted, but also by using 'maculate' for stained, reminding us of its opposite, immaculate. There is the same continuing experimentation with vocabulary—Shakespeare had not before used abandoner, unsentenced, or pretender, nor the hyphenated wind-fanned, bride-habited and maiden-hearted. There is the same felicity of phrasing as in the words 'thy rare green eye' and the description of Diana as 'our Generall of Ebbs and Flowes'.

Palamon's speech, addressed to Venus, is as masterly as the other two; but as Theodore Spencer has noticed,[71] it is very strange. It is quite unlike the corresponding speech in *The Knight's Tale*, and at first sight it seems to be inappropriate both to the romantic love-rivalry of the play and to the character of Palamon. It begins with conventional praise of Venus, but quickly develops into a satirical account of her power, becoming more and more grotesque as it progresses. Venus makes 'A Criple florish with his Crutch'; she makes the bachelor of seventy sing lays of love; she makes a gouty man of eighty, with one foot in the grave, marry and beget an heir, his wife swearing it was his, and who, asks Palamon, would not believe her? Venus is finally addressed

> O thou that from eleven to ninetie raign'st
> In mortall bosomes.

Although Palamon speaks of her as 'most soft sweet goddess', the picture we have of her is of an imperious and cruel creature who holds gods and mortals at her mercy. Palamon himself who bears her yoke 'As 'twere a wreath of Roses', finds it 'heavier than Lead it selfe, stings more than Nettles'. In the rest of the speech Palamon boasts that he has 'never been foul-mouthed' against Venus's law, that he has never betrayed a woman or committed adultery, that he has objected to bawdy conversation and that he avoids licentious company. The pleasanter side of love is not represented.

It is obviously absurd to suppose that Shakespeare, who not long before has written love-scenes for Perdita and Florizel and for Ferdinand and Miranda, was putting his own personal sentiments into Palamon's mouth. There would seem to be three good dramatic reasons for this satirical speech. In the first place, Palamon is rightly concerned with Venus's power—the power 'Even with an ey-glance to choke Mars's Drom'—because his rival is appealing to the power of Mars. And the power of Venus is most plainly displayed in the conquest of the gods, and in the miraculous reversal of nature's laws. Secondly there are indications—in the scenes of both dramatists—of Palamon's disillusioned temperament. Emilia, describing his portrait, speaks of him as

> Swarth and meagre, of an eye as heavy
> As if he had lost his mother.

The third reason why Shakespeare wrote this kind of speech is that Palamon has indeed found Venus's yoke heavier than lead. It has caused him to quarrel with his kinsman; and if he wins the fight the man he loves will be executed.

Mars, Venus and Diana all answer their votaries' prayers, but not in the way they expect. Arcite prays for victory—to be styled lord of the day—and he wins the fight and loses Emilia. Palamon asks for success in love, but he achieves Emilia not by winning the fight but by the accidental death of Arcite. Emilia prays that the one who loves her best should win her, and we are meant to suppose that Palamon, who had originally hailed her as a goddess, was a truer lover than Arcite, who immediately desired her. Arcite confesses he was false to Palamon, because Palamon was the first to see Emilia and proclaim his love. We are not meant, presumably, to take this too seriously.

The stage-directions in this scene are as elaborate as in the first scene of the play, and they show that there must have been a considerable element of spectacle. When Arcite and his followers fall on their faces before the altar of Mars

> there is heard clanging of Armor, with a short Thunder, as the burst of a Battaile, whereupon they all rise and bow to the Altar.

At the altar of Venus 'music is heard, and doves are seen to flutter'; and the entrance of Emilia is even more elaborate:

> Still Musicke of Records. Enter Emilia in white, her haire about her shoulders, wearing a wheaten wreath; one in white holding up her traine, her haire stuck with flowers; One before her carrying a silver Hynde, in which is conveyed Incense and sweet odours, which is set upon the Altar of Diana, her maides standing aloofe, she sets fire to it; then they curtsey and kneele.

These are probably Shakespeare's own directions, since the hind is the centre of one of his image-clusters.

The continual references to the gods by Shakespeare, are an appropriate preparation for this last act in which the gods appear to intervene in human affairs. Arcite resigns himself to the will of the gods. Emilia, believing that Palamon is to be executed, demands:

> Oh all you heavenly powers, where is your mercy?

Palamon, seeing the dying Arcite, exclaims:

> O miserable end or our alliance!
> The gods are mightie.

In the last speech of Theseus, Shakespeare attempts to round off his references to fortune and the gods by showing that the gods work through the operations of Fortune:

> Never Fortune
> Did play a subtler Game: the conquered triumphes,
> The victor has the Losse; yet in the passage
> The gods have beene most equall.

Later on in the same speech Theseus declares that

> the gods my justice
> Take from my hand, and they themselves become
> The Executioners.

And at the end he addresses the gods as

> O you heavenly Charmers,
> What things you make of us! For what we lacke
> We laugh, for what we have are sorry; still
> Are children in some kind. Let us be thankefull
> For that which is, and with you leave dispute
> That are above our question.                (V.iv.129–34)

These lines, unless Shakespeare wrote part of *Cardenio*, are probably his last dramatic poetry. They do not imply that all is for the best in the best of all possible worlds, but neither is there any of the boredom and bitterness which Strachey found in the later plays of Shakespeare. We are left with a sense of mystery, the impossibility for man to understand the workings of providence, and of gratitude for life.

In its theophanies *The Two Noble Kinsmen* conforms to the pattern of the plays of Shakespeare's final period. In other respects it differs considerably. Shakespeare is no longer obsessed with the necessity of forgiveness; he no longer deals with the reconciliation of parents through the love of the children, with the restoration of the lost wife or child, with the recovery of a lost kingdom. The one evil character, Creon, never appears.

The plot of the play does not really allow much depth or subtlety of characterisation. If, for example, Emilia's dilemma were allowed to be more than pathetic, if she were given a will of her own or the reality of an Imogen, the ending of the play would be more difficult to accept. In any case Fletcher lacked the poetic sensitiveness to develop Emilia along the lines of her portrait in the third scene of the play. But it is quite possible that the playgoers at the Blackfriars preferred the slickness, the smartness, and the sentimentality of the Fletcher scenes to the gnarled toughness of Shakespeare's final style.

# NOTES

## PART I

1 *The Mirror up to Nature* (1965), 10.
2 Roger Ascham, *The Scholemaster* (ed. 1934), 211.
3 Sir Thomas Elyot, *The Boke named the Governour* (ed. 1907), 58.
4 *Endeavors of Art* (1954), 160.
5 *Terence in English* (1598).
6 Erich Segal, *Roman Laughter* (1968).
7 *Complete Works*, ed. A. Feuillerat (1923), III.23.
8 Edward M. Wilson and Duncan Moir, *The Golden Age: Drama* (1971), 106.
9 Act II, scene ii.

## PART II

1 By W. Warner (1595), after the performance of Shakespeare's play. The earliest translation of a Terence play was *c.* 1520.
2 Cf. G. R. Elliott, 'Weirdness in *CE*' *(U.T.Q.,* LV.95ff.) and Harold F. Brooks, 'Themes and Structures in *CE*' in *Early Shakespeare*, ed. J. R. Brown and B. Harris (1961).
3 Q. in New Cambridge edition (1922), 77.
4 1965, 1976.
5 Shakespeare's three earliest comedies were not published until the First Folio of 1623.
6 In Shakespeare's play Sly makes his last appearance at the end of I.i. It is possible that there was an appearance at the end of the play, outside the inn where he had been found, but Richard Hosley thinks not. Cf. *S.E.L.* I (1961), 17–34.
7 It seems unlikely therefore that the author of *A Shrew* knew more than the plot of *The Shrew*.
8 Translated by Roy Campbell.
9 But see Hosley's article mentioned in n.6.
10 Cf. C. C. Seronsy, *S.Q.* XIV (1963), 15–30.
11 *TG, MV, AYLI, TN, WT, Cym.*
12 In some productions the badness of the verse here is emphasised by the actor, presumably to show that the play within the play is more remote from life than the stage-audience.
13 Cf. Richard Hosley's edition in the Complete Pelican Shakespeare, 82.
14 Ibid.

15 *Shakespeare: A Survey* (1925), 40.
16 *Shakespeare* (1911), 108.
17 New Cambridge edition (1928), xvi.
18 Developed from Luciana's advice to Adriana, quoted above.
19 Quoted by Hosley.
20 Paperback edition (1970), 209.
21 New Penguin edition (1968), 22.
22 *The Sources of Shakespeare* (1977), 18. Cf. E. K. Chambers, *Shakespeare Facts and Problems* (1930), I.331.
23 G. Bullough, I (1957), 215–16. Many critics have pointed out the differences between Proteus and Titus.
24 In all the modern productions I have seen, producers have seemed uncertain what tone to adopt.
25 *Elizabethan Sonnets*, I (1904), cviii
26 See, e.g. *MND*, *LLL* and parts of *RJ* and *AYLI*.
27 Cf. Harold F. Brooks, 'Two Clowns in a Comedy ...', *Essays and Studies* (1963), 91–100.
28 *RJ*, III.iii.
29 Something has gone wrong with the text for, as it stands, Proteus has seen Silvia in the flesh as well as her portrait.
30 *Shakespeare's Happy Comedies* (1962), 64.
31 *Dr Johnson on Shakespeare*, ed. W. K. Wimsatt (1969), 108.
32 Reprinted *Appreciations* (1889).
33 *Shakespeare: A Survey* (1925), 58.
34 *Prefaces to Shakespeare* (1947), 413. But he thought that by judicious cutting it could be a success on the stage.
35 *Shakespearian Comedy* (1938), 270ff.
36 Unless we accept Leslie Hotson's theories about Shallow and Silence in *Shakespeare Versus Shallow* (1931).
37 Chapman, *Poems*, ed. P. B. Bartlett (1941), 28.
38 Ed. R. W. David (1966), xlii.
39 Gustav Ungerer, *Anglo-Spanish Relations* (1956), 81ff. *A Spaniard in Elizabethan England*, II (1976), 377ff.
40 As comedians on television today often do.
41 IV.iii.290ff.
42 F. Yates, op. cit. 73–82.
43 Ibid. 202.
44 *Shakespearean Comedy* (1949), 131.
45 Parrott's theatrical experience was presumably in the United States.
46 Walter de la Mare, *Pleasures and Speculations* (1940), 295.
47 *Shakespeare's Happy Comedies*, 209.
48 De la Mare, op. cit., cited J. D. Wilson, 212.
49 *Shakespeare's Happy Comedies*, 213.
50 'A Plea for the Liberty of Interpreting', *Proceedings of the British Academy* (1950).
51 William Blake, Annotation to Swedenborg's *Heaven and Hell*.
52 C. F. E. Spurgeon, *Shakespeare's Imagery* (1935), 259.
53 I Corinthians ii.9.

54 *Shakespeare and his Comedies* (1957), 90.

## PART III

1 Morris U. Schappes, *Shylock and Anti-Semitism* (n.d.).
2 Paul N. Siegel, 'Shylock and the Puritan Usurers' in *Studies in Shakespeare*, ed. A. D. Matthews and C. M. Emery (Miami, 1953), 129ff.
3 *Shakespeare's Happy Comedies* (1962), 113.
4 Cf. E. Honigmann, *M.L.R.* (1954), 297–8.
5 Op. cit. 110ff.
6 In *Casebook on MV*, ed. John Wilders (1969), 29–30.
7 Variorum *MV* (1888)
8 *Character and Characterisation in Shakespeare* (1962), 30.
9 E. E. Stoll, *Shakespeare Studies* (1927), 312–13.
10 *Journals*, tr. J. O' Brien (1956), I.338.
11 New Cambridge edition (1926), xxvi.
12 R. Noble, *Shakespeare's Use of Song* (1923), 46.
13 Op. cit. 100.
14 *E.C.* X (1960), 119–33.
15 *S.Q.* II (1951), 369; *Moses and Monotheism* (1939), *passim*.
16 *The Meaning of Shakespeare* (1960), I.90.
17 *Collected Papers*, IV (1934), 328ff.
18 Denis Johnstone's play, *A Bride for the Unicorn*, is based on this idea of Freud's.
19 *Prefaces to Shakespeare* (1959), I.335.
20 G. Wilson Knight, *The Shakespearian Tempest* (1953), 129.
21 But, as Harold Fisch points out, many texts in the New Testament advocating mercy merely echo the Old Testament.
22 F. C. Kolbe, *Shakespear's Way* (1930), 71.
23 '*Hamlet,* the Prince or the Poem', *Proceedings of the British Academy,* 28 (1942), 145–7.
24 *Sussex Daily News* (15 Oct. 1937). I am indebted to G. Wilson Knight for this reference.
25 Ed. 1929. He is quoting O. Rank.
26 H. Granville-Barker, *A Companion to Shakespeare Studies* (1934), 70.
27 F. C. Kolbe, op. cit. 87; K. Muir, ed., *Macbeth* (1972), xxviii.
28 *Shakespeare* (1911), 134.
29 D. J. Gordon, *S.P.* XXXIX (1942), 284, suggests that Shakespeare may have been influenced by Della Porta's *Fratelli Rivali*.
30 Op. cit, 127ff.
31 Kirschbaum went a bit too far. It would be possible, though unprofitable, to show that the two Margarets are not absolutely incompatible. If we were to assume that Borachio was an occasional, but not an inverterate, drunkard, that he is courting Margaret but not her lover, that under the influence of the festivities in Leonato's house, Margaret agrees to their playing at being Hero and Claudio, her

behaviour, if not her absence from the wedding, would be plausible. But, of course, no audience requires such tortuous explanation.

32 C. T. Prouty, *The Sources of MA* (1950), 46.

33 Paul and Miriam Mueschke, 'Illusion and Metamorphosis in *MA*', *S.Q.* XVIII (1967), 53–65.

34 I Corinthians i.27. The point was made by an earlier critic.

35 We have all met similar cases in real life, and it is a cliché in comtemporary drama.

36 Op. cit. 52.

37 G. M. Hopkins, *Further Letters*, ed. C. C. Abbott (1938), 161.

38 *FQ* VI.7.4. A. F. Potts, *S.A.B.* XVII (1942) 103ff.

39 *Shaw on Shakespeare*, ed. E. Wilson (1962), 136–7.

40 William Congreve, *Complete Plays*, ed. H. Davis (1967), 449.

41 St John Hankin, *Dramatic Sequels* (1926).

42 *Ellen Terry's Memoirs*, ed. E. Craig and C. St John (1933), 175.

43 *The Comedy of Errors*, as we have seen, is not entirely farcical.

44 Proteus, Valentine, Juliet and many characters in *The Merchant of Venice* are bourgeois, but the plays in which they appear are not, partly because of their Italian setting.

45 The effectiveness of the satire in *Love's Labour's Lost* does not depend on our identification of the contemporary figures allegedly satirised.

46 Cf. Leslie Hotson, *Shakespeare Versus Shallow* (1931).

47 J. E. V. Crofts, *Shakespeare and the Post Horses* (1937); William Green, *Shakespeare's 'Merry Wives of Windsor'* (1962).

48 William Green in Signet edition.

49 J. M. Nosworthy, *Shakespeare's Occasional Plays* (1965) argues that Shakespeare hastily refashioned a lost play by Henry Porter, entitled *The Two Merry Women of Abingdon*.

50 Anne Page, it appears, was meant to take this role. Cf. IV.iv.70.

51 Ed. cit. 26. Cf. Ralph Berry, *Shakespeare's Comedies* (1972), 146–53.

52 See Sheridan, *The Critic*, II.2. 'Mr Puff, as he knows all this, why does Sir Walter go on telling him?' Sylvan Barnet has an illuminating article on the improbability of *AYLI*. See *S.St.* IV (1968), 119–31.

53 Shakespeare does not even use the expedient of French classical dramatists, where each hero is provided with a confidant, each heroine with a confidante.

54 This may be a hit at Marston and other satirists of the last years of the sixteenth century.

55 Cf. K. Muir, *Shakespeare's Sources*, I (1957).

56 *Shaw on Shakespeare*, 31.

57 Equalled, perhaps, by Millamant.

58 Shakespeare seems also to have read Ariosto's poem. Cf. K. Muir, *The Sources of Shakespeare* (1977).

59 J. Doebler, *Shakespeare's Speaking Pictures* (1974), *S.S.* 29 (1976), 159. Some directors, anxious to raise our opinion of Orlando's intelligence, have made him realise at an early stage that Ganymede is a woman. One needs the tongue of Thersites to comment on this.

60 *Shaw on Shakespeare*, 25.

61 *TNK* begins, and *LLL* ends, with music.

62 B. Evans, *Shakespeare's Comedies* (1960), *passim*.

63 Leslie Hotson, *The First Night of TN* (1954) suggests that the scene was based on an actual incident at Whitehall when Sir William Knollys, the Comptroller of the Household interrupted some noisy revellers. Cf. E. K. Chambers, *William Shakespeare*, I (1930), 405–6.

64 Charles Lamb, *Essays of Elia* (1911), 169.

65 Cf. I.v.

66 J. L. Simmons, however, *H.L.Q.* xxxvi (1973), 181–201, shows that the Elizabethan controversy with the puritans probably influenced the portrait of Malvolio.

67 Cf. Harold Jenkins, 'Shakespeare's *TN*', reprinted in K. Muir, *Shakespeare: the Comedies* (1965), 79. It is possible that Viola was originally meant to sing this song, but Shakespeare may have had second thoughts about introducing Viola to Orsino as a *castrato*, or have decided that Armin was the better singer.

68 Cf. *LLL*, V.ii.13ff.

69 W. H. Auden, *The Dyer's Hand* (1962), remarks: 'It would be painful enough for her if the man she loved really loved another, but it is much worse to be made to see that he only loves himself, and it is this insight which at this point Viola has to endure.'

70 Barrett Wendell, *William Shakespeare* (1898), 89.

71 E.g. J. Middleton Murry, *Shakespeare* (1935).

72 Leslie Hotson, op. cit. Moreover, even if the Orsino in the audience knew too little English to take offence at the portrait of his namesake, can we believe that Elizabeth would have liked to see herself as Olivia? It may be mentioned that the name Orsino is used in one of the plays which is thought to have served as a model for *TN*.

## PART IV

1 Cf. W. W. Lawrence, *Shakespeare's Problem Comedies* (1931).

2 Cf. F. Harris, *The Women of Shakespeare* (1911), quoted in A. Ralli, *History of Shakespearean Criticism* (1932), 303–4.

3 E. K. Chambers, *Sir Thomas Wyatt* (1933), 181ff.

4 Oscar J. Campbell, *Comicall Satire* (1938), 185ff.

5 I.ii.18ff. This is thought by some to be the purge administered by Shakespeare. See *The Return from Parnassus*, ed. J. B. Leishman, (1949), 1766–74.

6 I.iii.66.

7 Op. cit.

8 R. W. Chambers, *Man's Unconquerable Mind* (1939), 277. R. G. Hunter, *Shakespeare and the Comedy of Forgiveness* (1965), 204.

9 Roy Battenhouse, '*Measure for Measure* and the Christian Doctrine of Atonement', *P.M.L.A.* LXI (1946), 1029–59.

10 Romans vii.18–20.

11  Cf. Chaucer, *Parson's Tale*, ed. Robinson, 304, and T. M. Pearce, *N.Q.* (1960), 18–19.

12  III.i.120ff.; III.ii.327; V.ii.212.

13  Robert Stevenson, *Shakespeare's Religious Frontier* (1958), 44.

14  Walter Whiter, *A Specimen of a Commentary*, ed. A. Over and Mary Bell (1967), 203–4.

15  *MM* II.ii.180.

16  C. J. Reimer, *Der Begrift der Gnade in Shakespeare's MM* (1937).

17  Elizabeth M. Pope, 'The Renaissance Background of MM', *S.S.* 2 (1949), 66–82.

18  R. W. Chambers, op. cit. 286ff.

19  Shakespeare himself adapts Erasmus in urging the friend of the Sonnets to marry. Cf. J. W. Lever, *The Elizabethan Love Sonnet* (1956), 189.

20  Romans xi.5.

21  I have not been able to trace this.

22  v.22, vii.13–14.

23  Preface.

24  Cited in Variorum edition.

25  O. J. Campbell, op. cit. 213.

26  *Sunday Telegraph*.

27  Chapman has many words of Latin derivation, including some Shakespeare uses in *TC* (e.g. emulous, depravation, imbecility, transportance) and others of a similar kind (e.g. authentical, aversation, castigation, conformance, destinate, disjunction, confluent).

28  *Nashe's Lenten Stuffe* in *Works*, ed. McKerrow (1958), 141.

29  Cf. L. C. Knights, *T.L.S.* (1932), 408.

30  *R.II*, I.iii.298.

31  *The Wheel of Fire* (1949), 47.

32  1366ff.

33  III.iii.145ff.

34  *Luc.* 930.

35  Op. cit. 121.

36  Racine, *Athalie*, II.v.

37  Mark iv.21; Matthew v.15.

38  *E.C.* IV (1954), 282–96.

39  At a conference at Stratford-upon-Avon. *S.S.* 8 (1955), 28–39.

40  *The Frontiers of Drama* (1948), 73.

41  *Shakespeare's Problem Plays* (1950), 86.

42  Liverpool University Press (1968).

43  Cited Price, 57.

44  Op. cit. 43ff.

45  Cf. C. Leech, *E.L.H.* 21 (1954), 17; J. Price, *The Unfortunate Comedy* (1968), 83, 95, and Ch. 8.

46  The manners and morals of the Court had deteriorated.

47  *Shaw on Shakespeare*, ed. E. Wilson (1969), 34.

48  IV.v.14.

49  Cf. G. K. Hunter's Arden edition and M. C. Bradbrook's article, *R.E.S.* (1950), 289–301.

50 Cf. K. Muir, *Shakespeare's Sources,* I (1957), 99.
51 Cf. *AW*, ed. Barbara Everett (1970), 14ff. and G. Wilson Knight, *The Sovereign Flower* (1958), 107ff.
52 Knight, op. cit. 140, has a fine passage on this.
53 Bertrand Evans, *Shakespeare's Comedies* (1960), 165.
54 Ed. cit. 37.
55 Op. cit. 166. Katherine Mansfield disliked Helena: *Journal* (1927), 200.
   'I must say Helena is a terrifying female. Her virtue, her persistence, her pegging away after the odious Bertram (and disguised as pilgrim—so typical!) and then telling the whole story to that good widow-woman! And that tame fish Diana. As to lying in Diana's bed and enjoying the embraces meant for Diana—well, I know nothing more sickening. It would take a respectable woman to do such a thing. The worst of it is I can so well imagine ... for instance acting precisely that way, and giving Diana a present afterwards. *What* a cup of tea the widow and D. must have enjoyed while it was taking place, or did D. at the last moment want to cry off the bargain? But to forgive such a woman! Yet Bertram would. There's an espece de mothers-boyisme in him which makes him stupid enough for anything.'
56 I owe these quotations to an unpublished thesis by Rosalind Miles (Birmingham University). See also her book *The Problem of 'Measure for Measure'* (1976).
57 Una Ellis-Fermor, *The Jacobean Drama* (1965), 263.
58 Op. cit. 122.
59 *A View of the English Stage* (1975), 86.
60 Cf. *The Wheel of Fire, Man's Unconquerable Mind, R.E.S.* (1941), *P.M.L.A.* LXI (1946).
61 Op. cit. 93.
62 D. Traversi, *Approach to Shakespeare* (1938), 70.
63 New Cambridge edition (1922), xxx.
64 Op. cit. 290ff.
65 E. K. Chambers, *Shakespeare: A Survey* (1925), 215.
66 Elizabeth M. Pope, op. cit.
67 C. Leech, *S.S.* 3 (1950), 66–73.
68 James Black, *S.S.* 26(1973), 119.
79 J. W. Bennett. *MM as Royal Entertainment* (1966), 135ff.
70 I have argued (*N.Q.* 1966, 135–6) that Shakespeare wrote this soliloquy for the following scene while Isabella briefs Mariana.
71 Herbert Weil, *S.S.* 25 (1972), 27.
72 The ambiguities of the play are stressed in the following articles:
   Clifford Leech, *S.S.* 3 (1950) 66–73; Herbert Weil, op. cit. and Harriett Hawkins, *S.S.* 31, 105. Since this chapter was written Philip Brockbank in a review article (*T.L.S.* 26 Nov. 1976) has neatly expressed what I have been more clumsily suggesting:
   'Many of the play's specific puzzles can be solved by recognising the sleight of hand with which Shakespeare slips from the "human" to the "divine", and to the "theatrical".'

## PART V

1 F. J. Furnivall, cited in L. Strachey, *Books and Characters* (1922), 48–9.
2 E. Dowden, ibid.
3 L. Strachey, op. cit. 52.
4 *Shakespearean Comedy* (1933), 267.
5 A. H. Thorndike, *The Influence of Beaumont and Fletcher* (1901) 168.
6 Una Ellis-Fermor, *The Jacobean Drama* (1936), 268.
7 K. Muir, 'Theophanies in the Last Plays' in *Shakespeare's Late Plays*, ed. Richard C. Tobias and Paul G. Zolbrod (1974), 32.
8 But cf. P. Edwards, *S.S.* 11 (1958), 1–18.
9 Prologue to *Circe*: 'Shakespear's own Muse her *Pericles* first bore'.
10 K. Muir, *N.Q.* (1948), 362.
11 In an unpublished lecture.
12 Emrys Jones, Philip Brockbank, Glynne Wickham.
13 R. Warwick Bond, *Studia Otiosa* (1938).
14 *Johnson on Shakespeare*, ed. W. Raleigh (1925), 183.
15 *Prefaces to Shakespeare* (1946), 459.
16 James Sutherland in *More Talking of Shakespeare*, ed. John Garrett (1959), 144.
17 E, M. W. Tillyard, *Shakespeare's Last Plays* (1938), 68.
18 *Cymbeline Refinished*, reprinted in *Shaw on Shakespeare*, ed. E. Wilson (1962), 81.
19 *Shakespeare's Comedies* (1960), 285.
20 II.v.6.
21 E.g. the husband who kills his wife by kindness would never envisage the possibility that he was worse than her.
22 *Bernard Shaw—Ellen Terry: A Correspondence,* quoted in *Shaw on Shakespeare*, ed. E. Wilson (1962), 81.
23 Near the beginning of Juvenal's Sixth Satire there is a reference to a certain Postumus who, despite his personal experience of female depravity, is about to get married. Juvenal warns him that he will be cuckolded. Roy Walker once suggested to me that the juxtaposition of the name Posthumus and adultery was how the hero of *Cymbeline* got his name.
24 Helen Faucit (Lady Martin), *On Some of Shakespeare's Female Characters* (1891).
25 E. K. Chambers, *William Shakespeare: A Study of Facts and Problems* (1930), II.340.
26 K. Muir, *Shakespeare's Sources,* I (1957), 245 and 251.
27 J. D. Wilson, New Cambridge edition of *W.T.* 131. S. A. Brooke, *On Ten Plays of Shakespeare* (1925), 257–8. R. J. Trienens, *S.Q.* IV (1953), 321–6.
28 *S.S.* 22 (1969), 96.
29 Op. cit.
30 J. A. Bryant. *Hippolyta's View* (1961), 222.
31 S. L. Bethell, *The Winter's Tale* (1947), 103.

32  A. Bonjour, *E.S.* XXXIII (1952), 208.
33  The following quotations will be found in my *Casebook*. See also my
    essay in *The Morality of Art*, ed. A. N. Jeffares and D. W. Jefferson
    (1969).
34  *S.S.* 11 (1958), 38.
35  Cf. L. Sterne, *Tristram Shandy*, Book VIII, Ch. xix, where Trim tells
    Uncle Toby of the unfortunate King of Bohemia, unfortunate
    because
    > Taking great pleasure and delight in navigation and all sort of sea
    > affairs—and there happening throughout the whole kingdom of
    > Bohemia, to be no sea-port town whatever—How the deuce
    > should there—Trim? cried my Uncle Toby; for Bohemia being
    > totally inland, it could have happened not otherwise—It might,
    > said Trim, if it had pleased God.
36  Op. cit.
37  It was translated a few years later by Leonard Digges, the stepson of
    Shakespeare's overseer.
38  *The Defense of Poetry.*
39  See Variorum edition.
40  *R.E.L.* (1964), 98.
41  Preface to *The Tempest,* vol. 16, the Renaissance edition of Shakes-
    peare, ed. Sir Sidney Lee (1907).
42  *Defense of Poesy.*
43  Op. cit.
44  I.ii.
45  *S.S.* 25 (1972), 125.
46  R. Graves, *The Common Asphodel* (1949), 38.
47  Eleanor Prosser, *Sh. St.* I (1965), 261.
48  Shelley, *Defence of Poetry.*
49  *Works* (1614), 549, tr. T. Lodge.
50  R. G. Moulton, *The Moral System of Shakespeare* (1903), 325.
51  V.i.
52  *Life and Letters Today,* vol. 16, no. 7 (1937), 21–35.
53  See F. Kermode's Introduction to the Arden edition, xxxiv.
54  R. M. Rilke, *Poems 1906 to 1926,* tr. J. B. Leishman (1957), 140.
55  *The Court Masque* (1927), 342–3.
56  Isaiah xxxiv.4. 2 Peter iii.10.
57  Sir W. Alexander, *The Tragedy of Darius, Poetical Works,* ed. L. E.
    Kastner and H. B. Charlton (1921), 113.
58  So it has been assumed.
59  F. A. Yates, *Theatre of the World* (1969), 189.
60  G. L. Kittredge, ed.
61  K. Muir, Arden edition, *King Lear,* xxiv.
62  J. L. Hotson, *I, William Shakespeare* (1937), 222.
63  Cf. F. Kermode, op. cit.
64  Cf. Milton's *Areopagitica* (1645), 17.
    > 'To sequester out of the world into *Atlantick* and *Eutopian*
    > politics, which never can be drawn into use, will not **mend our**

condition; but to ordain wisely as in this world of evill, in the midd'st whereof God hath plac't us unavoidably.'

65 *English Miscellany II* (1960), 59.

66 Cited by L. Berthelot, *La Sagesse de Shakespeare et de Goethe* (1930).

67 Milton, *Second Defence.*

68 *Notebooks* (1947), 111.

69 Paul Bertram, *Shakespeare and the Two Noble Kinsmen* (1965). Cf. My article in *S.S.* 11 (1958) and my review of Bertram, *R.E.S.* XVII (1966), 432.

70 Theodore Spencer, *M.P.* XXXVI (1938–9), 255–76.

71 Ibid.

# INDEX